LEST MEMORY CEASE

Modern Jewish History
Henry L. Feingold, *Series Editor*

Henry L. Feingold

LEST MEMORY CEASE

Finding Meaning in the American Jewish Past

Syracuse University Press

First Edition 1996
96 97 98 99 00 01 02   6 5 4 3 2 1

The paper used in this publication meets the minimum requirements of American Na-
tional Standard for Information Sciences—Permanence of Paper for Printed Library
Materials, ANSI Z39.48-1984. ∞™

Library of Congress Cataloging-in-Publication Data
Feingold, Henry L., 1931–
    Lest memory cease : finding meaning in the American Jewish past /
Henry L. Feingold.
        p.   cm. — (Modern Jewish history)
    Includes bibliographical references and index.
    ISBN 0-8156-2710-6 (cloth : alk. paper). — ISBN 0-8156-0400-9
(pbk. : alk. paper)
        1. Jews—United States—History.   2. Judaism—United States.
    3. Jews—Cultural assimilation—United States.   4. Jews—United
    States—Politics and government.   5. Liberalism—United States.
    6. Secularism—United States.   7. United States—Ethnic relations.
    I. Title.   II. Series.
    E184.J5F3755   1996
    305.892'4073—dc20   96-25659

This book is dedicated to my mother, Frieda Feingold.
May her memory be as a blessing.

I thought I would make an end of them,
I would make their memory cease from among men;
Were it not that I dreaded the enemy's provocation.
—Deuteronomy 32:26, 27

Henry L. Feingold, a Professor Emeritus of history at Baruch College and the Graduate School of the City University of New York, specializes in American Jewish history and the history of the Holocaust. He is the author of the prize-winning *The Politics of Rescue: The Roosevelt Administration and the Holocaust, 1938–1944; Zion in America: The American Jewish Experience from Colonial Times to the Present;* and *A Midrash on American Jewish History. A Time for Searching: Entering the Mainstream, 1920–1945* was the fourth volume of his highly acclaimed five-volume series, *The Jewish People in America.* His most recent book is *Bearing Witness: How America and Its Jews Responded to the Holocaust* (Syracuse University Press).

Contents

Part Four
Secularism

LEST MEMORY CEASE

Introduction

A STORY IS TOLD of a sophisticated daughter of Jewish immigrants who takes her uneducated mother to a museum where they chance upon a painting of Madonna and Child. Patiently, the daughter explains the meaning of the portrait to the puzzled mother, only to overhear her murmuring to herself: "These Gentiles are truly funny people. Look! A husband she doesn't have, the child is illegitimate, she lives in a stable. . . . And what does she do? She has her portrait painted."

I related this story because it tells us at a glance the enormous cultural gap that had to be traversed between the Jewish immigrant culture and the culture of the host society. Not able to comprehend that she was viewing an icon of the Christian faith, the immigrant mother saw only profligacy. Hers was a generation with little to spare for portraits. In contrast, the daughter had already negotiated the difficult leap into modernity. Although it concerned a religion that historically was hostile to her own, she had learned to appreciate the aesthetic of the religious imagery of the majority culture. That detachment is part of the temper of modernity.

The adjustment of the Jewish immigrant was especially difficult because acculturation and modernization came in the same package and had to be negotiated simultaneously. Our mother and daughter were not only being Americaned, that is, learning their new country's language and ways; they were also being moderned, perceiving themselves first as individuals and only then, if at all, as members of an ethnic or religious community. The mother's response brings a smile to our lips. Her perception, rooted as it is in cultural dissonance, is so wide off the mark as to be comical. But that does not conceal the

1

pathos that is caused not only by having to give up so much so quickly but also by the generational dislocation that made parents into children and children into parents.

True, that abiding sense of loss was in some measure felt by all immigrants; but Jews, who often could not think of the punishing society they had left behind as homeland, carried an additional burden to the cultural denuding that is at the heart of the acculturation process. They could not be certain that they would be any more acceptable here than they had been in the old country. For a time, they truly belonged to neither culture, not the one they had chosen to leave and not the one they were anxious to join. The stress involved in such social dislocation can only be fathomed by those who have stood culturally naked and homeless in a strange and unfriendly world.

We can find in that forlorn condition a partial answer to why Jews clung so tenaciously to their culture, why they remained, longer than most ethnics, a lump in the melting pot. Jewish immigrants developed a community that generated its own distinctive political culture; its own remarkable intellectual establishment; an incorruptible labor movement; and a theater that, in its dramaturgy, and a press that, in its liveliness, often outdid those of the host culture. In Yiddish, the Jewish community had its own distinctive language, and with it came a bevy of writers. Had the writers been able to retain their language, they might have indefinitely remained "indigestible," as was said by one of them. Most important, having much historical experience in adapting to new cultures, they had an instinct for preserving their culture by weaving its strands into the new. The Jewish answer to homelessness was to build a community where they could feel at home. These *shtetlakhs*, ghettos, neighborhoods, congregations, *Landsmannschaften*, or any of the many forms that Jewish communalism assumed in its dispersion, were really homes that substituted for sovereign nationhood rooted in territory. They contain a clue to the remarkable survivability of Jewry, despite its dispersal.

What is that clue? It is that Jewish communal life in the Diaspora is organized through memory rooted in a widespread knowledge of group history and sacred text. The Jews of Israel live in Jewish space; and to the extent that the state is militarily secure, their survival is assured. But the Jews of America remain Jewish to the degree that they organize themselves communally on the basis of shared corporate memory. In their history is contained the signals from a distinct and separate religious civilization with its own myths, symbols, and claims. Loaded with such heavy cultural freight, the Jewish immigrant generation faced no ordinary challenge to an acculturation and modernization process that required the assumption of new values, perceptions, life-styles, and language. There was inherent conflict in such an accommodation because Jews could not be the malleable human clay that the Italians and the Irish might be in stepping out of their territorial space. Jews carried their group identity in their memories, which they could not dispel merely because the social and cultural landscape had changed. In addition to the expected stress of becoming modern and American, Jews also had to balance the claims of two cultures, the Judaic and the American. Often, the values, myths, and symbols of the new American society conflicted with those of the preexisting religious culture.

Since World War II, the values and claims of the American host society have proved to be irresistible. To a people who wanted desparately to be modern, America's post-Enlightenment culture was especially seductive. Its society was open and free, and individual development and achievement were cherished. Predictably, the absorption of such secular values weakened Jewry's sense of corporateness, the inherent sense of belonging to one people. The particularity of the Jewish community was diminished so that they became indistinguishable from other Americans; and as never before, they became acceptable as marriage partners. Each new problem posed by modernity, from questions of rabbinic authority to new techniques to perform circumcision, had an impact on the ancient legalistic religious structure of Judaism. Each of those ever-present problems of accommodation became a source of the survival anxiety that has become American Jewry's most prominent characteristic.

In America, which was organized on a centripetal principle, the absorption process worked like a powerful suction whirlpool. Unless, like African Americans, they were deliberately exempted, no ethnic communal group could long withstand its pull. For immigrant Jews, the historic memory that bound them gradually dimmed, and communal boundaries became porous. It is that process that serves as the motor force for the writing of these essays. Never far beneath the surface of the various subjects examined is a concern about the survivability of a Jewish community and culture in this benevolent, absorbing democracy. This concern goes beyond the historian's obligation to search for truth but can never conflict with it.

But why such survival anxiety when American Jewry is well established in a nation that allows the fullest expression of its energy and talent? Surely with the existence of Israel and its Law of Return, Jews no longer need worry about homelessness? Yet, thoughtful American Jews continue to be wracked by such fears. Israel is cherished and lovingly nurtured, but generations of acculturation in a nation that welcomed and made space for a "people that dwells apart" has made them feel fully at home. For most, the idea of having one day to leave it, as German Jews were forced to leave their beloved land, is unthinkable. True, these essays sometimes speak of anti-Semitism; but they speak even more of Jewry's remarkable climb to a high economic and social status. The mobility of American Jewry was so rapid and the energy and talent released after being pent up for centuries behind ghetto walls so explosive that they have been compared to the power of a released steel coil. Clearly, American anti-Semitism has had little braking effect and could not block Jewry's remarkable ascendancy.

The reader will not find an answer to the American Jewish survival conundrum in these pages. The basic reality is that historical processes like acculturation and modernization cannot be halted or wished away. Even if it were possible from on high to order Jews on which values of modern American culture to cherish and which to reject, there is no force in the Jewish polity to compel their adherence. The Jewish kings and subsequently their rabbis, who once could issue such commands, no longer exist. Modernity has altered the direction of governing authority from the governors to the governed. Like all Americans, Jews are a free people who dwell in a free society. But their historical experience also sets them apart from other Americans. There is, or at least for many years there was, something different in the terms set for their acculturation.

It is the source and the impact of that difference that these essays explore. They are offered to the general reader in the hope that they reinforce what has been discovered regarding the benefits of openness and tolerance. And they are also aimed at the Jewish reader, who is reminded that the rewards that came with becoming an American like other Americans also exacted a price. Today, Jews are not as secure in the knowledge of who and what they are and how to live life as were their immigrant ancestors.

These articles and essays, now fashioned into chapters, were published over two decades in various small Jewish journals and scholarly quarterlies that abound in the Jewish community. They are a sample of my general interest in all facets of the American Jewish experience. For convenience' sake, I have grouped them under four headings. The first concerns my basic concept about the writing of American Jewish history; the second deals with the problem of identifying American anti-Semitism; the third deals with American Jewish political culture, particularly Jewish liberalism; and the fourth deals with the impact of secularism on Jewish survivability. Because they are drawn from another time and context, some distillation of the problems they address and of the supporting ideas that have been brought to bear may be helpful to the reader.

The essays in part 1 present a historical explanation for a familiar characteristic of contemporary American Jewry: Why Jews developed a separate labor movement or how American myths and heroes are sometimes difficult to reconcile with those contained in the preexisting-coexisting historical stream that also sends signals to American Jewry. It is that separate historic stream that gives the American Jewish experience and therefore its history an abiding duality. For example, Henry Ford could be no hero to Jews; but Franklin Roosevelt was probably more of a hero to Jews than to other Americans. The disparity stems from the Jewish historical experience, which creates its own heroes and villains, its own distinct perception.

The writing of Jewish history cannot be easily separated from the omnipresent problem of how to survive as a distinct people, even while being settled in another people's space and culture. We note again the disparity of signals, this time in the historic myths that prevail in all history, such as the melting-pot myth, which encourages the total acculturation of immigrant culture and really serves the needs of the host culture. The Jewish myth, or story, on the other hand, features the image of the "wandering Jew," who is in fact a perpetual refugee. The former speaks of the wonders of America as the *goldeneh medinah* (promised land) that offers Jews success written largely in material terms. But the price is the eventual disappearance of a distinct Jewish culture. The refugee condition is not as comfortable but it permits such a separate culture to exist and even imagines that general economic success of American Jewry stems from the disequilibrium created by the need to discover over and over again the paths to security and comfort in the new land. That is what Jews, the perpetual immigrants, have had to do in the countries that received them. In the American experience, they have done so in three waves of immigration, each of which produced a commercial elite.

Until recently, American Jews lived in two cultures. The signals and fiat from each were usually complimentary, but there were also instances when the two could not be reconciled. A good example is the conflict that developed over the Sunday laws. The small Jewish population lived their daily lives in the Christian world that willy-nilly shaped civic life. Constitutionally, matters of church and state were separated; but often in practice, such things as the religious calendar or dietary restrictions could not always be accommodated. Preconditions for a tearing of the fabric of the minority Judaic culture were then in place. One writer describes the alienation and loneliness of a Jewish youngster in a small southern town during the Christmas holiday. It was to a Christian America that Jews had to accommodate.

Sometimes, the disparity concerned a shared ethos differently implemented. Judaism and Americanism both celebrate the idea of freedom, but the American concept of freedom is libertarian and unrestrained by the necessity to live in community or among strangers as are Jews. Jews also cherish freedom, but it is matched and limited by the necessity to be better human beings and by the constraints of Jewish law. Jews are never free of the need to improve the world by actual deeds.

The signals and claims of that coexisting millennial religious civilization to which Jews also adhere possess concrete economic, political, and cultural linkages. The link to Jewish communities in the Caribbean played an important role in developing the Jewish ethnic economy during the colonial and national periods. There is the so-called our-crowd phenomenon that is based on the ties of American Jewish banking houses to those of Europe. Similarly, the social democratic perspective behind the development of the Jewish labor movement came from the Jewish Bund in Poland. And of course, Zionism, the strongest shaping movement in recent Jewish history, is based squarely on the conviction of existence and need to strengthen a distinct Jewish peoplehood. Today, the strong ties to Israel and the protective mantle American Jews have cast over the Jews of the former Russian republics serve as evidence that the tie to the universal community of Israel, sometimes referred to as *K'lal Yisrael* in these essays, still exercises considerable influence.

Those who see only that American Jews use their freedom to free themselves of the bonds of tribe and religion might take heart in the health of its historical professional fraternity that has emerged in the past decades. That is a hopeful sign because it is partly the jealous possession of their history, from the Bible onward, that has allowed Jews to organize themselves bound only by historic memory of peoplehood. Like all communities of the Diaspora, American Jewry is anchored in time rather than space. The notion that there is a Jewish corporation that all Jews are commanded to safeguard stems ultimately from the Talmudic injunction *kol yisrael arevim zeh b'zeh* (all Israel is responsible one for the other). In a real sense, Jews are commanded to act as a community. But in the sense that many Jews no longer know their history and can no longer be commanded, the injunction has become more of an aspiration than a reality. In a democratic society, they can still be persuaded, however; and there historians bear a special responsibility.

The notion that a people can be organized through its historic memory is by no means an established truth. The creation of Israel after the Holocaust was a sad confirmation that in the modern world it was not yet possible to survive without protective territorial space. But the universalist dream that one day all mankind will become citizens of the world is nevertheless deeply embedded in the historic Jewish diasporic experience. The sense of homelessness, of belonging nowhere and therefore everywhere, feeds the universalism that persists in Jewish political culture.

In order for a community that develops within the culture and space of another nation to survive, it needs to be aware of its special historic experience, which contains its sense of worthwhileness. Such a history also needs to contain a full and truthful vision of what Judaism was in the past. In a word, Jewish history itself is an essential instrument for communal continuity. But it also bears the responsibility of all modern professional history. That dual role is yet another example of how the uniquely Jewish situation in the world serves to differentiate its historiography from that of land-rooted peoples.

That America has been hospitable toward Jews does not mean that it has been completely free of anti-Semitism. That would be highly unlikely in a derivatively Western Christian culture, where anti-Semitism is part of the socialization process. The incidents of anti-Semitism recorded in its history show that America was not exempt from this malady. But because of its pluralistic identity, anti-Semitism in America poses unusual problems of authentication. In a well-researched book of its history (*Antisemitism in America*, 1995), Leonard Dinnerstein observes that, like all anti-Semitisms, the American variety grows directly out of Judaism's troubled place in the

Christian schema. And although Americans are perhaps the most devout Christians in the Western world, Dinnerstein concludes that it nevertheless has the lowest quotient of anti-Semitism. Considering the high status Jews have achieved, the conclusion that such anti-Semitism as exists does not appreciably interfere with Jewish access to the promise of American life seems unavoidable. In fact, the burgeoning intermarriage rate may serve as evidence that the danger to American Jewish continuance stems less from anti-Semitism than philo-Semitism.

Evidence of this society's unthreatening character is that, unlike Europe, there have been relatively few examples of political anti-Semitism, the kind that results in government acts and laws that officialize and amplify it. A "Jewish question" that sets limits to how much wealth or power Jews should be allowed to possess has rarely appeared on the American political agenda. That has not been true of American Catholicism, which arrayed against it the Know Nothing Party in the 1850s. With the exception of General Order Number 11 (1862), which singled out Jews for collective punishment, and other questionable incidents like the restrictionist immigration laws of the twenties, anti-Semitism in America has been confined to the private realm; that is, it is exercised by private citizens or institutions against other private citizens, as in the well-known Harvard *numerus clausus* case, which restricted Jewish enrollment. That American anti-Semitism is largely private does not of course mean that it is less dangerous or that its sting is less felt. In a society that has raised the market economy mechanism to an almost sacred position, what happens in the private sector is often more important than what happens in the public. The absence of Jews in the top management of America's railroads, for examples tells us something about the distribution of power in nineteenth-century America, when Jews were simply not considered for managerial positions in basic industry. But historically, it is when anti-Semitism is amplified through public policy, when it becomes part of the political agenda, that it tends to become lethal. That is what happened in the Germany and Poland of the thirties.

There is a conventional wisdom among Jews that as long as the primary hatred of the American people remains racial, it will act to deflect the hatred against Jews that is normative in other Western societies. Whether or not that is true, there is little doubt that the multiethnic nature of American society poses problems for the anti-Semite, who needs to single out Jews from a welter of other groups who may appear more religiously aberrant. Target centering Jews poses similar problems for the researcher, who may encounter difficulty in distinguishing anti-Semitism from the normal intergroup tensions that one can expect in such a heterogenous society. When African Americans oppose increased aid to Israel and insist that such money be funneled to the inner city, are they being anti-Semitic? When Congress restricted immigrants from southern and eastern Europe by using a screen based on the notion of Nordic supremacy, were they aiming to restrict only Jewish immigrants, or did they have antipathy for all immigrants that stemmed from those regions? In short, is there a way of opposing the Jewish interest without appearing to be anti-Semitic? In the absence of a taxonomy for identifying anti-Semitic incidents, the cry of "wolf" may be sounded so often that, when a real danger develops, it might go unheard.

The Harvard *numerus clausus* case serves at once to illustrate the peculiar public-private dichotomy and the difficulty of clearly identifying American anti-Semitism. The fuss made over Harvard's restrictive enrollment policy is puzzling because only a handful of Jewish students were excluded and Harvard was not the first elite school to adopt such a policy. Why then did Harvard's policy become a *cause célèbrè?* The answer has something to do with the fact that formal education and the professional certification to which it could lead had become a favorite route to achieve middle-class status for the children of the Eastern immigrants. Jews quickly realized that an investment in their own human capital through formal education would reap high returns. It was Harvard that set the conventions for American higher education. If its limitation policy went unchallenged, it would have a long-range impact on the drive of the second-generation Jews to establish themselves.

Yet, as in the immigration laws that effectively restricted other immigrant groups, there was also an indeterminate quality when Harvard's exclusion was viewed as merely another example of anti-Semitism. Harvard could in fact rightfully claim to be the most liberal minded of the Ivy League universities and actually was last to come to the *numerus clausus* policy. Its student body and most of its Board of Overseers thought of the institution in proprietary class terms. From that perspective, Jewish student culture was at odds with Harvard's genteel culture, which sought to mold character as well as minds. Far more interested in the latter, Jewish students of eastern European parentage did not lightly surrender their souls to Harvard. The university needed quotas, President Abbott Lawrence Lowell claimed, to prevent a rise in the level of anti-Semitism that inevitably occurred as the percentage of Jewish students increased. He often pointed out that Harvard had not discriminated against the less numerous sons of the preceding German Jewish immigration, who seemed to fit much more smoothly into Harvard's student life. What was meant, of course, was that the sons of the former German immigration were less identifiably Jewish.

A solution that, for the moment at least, satisfied both Harvard and Louis Marshall, who had worked to undo the Jewish limitations policy, was agreed upon; but the private-public dichotomy was never really solved. Harvard's quotas were a case of private anti-Semitism, yet Harvard also had a public mission to develop the nation's talent for which it had been granted the power of certification backed by government authority. That a national interest was inevitably involved in using such power came to the surface during the cold war, especially after *Sputnik,* when there was a realization that it benefited the nation to recruit talent wherever it might be found. At that juncture, Harvard's admission committee opened its gates to all who qualified. It, however, became a different Harvard, no longer the exclusive training ground of a would-be hereditary ruling elite but rather an incubator of a Jeffersonian natural aristocracy based on talent. The Harvard case also contained a lesson for Jewish leaders. It taught them that anti-Semitism could be challenged and beaten back.

When political scientists examine a group's political culture, they are primarily interested in determining why it votes a certain way. In order to make such a determination, political scientists require knowledge of the group's ethos; its assumptions about society; its values and habits; and above all, the historical experience it brings into the political arena.

In the three-and-a-half centuries that have passed since a group of Sephardic Jews first entered the spacious harbor of "Nieuw Amsterdam," most things that made Jews distinctive have disappeared. They can no longer pride themselves on their determined adherence to their religion or the high cohesiveness of their family and communal life. Their tendency to congregate on certain areas of the economic and geographic checkerboard has lessened, and their remarkable social mobility is today matched by other ethnics. Such cultural markers that might make up an American Jewish fingerprint have been melded away. The one characteristic remaining that still marks Jews off from other groups is their distinct political culture. They are America's liberals par excellence; and if no longer the most liberal, they remain the wealthiest constituency to make their political home in the left wing of the Democratic Party.

That proclivity for being liberal has been a source of chagrin and puzzlement for a group of neoconservative Jews like Irvin Krystol and Norman Podhoretz, one of whom humorously speculated that there may be an anatomical peculiarity behind it. Once Jewish voters are alone in the voting booth, they discover that, try as they will, their arms will not pull down the Republican lever. Nearer to the truth, as the German-Jewish statesman and industrialist Walter Rathenau observed, the fact is that Jewish voters are actually profoundly conservative, so much so, that they cannot easily break with generations of a liberal tradition or the nearly equivalent social democratic tradition that directs them to the moderately left side of the political spectrum. What seems most paradoxical is that, after all else has been acculturated, a political culture incubated largely after the European Enlightenment is what remains most identifiably Jewish about American Jewry.

Yet, that linkage to the Enlightenment in Jewish political culture should not come as a surprise. The ideals behind the emancipation of European Jewry that granted them civil and political rights are cut from the same cloth as are the founding principles of this new nation. Commitment to these principles accounts for Jewry's forthright position in support of the American Revolution. But there is also a puzzling indigenous component of Jewish political behavior. The influence of the Enlightenment can hardly account for its aberrance in supporting Jefferson over Hamilton. The former, after all, was a physiocrat who favored a simple rural life, whereas Hamilton supported the very commercial-urban sector where most Jews had located themselves. But then as today, a peculiarly broad interpretation of their group interest did not permit the Jewish vote to be dictated by the pocket-book interest. Today, rich Jews are as liberal as poor ones, perhaps more. That altruism, which some believe to be suicidal, was characteristic of Jewish political culture from its earliest settlement in America.

For our purposes here, liberalism is viewed as that interest which confronts the regnant societal injustice. It has at various times sought to liberate slaves, exploited workers, duped consumers, women, gays, the handicapped, even entire species facing extinction. Because there seems always to be such a group in need of liberation, that is, an injustice is always present in organized society, liberalism acts as the motor force of American politics. More a political posture than an internally consistent programmatic ideology, liberalism plays an important role in determining what the political agenda will consist of at any given historical juncture. Democrats and Republicans may argue about how far government concern should extend, but that the issue comes up at all can be traced to the liberal assumptions that are embedded in secular democracy. That fact hardly explains why liberalism has sustained itself so long among American Jews, however. It may be that liberalism is also indigenous to Jewish political culture, that it is nourished by Judaic as well as American sources.

In the conflicting amalgam of ideals that make up American liberalism, there are both a libertarian principle, based on a quest for ever more freedom, and an egalitarian principle, rooted in a quest for justice and equity. In the past, Jewish allegiance has been more to the latter. Support of the egalitarian principle exists because the religious civilization to which Jews also adhere places strong emphasis on the justice ideal and proposes a more limited and community-oriented concept of liberty or freedom. Add to this situation the fact that the immigrant group that gave American Jewry some numerical weight carried in its eastern European cultural baggage the egalitarian and statist ideas embodied in socialist ideology. Once in America, that core systemic ideology was gradually reshaped through the Jewish labor movement and Jewish social workers to bring it within striking distance of reformist Progressive and later New Deal welfare-state liberalism. It was during the New Deal period that the two became fully joined, and Jewish liberalism came into its own. It was the Jewish labor movement that sponsored the organization of the American Labor Party, which became the Liberal Party in New York State in 1940. It is the only example in American history in which a party actually designated *liberal* appeared on the ballot. But it was an Americanized liberalism that had been refashioned to tone down its statist thrust.

Liberalism is dynamic and therefore proffers a continually changing political interest. That change is especially apparent in its Jewish component. In the post–World War II period, it has evolved from its former egalitarian position to one much closer to the libertarian position of the non-Jewish liberal voter. Jewish voters, who at one time supported the kind of social engineering involved in welfare-state programs like affirmative action, no longer do so today. Yet, they remain chary of any attempt by government to censor on the basis of an abstract standard of morality. They remain strongly in favor of choice on the abortion issue; and they have joined, by a slight majority, other American voters who favor capital punishment. But the broad approach to their group interest that occurred during the national period continues. Despite their high per capita income, contemporary Jewish voters favor entitlement programs, such as aid to dependent children, and use of the progressive tax to narrow the growing gap between rich and poor. Jews are also far more prone to favor government support of the arts and research through agencies like the National Endowment for the Arts (NEA) and the National Endowment for the Humanities (NEH).

The reason for their change to libertarian liberalism may stem from their raised socioeconomic status since the turn of the century. Yet, the fact that they are no longer a have-not group does not help us explain the altruism Jews continue to display in their liberal politics. It may be rooted in the Judaic faith, whose tenets of social justice remain latent in communal memory, even though few Jews are religiously observant. A more immediate reason for the change to a libertarian liberalism is because the institutional engines that moved Jews to liberalism, especially the Jewish labor movement, have become weaker. Today, it is the vicarious liberalism taught in the university that has become its new engine. Survey research informs us that the political positions Jews assume are correlated most highly with their level of education. The higher the level, the more liberal. Jews boast America's highest level of formal education. Beyond that, the Jewish liberal imagination, which customarily underplays the role of power in human affairs, was confronted with the practical need to support and nurture Israel. American Jewry acts as Israel's advocate before the American government. That has compelled Jewish liberals to confront the realities of political power in the world. Israel's need for loans, military equipment, and diplomatic support have lent a temporal sectarian cast to its political culture that is often at odds with the universalist temper of the liberal sensibility.

Jewish voters were as loath to abandon the merit system as they were Israel. The conflict with African Americans that began with the Ocean Hill–Brownsville debacle in 1968 reflected the new-found sense among Jews that group interests must be protected. When American liberalism came to occupy itself almost exclusively with the problem of racial justice during the Johnson administration, Jewish voters did not quite make the turn. It was at that juncture that they gave up their claim to being the most liberal constituency in the electorate.

But the actual change began two decades earlier with the American Jewish reaction to the Holocaust. Central to the liberal imagination is the assumption that there is some place in the political world—the Oval Office, the Vatican, the corridors of the League of Nations or the United Nations—where a civilizing spirit can be mobilized to protect any group's being read out of the "universe of obligation." That universe is based on a recognition that all human beings are members of the human family and therefore worthy of concern. The absence of such recognition is a familiar attitude preceding genocide. But during the Holocaust, this central tenet of liberalism was not operative. One out of every three Jews was allowed to perish while witnessing governments and institutions like the churches stood idly by. Liberalism was exposed as an empty, powerless sentiment that could not be relied upon to fend off evil intent. Such exposure should have been sufficient to shake Jewish faith in liberalism. That Jewish liberalism nevertheless emerged from the war is evidence that its roots went deeper than the Enlightenment to Judaic sources.

Historically, liberal democracy has been closely associated with the process of secularization, which we examine next. In its penchant for individual rights and freedom, American liberalism resonates the core assumptions of America's "hard" secularism. It is that mindset that has caused American Jewry to face its most difficult challenges.

Moderns view the world through a secular prism. But when viewed from the Jewish context, that seemingly simple truth encounters problems because secularism already has a specific reference in Jewish history. Like the general phenomenon, it pertains to the movement that broke with religious tradition and rabbinic authority in favor of some form of worldly ideology, like the socialism carried forward by the Bund or the Zionist-oriented labor parties (Poale Zion). But as used in these essays, the term *secularism* encompasses all the contradictory values and aspirations that are contained in modernity. It is that desire in modern persons to be free, autonomous individuals, able to achieve self-realization in an open, democratic society in which they participate voluntarily. Their mentality is temporal and scientific; and above all else, secular persons are involved in the "pursuit of happiness."

No American subculture has been more receptive to secularism than American Jewry; and in survey after survey, it is shown to be America's most irreligious subculture. Jews tend more often to consider themselves atheists or agnostics, and they are less likely to be members of a religious congregation or attend religious services. Some find the roots of American Jewry's survival crisis in that overweening desire to be modern and secular. It has left its synagogues empty, its rabbis without authority, and its once extensive network of organizations ineffectual. It was partly the individuation and privatism inherent in secularism that caused the disunity that prevented American Jewry from adequately responding to the Holocaust. Nor was it able to regain community cohesiveness even after its successful effort to establish Israel. Today, its fragmentedness is again apparent. Its family life, whose high quality had assured that there was a ready instrument to transmit Jewish culture to the next generation, has been subject to all the stresses of modernity. The once comparatively low Jewish divorce rate now matches that of the majority culture. Each new problem raised by secularism, whether it is intermarriage or the acceptability of female or gay rabbis, buffets the fragile synagogue structure, leaving it still weaker.

Yearly, the gap grows wider between those who are observant and those who consider themselves secular and therefore free of the strictures of religious law. Just as in the Christian world, in which art was separated from religion, church from state, and ethics from etiquette, so Judaism, the religion, became separated from Jewishness, the living culture of the Jewish people. Modernity fragmented the holistic fabric of premodern Jewish life, much the same way it fragmented Christianity. It was in the sense of Jewishness, now separated from Judaism, that the secular spirit anchored itself. A secular Jew is one who believes it is possible to be Jewish without being Judaic.

Judging from the weakened Jewish condition in America, that assumption seems not to be born out by reality. A recognizably Jewish ethnic culture with its own language was not able to sustain itself beyond the immigrant generation. America's powerful solvent of acculturation undermined not only religious institutions, schools, and rabbinic academies but also ethnic institutions like the Yiddish theater and the press. Today, American Jewry no longer produces a culture of its own but lives on a memory sometimes transmitted through American popular culture in whose development and marketing Jews play a prominent role. Its best known artifact may be the musical *Fiddler on the Roof*.

The loss of the immigrant Yiddish-speaking culture meant that a secular Jewish cultural net, which might somehow have held Jews who could no longer adhere to the faith but wanted nevertheless to live within Jewish communal bounds, no longer existed. Such a world existed in prewar eastern Europe and permitted a secularizing Jew to live a full, albeit secular, Jewish life. In contrast, when American Jews abandoned the congregation, they frequently fell out of the Jewish world altogether. A powerful Jewish secular current first swept away much of the religious tradition only to find itself undermined by America's seductive popular culture.

By the twenties, signs that all was not well within the Jewish community were everywhere, from the decline in the number of Jews observing the dietary laws to the falling readership of the Yiddish press and declining attendance at the Yiddish theater. But measuring the well-being of the Jewish enterprise by a spiritual or cultural yardstick had itself become a victim of modernity. Success was now measured in secular terms like per capita income, degree of professionalism, years of schooling, and standard of living. Judged by such a measure, Jews were doing well. The anti-Semitic rhetoric of Henry Ford in articles in the *Dearborn Independent* and the exclusionary admission policy of Harvard notwithstanding, they shared fully in the prosperity of the twenties.

From his position as a professor of homiletics at the Jewish Theological Seminary, Rabbi Mordecai Kaplan, the founder of the Reconstructionist movement, could sense American Jewry's deep spiritual malaise. For him, as for others, the answer was somehow to accommodate the faith to the new secular mentality, to take it to where the Jewish people had located themselves. But like other endeavors that sought to bridge the gulf between Judaism and Jewishness, between the religious and the secular, it proved to be unpersuasive. Budgets in the Jewish Centers, which had also become popular in the Reform movement, appropriated more money for secular activities, such as maintaining a ballroom dance program or swimming lessons for the younger set, than for maintaining the religious sanctuary and school. Second- and third-generation American-born Jews were no longer as knowledgeable as their parents about Jewish texts and traditions. They often seemed unable to maintain their cultural portfolio with the same care as they did their financial investments.

There was something in the freedom that secularism generated, especially the "hard" libertarian secularism of America, that made finding a middle road between the religious tradition and the modern life-style difficult. Not only was church separated from state but for American Jewry, it was also separated from the interior life of the

Jewish people. They used their freedom to throw off the constraints of a religion that had laws about everything from what to eat to the fulfillment of marital obligations.

The new secular persons, who placed themselves in the center of the universe and who were convinced that modern science would allow humankind to control it, could not take the supernatural character of religion seriously. Convinced of the equality of all human beings, talk of special covenants and chosenness smacked of a premodern tribalism. These new free Jews, who were not really free at all, would not allow themselves to be fettered by religious fiat, although they sometimes bound themselves with political ideology whose claims on the self were no less demanding. Some theorize that these ideologies were in fact substitutes for religion and, as in the case of socialism, shared some basic ethical principles. But ultimately, it would not only be the churches and synagogues whose hold had been weakened but all institutions and ideologies that demanded total commitment. In today's America, there are few recruits for monastic orders.

Still, when a community has survived for millennia, it would be foolish to underestimate the vitality of its underlying now-latent ethos. This is not the first instance in its long history that Judaism has had to adapt to difficult circumstances. Hellenism as a cultural force has faded into the past while Judaism, after adopting some Helenistic elements, survives. For a similar outliving of secularism, some means of retaining its corporateness must be found. Judaism must go beyond the rhetoric of the United Jewish Appeal (UJA) slogan, "we are one," which fills the air though Jews can see eye to eye on very little. Yet, secularism has not affected the extraordinary philanthropic largess of such Jews, though the mandate for giving stems from a religious commandment they no longer know. Most American Jews today still remember something because they have in practice located themselves somewhere along the axis at one end of which is the extreme secular position, on the other, the ultra Orthodox. Where that point may be depends on family history and the search for comfort that is also central in modern life. Still, the individuating impulse inherent in the secular life style goes forward among all modern persons, including the Jews of modernity.

Jacob R. Marcus has called this period the Golden Age of American Judaism. Jews are secure in their middle-class status. They consider themselves to be Americans and are fully accepted as such. They play a disproportionate role among the managerial, scientific, cultural, and opinion-making elites who shape and manage American society. The scientific and cultural enterprise in America makes full use of Jewish talent and energy. Some believe that, even when considered in terms of Jewish culture and religious tradition, the picture is not without hope. It is based on some unpredictable things that have happened. For example, with the decline of the public school system, which served earlier Jewish generations well, Jewish day schools are growing in number and impact. Jewish rabbinic academies suffer no dearth of enrollment, and university presses and commercial publishers produce more books on Jewish subjects than ever before in Jewish history. For the first time in millennia, with the creation of Israel, Jews are again organized in time and space. Half a century after having suffered radical biological and cultural losses during the Holocaust, Jews seem to have regained the confidence to go forward.

What we are witnessing, argue some, is not disintegration but transformation. That does not mean an abandonment of faith but rather the transmutation of its basic principles to accord with the modern sensibility. The messianic impulse appears again as the search for justice and world peace, exile is transformed into a priestly mission to the nations, choseness becomes avocation. Most important, the religious sensibility that was once public, commanding, and communal becomes, in modernity, internalized, private, and searching.

To balance the loss of communalism, the secularized Jew boasts a high level of professional skills that can serve as a new source of power and influence as the proportion of Jewish voters declines. Jews are America's earliest and most efficient contraceptors, and their proportion of the population has declined from a high of 3.7 percent to less than 2.5 percent today. In numbers and urgency of agenda, they are overshadowed by African and Hispanic Americans. In contrast, the proportion of Jews in medicine, law, the professoriat, and the sciences, a source of influence and power in modern societies, is disproportionately high. During the Holocaust years, the numerous secular Jewish scientists involved in the development of the atomic bomb in the Manhattan project or the prominent secular Jews around Roosevelt were not mobilized. But today, such Jews can often be persuaded and even educated to recognize a Jewish need and to use their personal influence in its behalf.

The fear that secular Jews, unanchored to the ethical system embodied in Judaism, would lose their moral compass has not been borne out. But recently the large number of Jews who were involved in inside trading and other financial scandals did cause apprehensiveness among American Jewry. For a group that prides itself on its civic virtue and also retains some fear of rejection, that disgraceful behavior was a hard pill to swallow. Nonetheless, secular Jews are as likely to be persons of moral stature as are observant ones. Natan Scharansky, the "prisoner of conscience" whom many consider the most heroic Jew of this generation, drew his moral strength from secular sources.

There may also be something in the formation of secular identity that, by eschewing the benefits that come from a sense of belonging, by its inner-directedness, becomes immune from the greatest evil of our time: human beings' enthusiastic participation in genocidal murder. Because of their need to belong only to themselves, such Jews have been disparagingly called "rootless cosmopolitans." Strangely, they are considered a bane by both the nativist anti-Semite, who questions their loyalty and patriotism, and by some religious Jews, who see in them all the deracination inherent in the modern. Yet, as the most advanced representatives of secular identity, they offer to society and to the Judaism from which they are once removed, a productive, unthreatening, tolerant element. True, it is unlikely that they will be found in the religious congregation or deeply involved in the study of Jewish texts. But they are also absent from the howling mobs of Hitler or Khomeini followers at Nuremberg or Tehran party rallies. They cannot be commanded, but neither can they be misled by charismatic figures.

Whether American Judaism can survive in the free secular atmosphere of America is a question more inherent than openly stated in these essays. The answer ultimately depends on whether Judaic values, laws, and practices can be passed on to the next generation. Historians make poor prophets, and so only partial and qualified answers will be found here. But one thing is apparent: there can be no continuity without adjustment by both secular change agents and observant guardians of the faith. Young secular Jews are not ready to surrender the freedom and the opportunity for self invention proffered by a free, secular American society that accepts them. Their religious spirit has been internalized and lacks the specificity of Judaism. But they are open to change and would involve themselves in religion if they could do so on their own terms. They have become searchers.

They realize that something is amiss in the postmodern world of which they are part. It is a world in which the agencies of social control—the family, the church, the school, the fraternal orders—that together compose the weave of civic society have become weaker. At the same time, the development of internalized controls that were posited as part of the maturation process of the secular person are little in evidence. Varying with the community, a given percentage of the population never develops such controls, that is to say, never achieves the secular model of *citoyen,* an autonomous, self-actualized, yet responsible individual. The rising tide of violence in our cities correlates most highly with the ever-increasing degree of freedom that is the perennial quest at the heart of secular political culture. The result in the postmodern American world is that there are neither extrinsic nor intrinsic controls, a sure formula for chaos. That lack of controls is already observable in the cities with which Jews have cast their lot.

The new generation of Jews seeks to regain that sense of belonging that Jewish communalism provided heretofore. That is perhaps the reason why they are so prominent as members of communes and cults. Yet even when they long to hear a commanding voice, they can no longer heed it. And the internal voice they are supposed to have developed, when it exists as all, is weak. That is the essence of the impasse that secularized American Jewry faces.

This impasse leads to the survival dilemma described in the final group of essays. In Judaism, we have a corporate, highly legalistic faith that intrudes deeply into the psyche of the adhering self. But modernity assumes that modern persons can develop their own moral compass and, in the name of personal freedom, prohibit such a deep intrusion. The survival dilemma posed by secular modernity is whether the corporate communal character at the heart of Judaism can accommodate the individuation that is the quintessence of modern secular life. It is whether Jewishness can become again a living culture without its primary religious ingredient, Judaism, from which it has become separated.

PART ONE

History

1

Jewish Survival in America

> Remember the days of old,
> think of the generations long ago;
> ask your father to recount it
> and your elders to tell the tale.
> —*Deuteronomy* 32:7

THE AMERICAN JEWISH HISTORICAL SOCIETY is the oldest "ethnic" historical society in America. How strange then to note that, notwithstanding a surfeit of scholars trained in the historian's craft, a growing network of local societies, and a remarkably sustained presence in America of over three centuries, until recently the American Jewish community did not possess an adequate historical portrait of itself. The thoughts that follow are about the implications of that missing history for Jewish survival in America. Jewish communities in the Diaspora have traditionally relied on history to invent themselves. The Jewish God is present in history, and it is in history rather than in territory or sovereignty that Jews discover reasons to remain a people. Today, American Jewry is involved in a melancholy search for exemption from the gradual erosion of group identity that seems to be the fate of all America's subcultures. Such exemption is inconceivable without the possession of a "usable past." Seen from that perspective, the work of historians becomes more crucial than generally believed, and historians are thus a crucial component in the struggle for Jewish survival in America.

This essay appeared originally in *American Jewish History* 71:4 (June 1982). A new conclusion has been added.

The founders of the American Jewish Historical Society did not think in such dire terms. They were intent on making Jewish life in America more secure and comfortable by demonstrating that American Jewry was "present at the creation." That would legitimize the Jewish presence in America, which was challenged by the virulent anti-Semitism of the 1890s. Their purpose was frankly apologetic. Oscar Straus, founder of the society in 1892 and its first president, commissioned Meyer Kayserling to write a book on the Columbus voyage of discovery with special attention to Jewish involvement. The result was the still well-known study *Christopher Columbus and the Participation of the Jews in the Spanish and Portuguese Discoveries*, which was published in 1894. For the German Jewish stewards like Strauss, history was assigned the task of facilitator and ameliorator.

The rationale of that role is still apparent today. The decade of the nineties was a troubled one in America. It began with the announcement by the Bureau of the Census that the frontier, the "cutting edge" between civilization and the "wilderness," no longer existed. The Westernization process which had shaped the American experience and formed its national character for over three centuries was no more. For the first time, America was locked in. It would spend the next century seeking an equivalent seminal experience to call forth its energy and release its latent talent. More immediate was the effect of the loss of a "safety valve," which syphoned off the superabundant energy of the American people. Now, turned inward upon itself, it would generate the turbulence that marked the nineties. The new anti-Semitism that Straus and his cohort saw evidence of everywhere was undoubtedly a symptom of that larger "psychic crisis." The bitter labor-management conflict that marked the silver miners strike at Cour d'Alene, the Homestead Steel strike and the Pullman strike in the first half of the decade seemed to bear out the Marxist exhortations regarding "class struggle," a sensibility clearly enhanced by the class-conflict character of the election of 1896. Projected against the steep downturn of business activity and full-scale depression in 1894, after more than a decade of business expansion and consolidation, the portents for trouble were ominous. There were no "cushions" or "nets" during the depression of 1894 nor was the suffering endured in silence, as the march of Coxey's army on Washington seeking government relief indicated.

There were puzzling factors about the strident anti-Semitism that Straus and his fellow stewards witnessed. There had rarely been a paucity of anti-Semitic rhetoric from all quarters of American society. But why did the protesting farmers of the South and West, who were least in contact with the highly urbanized Jewish population, nevertheless pick them out for a special animus. Moreover, the leaders of the Populist revolt combined traditional anti-Semitic images (moneylenders in temples, crucifixions upon crosses of Gold) with primitive socialist conspiratorial ones (the Rothschild banking conspiracy, parasitic Jewish middlemen) in such a poisonous amalgam that its force would fuel the anti-Semitic imagination for the first half of the twentieth century. When added to the news of depredations in Russia, Romania, and other nations as well as the Dreyfus affair in France (1894), there was sufficient evidence to convince even the most skeptical that the threat to Jewish well-being was omnipresent. Straus was perhaps naïve in believing an exposure to a heroic version of Jewish history would correct the mistaken image of Jews in the minds of the Gentile population. Underlying it was the assumption that anti-Semitism could be eliminated by changing the characters of Jews or the image of what they were thought to be.

Jews living in the 1890s might also take note of a disjuncture between the perceived threat and the reality of what was happening to the American Jewish enterprise. Although not as accelerated as popularizers would later claim, the German Jewish climb to affluence was as remarkable as it was atypical. By 1890, peddling, which served for many as the entry-level occupation, had been replaced by storekeeping. A small group had gone further to large-scale merchandising and garment manufacturing. Their talent for "courageous enterprising" had attracted them to a wide variety of businesses. A still smaller group, joined and buttressed by a similar group in Europe, went on to become private commercial bankers. It was the only subculture on the American scene to generate a commercial elite on such a scale. It was a singular phenomenon, the visible peak of a Jewish success story amply, if reluctantly, documented by the Dunn ratings. This commercial success was paralleled by equally impressive achievements on the community level. In 1889, Isaac M. Wise, the founder of the Reform movement in America, placed the organizational capstone, the Central Conference of American Rabbis, on that burgeoning new branch of Judaism. The establishment of new congregations, especially in the growing cities of the West, suggested to adherents that the Reform branch was peculiarly suited to confront the problems Judaism faced in American society. Even the most crucial problem, whether a quarter of a million dispersed Jews adhering to Reform Judaism would be able to transfer a distinct Jewish culture to the next generation, was being solved by the arrival of masses of Jewish culture carriers mostly from Eastern Europe. For the German Jewish natives, the new arrivals were not precisely the kind of human clay they would have preferred, but they were optimistic that these new Jews, who appeared so strange, could be reshaped in their own image. (They were destined to be disappointed.) Finally there was the great pride felt when the founder of the society, Oscar Straus, became secretary of commerce in 1906. For many, it was all the evidence required that America's ruling elite had finally become convinced of what the society had been saying all along; Jews did indeed belong.

What a paradox then to note nine decades later that the American Jewish Historical Society, like all American Jewish agencies and organizations, confronts problems that, in some measure, are directly traced to that same sense of acceptance and belonging so much desired by the founders. Ultimately, it is that acceptance, the willingness of American society to fulfill and even go beyond the emancipation transaction, which lies behind the waning sense of identity as a distinct people that is manifest everywhere in Jewish America. Looking at the Eastern immigrant, Oscar Straus and his colleagues might have felt that they were blessed with an excess of Jewish culture or at least one whose potential for becoming American could be questioned. How contemporary survivalists wish we possessed that excess of cultural energy. What was then perceived as a challenge to the Americanization process could be used today to reenergize the waning sense of Jewish group identity. They felt a special need to fill out the American component of the dual American-Jewish identity. Ninety years later, we need to revitalize the Jewish half. There is a perpetual tug-of-war between the two. The problem remains survival, but it is no longer from the threat of a hostile world; it is from the weakening of the internal group bonds, grown slack in a benevolent host society.

What American Jewry together with other Jewries living in "modern" cultures no longer possess is the ability to create the total environment that produces a Jew who follows the tenets of the faith as if prompted by an internal Pavlovian bell. Modern Jews do not learn the richness of their cultural tradition with their mother's milk. The worthwhileness of the tradition must be taught, and many will argue that it is precisely on those who are guardians of its history on whom that special mission devolves. The special sense Jews have of their identity is in good measure contained in their history. "For modern Jews," observes the historian Michael Meyer, "a conception of their past is no mere academic matter. It is vital to their self definition. Contemporary forms of Jewish identity are all rooted in some view of Jewish history which sustains them and serves as their legitimation." The uniqueness of Jewish history stems not only from its substance but also from the role it plays in generating a sense of peoplehood. The Jewish presence in history is not dependent on the normal accouterments of power—national sovereignty, territory, military force. In its stead, history is compelled to play the binding role that these more tangible factors play for others. Jewish identity is an idea embodied in its history.

The noted Islamicist Bernard Lewis speaks of a "corporate memory" binding the Jewish people together by shared experience. Similarly, Franz Rosenzweig (1886–1929), the founder of the influential "Jüdishes Lehrhaus" in 1920 saw the Bible as a form of history and the writing of Jewish history as a continuation of the "holy work of writing Torah." Simon Dubnow (1860–1941) became convinced that it was the absence of a spatial dimension for much of the history of the Jews that gave them an especially strong sense of their history. Its high moral content and "soulfullness" he attributed to the travail Jews experienced throughout their long disparate history and to the fact that Jewish national consciousness was based on the spiritual rather than the mundane ideas of race and territory. Virtually all postemancipation Jewish historians have sought in history a clue to Jewish distinctiveness and the mystery of their millenial survival. Salo Baron, the late doyen of contemporary Jewish historians, defined his subject matter as simply the examination of the idea of Judaism as it was developed and carried forward by the Jewish people. He believed that the Jews, rather than the ancient Greeks, were superior practitioners of the historian's craft. Their history demonstrated "that fine combination of factual statement, pragmatic interpretation, and charming presentation." The intricate formulations of the historian stand in contrast to those of Daniel Bell, who lays aside his mantle as an outstanding secular intellectual to reveal an emotional attachment to his Jewishness that he defines as being part of "a community woven by memory." It is embodied in Jewish ritual and prayer. "In the Yiskor," he acclaims, "through memory, I am identified as a Jew."

For Jews, then, history is compelled to carry a heavier burden than merely to record what happened to their people. Historians have traditionally sought to find in that story the rationale, whether it was the idea of the one God or simply a sense of moral elevation to spur the Jewish enterprise forward. What happens when such a history is not available, as it was not for American Jewry? It is then not only a reflection of a lack of group identity but also becomes an accelerator of its demise.

Few can doubt the crucial link between Jewish history and identity, especially in the Diaspora. What is puzzling is that American Jewry, a community of 5.6 million whose over three centuries of history has had considerable impact on both the American and the Jewish world, does not yet have a historical portrait of itself that might inform its adherents about who and what Judaism is and where they belong. The absence is not caused by a scarcity of trained historians. The number of Jews who practice Clio's art is disproportionately high in writing all kinds of history. Moreover, we are actually embarrassed by a surplus of riches as is reflected in the growing number of local Jewish historical societies. (Probably no other subgroup in America has sprouted so many local historical societies.) There are also two major agencies and archives, each with a respectable journal. Any other subgroup would be satisfied to have one such agency. Withal, a complete and satisfying history of its American experience was not available until recently.

The reason for its late appearance lies partly in the special problems the scholar encounters in writing the history of a Jewish community ensconced in a society so plastic and absorbent of other cultures that the researcher is continually faced with questioning the validity of his scholarly assumptions and determining the precise boundaries of his subject. The matter of the application of the assumptions of modern scholarship is especially interesting. Historians of the American Jewish experience undergo normal university training in the liberal arts, where emphasis is on universalism and where at one time the study of an ethnic group may have appeared to be too sectarian. The specialized training in history stresses value freeness, detachment, and objectivity. The assumption is that, equipped with proper training and other necessary skills, the modern scholar can force Jewish history to yield its truths much the way other histories have been compelled to do. A well-trained French or English historian can write Jewish history much as Jews can write French and English history. In fact, an outsider who need not struggle for objectivity and detachment might, in theory, do better. Yet, one can question whether the tenets of modern scholarship as taught in the university are appropriate and useful for studying Jewish history, whose role in the Jewish community is more than simply knowing the Jewish past. Is it possible that there is something so idiosyncratic about the Jewish presence in history, considering the fact that it is a community based on an idea and on history itself, that it resists the tools and thwarts the assumptions of modern scholarship? The answer to the enigma that millenial Jewish survival poses for scholars, for example, surely lies not in what Judaism shared with other civilizations but in how it was different, something it possessed internally not discoverable by historians. Had the "laws" of history applied, as Arnold Toynbee sought to make them apply, then by all rights the Jewish presence should have vanished from the historical stage long ago. It is then not necessary to be Jewish to be a student of Jewish history, but it is necessary to be aware of the peculiar resistance the Jewish experience offers to the tools and tenets of modern scholarship. The latter point is especially true in the study of American Jewish history because American historiography, from which it partly derives, is craft-oriented and unaccustomed to handling an idea-oriented subculture.

In the social sciences, it is assumed that everything should be subject to examination. They do so by mimicking the process of science, which is based on separating things into component parts and by endless classification. It is at that juncture that the difficulty starts. Just as Judaism itself has traditionally been holistic so that it resists the separations of modernity, theory from practice, ethics from etiquette, public from private, art from religion, and so forth, so the history of the Jews resists the separation of scholar from subject essential to modern scholarship. If the truths of Jewish history lie in its wholeness, then the required distancing leads to distortion and fragmentation.

The problem of classification, that is of objectifying the Jewish historical experience so that it can become a finite object of study, similarly eludes the net spun by modern scholars. It seems impossible to classify modern Jewry. In America, they have been known as a race, a hyphenate group, an ethnic group, and a religious denomination. That resistance to classification is itself evidence of an idiosyncratic history. Like all history of diasporic communities, American Jewish history has a basic duality. On the one hand, American Jews have adapted to as well as adopted the culture, the language, the very tone of American society, so much so that they sometimes appear to

be "exaggerated" Americans. On the other, they retain something dis-
tinctive that is especially conspicuous in their abiding interest and
concern for beleaguered Jewish communities abroad. The attempt to
get diplomatic intercession for their brethren has been more sus-
tained, more systematic, and more persistently sought than by any
other ethnic group acting in the political arena. So tightly entwined
are these two strands that the historian has difficulty determining
what belongs to the preexisting stream of Jewish civilization and
what to the American. Few would gainsay that what transpires in
American society, whether it is a recession or a loss of direction, af-
fects American Jews, "When the Christian world sneezes," a Jewish
proverb has it, "the Jewish world catches a cold." Yet, the same Jewry
so deeply and comfortably ensconced in American society takes
many of its signals and defining myths from the stream of general
Jewish history. Its history is periodized by the waves of immigration
spurred by events in Iberia, central Europe, and finally eastern
Europe. The colonial Sephardic commercial elite and the nineteenth-
century German Jewish banking group ("Our Crowd") owe their ex-
istence in part to a link to Jewish communities elsewhere. Similarly,
the basic political and religious ideas that have shaped American
Jewry's thinking were incubated in the Jewish communities of Europe
and carried here by immigrants. American Jewry recognizes that link
by its overriding concern for the welfare and security of beleaguered
Jewish communities abroad. That concern is perhaps the most Jewish
aspect of the American Jewish identity. It is a community leaning out-
ward as if better to hear the signals and to address the needs of less
fortunate Jewish communities. From one point of view, American
Jewry is merely another Diaspora in a history full of Diasporas; from
another, it is an American ethnic group adrift in a pluralistic society
seeking some mooring that might exempt it from "melting." The two
strands are so tied together that it is almost impossible to determine
to whose history the American Jewish experience belongs. Separating
them will produce a distorted history. The historian must be content
somehow to approximate the peculiar amalgam of two cultures and
histories, which in reality American Jewry is.

Finally, as if the problems of writing American Jewish history
were not sufficiently vexing, there are some Zionists who maintain
with considerable fervor that such a history does not exist because
diasporic Jewish communities can only be the object of someone
else's history. The Israeli novelist Hanoch Bartov has one of his char-

acters declare, "a people that doesn't live in its own country and doesn't rule itself has no history." He goes on:

> You see we never made our own history, the Gentiles always made it for us. Just as they turned out the lights for us and lit the stove for us and milked the cow for us on the Sabbath, so they made history for us the way they wanted and we took it whether we liked it or not.[1]

Even had Mr. Bartov's character been a faithful reader of *American Jewish History*, there is little likelihood of a change of mind. It is not a matter of evidence but of definition. It is part of the notion, held by a small number of Zionists of extreme persuasion, who maintain that Jewish life in the Diaspora is in any case doomed. They construct a vicious circle from which there is no out. Powerless and without specific identity, American Jewry they insist, can have no history and therefore lacks identity because it does not possess the history in which it is contained.

If there can be no American Jewish history then, the growing number of scholars who are today writing the best history thus far produced for American Jewry are unaware of it. They are in fact faced with the opposite problem: an information explosion of such magnitude that merely screening the amount of data available and separating them from pseudo data poses extraordinary difficulties. The impact of that explosion is twofold. It directly effects not only how the future history of the American Jewry will be written but what will be written about. Secondly, it makes the role of support institutions, most notably well-managed archives, more crucial than ever. The "new" history is less concerned about the beauty and elegance of the historical narrative and more about bringing facts to bear. Its slogan might well be "one fact is worth a thousand well turned phrases." Because so many things that were merely speculative or intuitive can now be confirmed, the story in the historical narrative, which was often its most compelling aspect, is overshadowed. Instead, there are tables and charts and quantifications that describe a discreet phenomenon. That is the primary reason why a one-man tour de force such as that undertaken by Salo Baron has grown rare. Few working historians have the sense that they have mastered the entire historical canvas or that it can be known in its entirety. Most research works today are characterized by discreteness. They probe one de-

cade in depth or one generational cohort, one episode, even one lo-
cality, such as Harlem. If the historian is really ambitious he may
work on one process, social mobility in a city, or family life and the
process of acculturation in a specific community.

The deluging of a particular historical event or process with
data makes it "source intensive." The historian requires many more
original sources before the narrative can be shaped. That means that
historical archives, or whatever data retrieval agencies will be called
in the future, will be more crucial than ever to the historian. Because
much of the new data must be retrieved from various sources and are
quantified, computers and other "machines" will be required to dis-
till, order, and present the information. In the future, history will
more than ever be produced out of raw material. That has a special
impact on American Jewish historiography. As our archivists in Wal-
tham and Cincinnati and other places work feverishly to catalog and
inventory newly received material, it becomes increasingly apparent
that they must run merely to stand still. If an investment to computer-
ize the archives is not soon made, they will become obsolete in one
generation. Moreover, "source intensity" virtually requires an overall
accession policy to apply to the entire Jewish community. That re-
quirement contains the greatest irony of all because American Jewry,
traditionally lacking coherence and cohesiveness, needs to produce a
history that requires an organized community at least as far as record
maintenance and collection are concerned. That would prevent the
discarding or simply the rotting away of precious records because
their value for the historian is not known. Paradoxically, the reverse
process, the awareness that maintaining control of one's records
means controling the writing of one's history, is equally problematic
from the historian's point of view. Many Jewish agencies—the United
Jewish Appeal, the American Jewish Joint Distribution Committee,
the American Jewish Committee, and doubtlessly other agencies—
have chosen no to deposit their records in a central archive. For the
archivist, the problem of having sufficient space and monetary re-
sources to put such records in working order is solved; but for the
historian, crucial original source material could become inaccesible.

The founders of the American Jewish Historical Society linked
the writing of history to the ever-present Jewish survival problem.
The history of triumphs and contributions they preferred was meant
to disarm would-be enemies. That perception of needing to earn one's
right to the promise of America has changed. Their burgeoning inter-
marriage rate and their high economic and social status are signs that

Jews live in a society that beckons them to enter and amply rewards their skills and energy. Yet, the anxiety about survival (the term *continuity* is used today) seems more urgent than ever, as is its link to the writing of its history. What has changed is our way of organizing and producing that history. The apologetics and self-celebration characteristics of the society's early endeavors have given way to a historiography that renders the American Jewish experience with its failures as well as its triumphs. The historian's role today is to furnish American Jewry and the host nation to which it is committed a full and objective portrait of what it once was and where it has been. But in the case of American Jewish history, we go beyond producing another ethnic history. A full and objective history also inevitably serves the twin requisites of group survival, for only by being armed with such self-knowledge can American Jewry become aware of where it is going and how it will get there.

2

Jewish Exceptionalism

GEORGE SANTAYANA once observed that "American life is a powerful solvent,"[1] and so it was for the millions of immigrants who have been reshaped in America's image for over three centuries. For the most part, it was a benevolent, slow process achieved more by seduction than by coercion. Once Jews had left the "old home," America substituted its own culture, which was tolerant enough to allow for the retention of some of the sentimental facets of the old. Much ethnicity today reflects that sentimentalism.

A major theme of this discussion is that the Americanizing solvent did not work the same way for Jews, and it is that fact that continues to differentiate them in the American culture. To be sure, Jewish immigrants became Americanized, even "exaggerated Americans," but they did so on different terms than other immigrants who, having abandoned the territory of the "old home," became malleable human clay ready for remolding. Jews also have an "old home," but it is not the country from which they emigrated. It was because the society from which they fled despised them that they were compelled to set out on their perilous journey. Jewish immigrants were shaped by a culture not rooted in territorial space, and mere physical removal could not separate them from it. It is a residual feeling of belonging to the Jewish people that gives American Jewry a strange and persistent duality that is reflected in virtually every facet of their experience in America. They are in America but never completely of it. Something

This essay appeared originally in *Jewish Life in the United States: Perspectives from the Social Sciences,* ed. Joseph B. Gittler (New York Univ. Press, 1981), under the title, "Jewish Life in the United States: Perspectives from History."

is held back. American Jewry seems always to be trying to achieve a delicate balance between two cultural pulls, the tangible American, with which they have cast their temporal lot, and the preexisting Jewish, which continues to lay claim to much of their spirit.

I have called that phenomenon "American Jewish exceptionalism," by which I mean not its superior achievement but the unique duality it possesses.[2] It bedevils those social scientists who naïvely seek a classification, ethnic group, religious denomination, and hyphenate to make their task easier. I leave these problems to them in the certain knowledge that none of their categories will precisely fit American Jewry. Instead, let us examine how this internal tension between the American and the Jewish plays itself out, first in the writing of American Jewish history and then in the actual Jewish experience in America.

Confronted by two independent historical streams, the historian of American Jewry faces unique problems of perspective. To whose history does American Jewry belong? Is it part of American migration, or ethnic or urban history, or a brief and as yet unheralded chapter in the millenial stream of Jewish history, another Diaspora in a history full of Diasporas? One can, for example, compare the American Jewish historical experience to that of other Jewries in the Western Hemisphere.[3] Previously, comparison of American Jewry with German Jewry was popular, especially during the Weimar Republic.[4] At the same time, one can read the American Jewish experience as being solely part of the American historical canvas. Two of the most prodigious workers in the field, the late Bertram Korn and Rudolf Glanz, used such an approach with fruitful results. But most historians find it impossible neatly to separate one from the other. They find that some amalgamation or at least some reference to the other stream is necessary if a full historical picture is to emerge.

Problems of historical perspective in viewing the history of the host culture can be especially vexing for the Jewish-conscious historian. As part of the process of self-identification, all cultures produce heroes and myths that define the values they hold dear. As members of the community, historians must take these elements into account because they are themselves subject to their impact and because heroes and myths tell us something about the society under study. But the Jewish historical perspective, which is richly furnished with its own heroes and myths, can find itself in conflict with what the host culture deems as heroic or important. Salo Baron uses the illustration of the Roman emperor Titus, who was favorably considered by Roman historians but who is rarely mentioned in rabbinic sources without the epithet *ha-rasha* (the wicked) because he is held responsible for the destruction of the temple.[5]

Such a lack of confluence abounds in a Jewish view of American history. What, for example, shall we do with Henry Ford, whom American historians consider an ingenious, if somewhat eccentric, mechanical whiz who successfully produced an automobile within the purchasing power of the average American and thereby changed the face of America? But from the Jewish perspective, he is also the man who fueled the anti-Semitic imagination in the xenophobic 1920s by publishing *The Protocols of the Elders of Zion* in the *Dearborn Independent*.[6] For most Americans, Charles A. Lindbergh may be a folk hero. His 1927 transatlantic flight symbolized the values small-town America held dear—coolness in the face of danger, love of nature, self-reliance, even inarticulateness. But Jews also noted in Lindbergh an easy ability to fall into Nazi-type racial attitudes, which held their group in low esteem.[7] General Ulysses S. Grant has gone down in American history as a somewhat mediocre president but nevertheless the military leader who saved the union by developing the strategy that finally brought the Confederacy to its knees. For Jewish historians, however, he is also the leader who issued Federal Order No. 11, the only instance of government-sponsored collective punishment of Jews in American history.[8]

Sometimes, an incident barely mentioned in American history books, such as the lynching of Leo Frank or the harassment of Jewish merchants in the Confederacy, warrants special attention from the Jewish perspective.[9] Every student knows the dramatic story of how William Jennings Bryan stampeded the 1896 Democratic convention in Chicago with his famous "Cross of Gold" speech. But the innocent use of that Christian metaphor, "You shall not crucify mankind upon a cross of gold," may strike the Jewish historian, who is aware of the deicide polemic and the link many Populists sought between the currency problem and Jewish moneylenders, as far from innocent. Much depends on how one looks at things and from what vantage. Thus, the outspoken editor of the *Jewish Spectator* maintained that much of what consists of American Jewish culture should not be sought in its contribution to American *belles lettres* or in its impact on popular culture, that is to say the culture actually generated by American Jews, but in the humanistic values like the love of learning, which originate in the Jewish religious tradition.[10]

An entire episode may look different from a Jewish perspective. For example, American historians may have given little attention to the role played by organized anti-Semitism in the isolationist trend of the 1930s. To be sure, an ethnic component has been found in the Midwest, but disillusionment with America's entry into World War I and other factors have been stressed.[11] A work by Gerard Smith emphasizes the link between isolationism and anti-Semitism. Spokesmen like Gerald L. K. Smith, William Pelley, Charles E. Coughlin, and Fritz Kuhn cloaked their cause in legitimacy and amplified their voice by successfully linking themselves to the isolationist nexus.[12] Then Charles A. Lindbergh, in Des Moines in September 1941, warned that Jews and anglophiles were pushing the nation into a war against the national interest. Jewish historians long ago noted a possible linkage between the thirties isolationism, the antirefugee policy, and anti-Semitism.[13]

In European history, the classic example of how a Jewish historical perspective differs from that held by non-Jewish historians can be gleaned from a prize-winning book by Lucy S. Dawidowicz.[14] She gives the Holocaust a centrality in World War II that is shared by few specialists in the field. It is not possible to dismiss such views as failure by the Jewish historian to muster sufficient detachment to write value-free history. There are many areas in American history—the abolitionist movement, the Populists, the Progessive movement, the Red Scare, and even the New Deal—that simply look different when viewed through Jewish eyes. That vision stems from a separate Jewish historical experience and identity that many Jewish historians, by no means all, carry with them. This combination of experience and identity is an example of how the duality of the Jewish presence penetrates even to the writing of history.

History is not a seamless garment. Historians divide the stream of events into periods, and how they do so indicates what they consider important and what ephemeral. Nowhere is the interaction between two separate historical streams, the American and the Jewish, more evident than in the different periodizations employed. The major periods in antebellum American historiography are the colonial period (which can be subdivided further), the revolutionary period, the national or federal period, the Era of Good Feeling, sectionalism, Jacksonian democracy, the Civil War, and so on. Of course, things are really not so neat because, at the same time, historians may employ topical ways of breaking up or organizing the time stream into such classifications as labor history, women's history, urban history, slavery, and the history of reform movements, among others.

Now, although American Jewish history also deals with such sequences, its major periodization originates in the stream of Jewish history. As outlined by Jacob Marcus, the dean of American Jewish history, the first period of Sephardic hegemony (1654–1820) is linked to the Iberian expulsion and the subsequent growth and influence of Jews and Maranos in the viceroyalties of Spanish America. The second period (1820–1920) is one of German-Jewish dominance and is again linked to the mass emigration of Jews triggered partly by the new wave of anti-Semitism during the Restoration period. The period of eastern Jewish predominance (1881–1920) is again related in part to the strident anti-Semitism of the governments of that region. Only the last period, which starts in 1921, called by Marcus simply the "American period," tested the strength of this linkage during the Holocaust.[15]

The existence of a periodization scheme whose reference points relate to Jewish rather than American history reflects the natural tension in American Jewish historiography created by two separate and independent pulls. That tension does not exist in a vacuum. It is a reflection of the duality that is present in the actual Jewish experience in America. Like all history, American Jewish history relates closely to the people whose story it seeks to tell. How could it be otherwise?

We turn next to four developments in that story—Jewish mobility, the Jewish labor movement, Jewish organizational life, and Jewish interest in foreign affairs—to demonstrate how a link to Jewish peoplehood, the memory of corporateness, has come virtually to define what remains Jewish about American Jewry. Under ordinary circumstances, the amazing success story of American Jewry would best be left to the sociologists or historians, who gleefully toll the numbers to prove their case.

But the story of Jewish mobility is so quintessentially American and, at the same time, so apparent in many Jewish communities the world over that it serves as an almost irresistible illustration of our theme of duality. Yet, describing its precise contours in America remains problematic. Few have been able to state with any precision how much more mobile Jews were than other subgroups in America. We know today that other immigrant groups have now also "made

it"; that is, they have gone beyond the founding Protestant denomina-
tions in income and job status.[16] Moreover, the Jewish climb "from
rags to riches" has not been nearly as uniform as has been imagined.
That much the discovery of the Jewish poor attests. But a consensus
has developed that Jews were somehow faster in their climb; they
leaped over the generational increments in income and job status to
which most other immigrant groups were heir.[17]

It seemed as if this society had released energy and talent that
had been stored up for millenia. But because the lovers of statistics,
paradigms, and trends have been primarily focused on the contempo-
rary picture, they have not realized that, during a three-century resi-
dency, American Jewry has actually repeated the success story three
times and has also produced three separate commercial elites. It did
not matter if it was an agricultural, preindustrial economy, as in the
colonial period, or a postindustrial one, as today; Jews were success-
ful on the terms laid down by the society. More interesting is the fact
that, to some extent, their success was contingent on connection with
a Jewish nexus.

The Sephardic Jews of colonial America produced a commercial
elite by doing many things, including the manufacture of spermaceti
candles and merchandising. But their greatest wealth came from their
participation in ocean commerce, which touched Africa and the West
Indies and found its American anchor in Newport, which, for a time,
boasted the largest Jewish community in colonial America. The suc-
cess of merchant princes like Aron Lopez was, in some measure, the
result of a strategic and profitable connection with the equally suc-
cessful Jewish merchants of the original Jewish communities in the
Carribean. The second elite, called "our crowd" by Stephen Birming-
ham, attached themselves to the westward movement, where they
filled a merchandising vacuum by peddling and by establishing stores.[18]

By the final decades of the nineteenth century, a small group of
the most successful merchants made their way into investment bank-
ing, where they were joined by an equally successful group of Jews
stemming from the banking houses established by Jews in Germany.[19]
Again, it was a conduit furnished by the connection with German and
European Jewish banking houses that contributed to their success.
These houses were important because they could supply the risk cap-
ital required by intense industrial development that occurred in
America after the Civil War.

The third wave of eastern European Jews repeated the success
story on different terms. First, they dominated the rapidly expanding

ready-to-wear garment industry that was previously the scene of German Jewish commercial activity. At the same time, they entered and developed many marginal industries, such as the second-hand business. Eastern Jewish involvement in commerce was, for various reasons, destined to be less sustained. A good number of the second and third generation chose to enter the professions rather than small business; so that today medicine, law, dentistry, and the professorial ranks are disproportionately practiced by Jews.[20]

In all three cases, we may take note of a phenomenon called "courageous enterprising," the peculiar ability of American Jews to strike out as pioneers into relatively new fields—such as fur trading in the colonial period or plastics today—or to take old components and combine them in a new way.[21] Many of the so-called egg-head millionaires, new Jewish millionaires of the post-World War II period, combined a professional skill, such as chemistry or engineering, with traditional business acumen to make their fortunes in plastics or transistors.[22]

Most important for our story, however, is not that a disproportionate number of Jews were successful in America but that such success stories were not confined to America. To some extent, Jewish success was a phenomenon that could be observed in all developing Western economies during the postemancipation period. The rapid mobility of Soviet Jewry in the 1920s, although it came about in "socialist" terms, indicates that we need not confine our story to the West. That is noteworthy because it raises the question of the sources of Jewish mobility. Does it stem from the relative openess of the American economy, or does its driving force come from within the Jewish culture and condition in the Diaspora? Or was it caused by the linkage of the two at a particularly fortunate historical juncture? We have seen how the success of the Sephardic and German Jews was based, at least partly, on a strategic position vis-à-vis other established Jewish communities. To some extent, even the dominance by eastern European Jews of the garment industry, which served as their principle economic base, was contingent on the prior role of German Jewish entrepreneurs.

When the full story of American Jewish mobility finally comes to light, it will be difficult to overlook the dual cultural generating force that was at its heart and that the historical focus reveals. Like so many facets of the American Jewish experience, Jewish success in America appears to rest partly on the preexisting Jewish culture (which gives it behavioral cues, a unique entrepreneurial vision, plus connections and capital); and American culture (which gives it a success ethos, economic opportunity, and an open society).

A parallel interconnectedness of the Jewish and American cultural stream can be noted in the remarkable development of the Jewish labor movement. The Jewish contribution to the business sector is matched by its contribution to American organized labor. The eastern European Jews were one of two American subgroups (the other was the German Americans) who organized their own labor movement. The existence of organized Jewish workers is a strange phenomenon related to the rapid proletarianization of Jews in the Russian Pale in the final quarter of the nineteenth century.[23] The process was intensified by the immigration and transplantation experience that converted many Jews from artisans, craftspersons, and petit merchants to mere "hands" in shops. The skills they possessed in the Pale were frequently not usable in the more advanced industrial economy of America. They were unaccustomed to thinking of themselves as factory workers; nor did they readily abandon aspiration levels, often reinforced in the new environment, that might more readily be associated with the middle class. We know that it was extremely difficult to organize them and keep them organized.[24] Indeed, their sojourn in the working class, which so won their loyalty, was temporary. It lasted but one generation. But during that eye blink in American history, the Jewish labor movement had a profound impact.

For the historian, the movement represents something of a paradox, for although the ideology it advocated and the methods it employed had a distinctly foreign, if not precisely Jewish flavor, it also served as a prime Americanizing agency, especially through the press. It was also the Jewish institution in America that came into possession of real power that could directly effect the lives of thousands of people. How that power was used, rather than the radical rhetoric it projected, tells the historian a great deal about its real character.[25]

For men like Samuel Gompers, the English-born Jewish cigar maker who came to lead the American Federation of Labor (AFL), the very idea of a separate labor movement based on the Jewishness of its rank and file smacked of a narrow parochialism. Undoubtedly, patrician "uptowners" shared that view because it resonated what they felt about all manifestations of Jewish separatism. But for individual Jewish immigrants, who perceived that they were different, separate Jewish locals seemed the most natural thing in the world. It did not mean that they did not want to be American. That wish was very dear to them. But they wanted to be Americans on their own terms, and their conception of how much of their original culture could be maintained in the New World was simply more optimistic. The Jewish labor movement therefore not only espoused a philosophy at odds with that of the mainline unions but its methods of organization from the top down also departed markedly from the normal local craft unions, which were the most enduring components of the American labor movement. The priority given by Terence Powderly's Knights of Labor to fraternalism and the cooperative movement seemed merely ameliorative to the radical intellectuals who organized the Jewish labor movement.[26]

The idea of business unionism based on "bread and butter" objectives lacked ideological depth. More crucial was the restrictionist position taken by the mainline organizations, which flew in the face of the Jewish interest. But it was the socialist approach of Jewish labor leaders that was the primary source of contention. Leaders like Samuel Gompers were convinced and so testified before congressional committees that the "pie in the sky" instrumentalist approach to unionism advocated by Jewish labor leaders was cynical and based on a fundamental misunderstanding of the American economy and culture.

Although men like Abraham Cahan, Louis Miller, and Daniel De Leon believed that organizing workers was not an end in itself but merely a step toward the day when a new order of society would give workers the fruits of their labor, they also realized that steps to improve workers' conditions in the "here and now" were necessary. They fought against the sweating system and for some job security for the workers. But ultimately, the "new day" of socialism would have to solve the basic problems of the working class. In the heavy moral responsibility these labor organizers bore, they were quintessentially part of the Jewish political culture.

It was primarily that socialist instrumentalism coupled with moral righteousness and separatism that alienated them from the mainline unions. One of the largest units of the Jewish labor movement, the Amalgamated Clothing Workers, did not join the American Federation of Labor until 1933; and those unions who were affiliated, like the powerful International Ladies Garment Workers (ILGWU), had almost no influence in the inner councils of the federation. Robert Asher concludes that "until the period of the 1930's the Jewish unions were largely in, but not of, the mainstream of the American labor movement."[27] As we have seen, that condition is not unlike that of American Jewry in general.

Yet, such apartness did not mean that the movement could avoid the effects of the pull of Americanization. Indeed, one way to view the internal tensions within the movement is to see them as generated by the conflict between European secular-Jewish and American modalities. The *Forverts* (Forwards), like other popular Yiddish dailies,prominently featured columns on citizenship education and presented news of the American environment, even if it was viewed through socialist eyes. Moreover, the socialist ideology and other factors that kept it separate were not destined to endure when pressure to Americanize became fully operative. The socialist rhetoric could fly high only before it was tested in the real world. It was linked to powerlessness. But once power came, once the triad that served as its base—the *Forwards*, the United Hebrew Trades, and the Workmen's Circle fraternal order—were firmly established, that rhetoric had to be muted. In the real world, there were "bosses" with countervailing power whose truths derived from the ledger sheet, not from socialism. And there was a perpetual threat from the extreme Left, which wanted to co-opt the movement.

To be sure, the influence of socialist ideology did not disappear entirely; but its preeminence gradually gave way to a pragmatic operationalism that was recognizably American in its problem-solving approach. The radical intellectuals who founded the movement remained dedicated and incorruptible, but much of their creative energy was now devoted to conceiving the ameliorative steps that some had previously opposed because they would dull the edges of the class struggle.

Initially, the struggle to reorganize the garment industry was especially bitter. Both the shop owners and the workers were Jewish, and conflict between brothers sometimes takes on a more passionate quality. But ways were ultimately found to bring peace to the industry. In the early days of the depression, when Hart, Schaffner, and Marx contemplated liquidation and thereby threatened the jobs of four thousand members of the Amalgamated, Sidney Hillman gave the firm an extraordinary "loan" in the form of a voluntary wage cut for one year.[28] During the contract negotiations, the management team was sometimes astonished by the expertise brought to bear by the "professionals" of the union team, who often had a better knowledge of what ailed the industry than did management.

In one sense, it was the ameliorative measures first recom-

mended by Jewish unions that found their way into Roosevelt's wel-
fare-state program, especially the program for labor. It was Sidney
Hillman who urged upon Roosevelt the idea of minimum wages and
maximum hours. The provisions guaranteeing the right to organize
and bargain collectively, which found its way into the path-breaking
clause 7a of the National Industrial Recovery Act, had its prototype in
contracts negotiated by Jewish unions during the previous three de-
cades of the century.[29] Roosevelt's appointment of Sidney Hillman
and Leo Wollman to the Labor Advisory Board was in recognition of
what garment unions had contributed.

Other facets of the welfare-state program, such as unemploy-
ment insurance, codes of fair competition, and old-age pensions,
stemmed directly from contracts negotiated by Jewish unions.[30] The
Amalgamated and Cloakmakers pioneering unemployment compen-
sation plan of the twenties was precedent for the Federal Social Secu-
rity Act of 1935. Jewish unions also pioneered in other areas. The
International Ladies Garment Workers Union was first to operate a
health center, a prototype for other unions. The "cradle to the grave"
total approach to social services of the Workmen's Circle, including
old-age medical care, is suggestive of the direction government policy
is taking today.[31] Cooperative housing, credit associations, super-
markets, paid vacations, and scholarships for the children of mem-
bers, now a normal part of the program of established labor unions,
were pioneered by the Jewish labor movement.

Except that these programs were conceived by secular Jewish
unionists from eastern Europe, there is nothing in them that makes
them substantively Jewish. On the contrary, because Jewish labor
leaders were addicted to universalism as a solution to the Jewish
problem, one might argue that they advocated an end to Jewish par-
ticularism. Yet despite its ideology, the Jewish labor movement some-
how remained bound to the Jewish people. Within the socialist ideology
of the leaders, one could often find a "folk religious ethic" that was
sometimes buttressed by scriptural references.[32]

Eventually, the connection to American Jewry was reestablished
through a secular labor-Zionist conduit. Although the Jewish labor
movement refused to support the American Federation of Labor's
pressure on behalf of the Balfour Declaration and other Zionist causes
in 1917, that policy soon changed.[33] By 1924, the United Hebrew
Trades, led by Max Pine, joined with Labor Zionists in forming the
Geverkshaftn campaign on behalf of *Histadrut* (the labor federation of

the Jews of Palestine). By the mid-1930s, Jewish unions contributed an ever-increasing outpouring of funds and support. After the Holocaust, support of the now much changed United Hebrew Trades was unstinting.

In 1934, the Jewish Labor Committee was established. It played an important role in the struggle to recognize the State of Israel in 1948 and has been active in supporting programs in Israel since that time. Jewish labor had found its way back. Although much of what was once alien in the Jewish labor movement had been melded into an acceptable American pattern by the 1930s, its approach to politics and political action continued to be different. It favored more direct political action by the labor movement. When John L. Lewis organized the Congress of Industrial Organization (CIO) in 1935, some movement in that direction could be noted in the establishment of the Political Action Committee.

Under David Dubinsky, the ILGWU and other elements the liberal coalition went one step further by organizing the American Labor Party in New York State. What was desired was not so much a party that could enact a labor program. Under the governship of Roosevelt and Herbert H. Lehman, a good part of their objectives had been made into law.[34] What was needed was a party ticket whereby socialist-oriented Jewish voters could cast their ballots for Roosevelt, a high-born patrician Episcopalian, without compromising their socialist principles.

Like other facets of the American Jewish experience, the Jewish labor movement had become part of America; and yet it kept something apart. Asher notes that, "the Jewish labor movement had become 'Americanized' and the American labor movement had assimilated many of the 'foreign' ideas and practices of the immigrant Jewish labor movement."[35] That attitude can be observed in many other areas of the Jewish relationship with America.

We come next to a discussion of one of the major differentiating characteristics of American Jewry: its rich organizational structure. At the turn of the century, the elaboration of Jewish organizational life had two basic objectives: to evolve a strategy for survival that called for the reestablishment of some kind of Jewish corporateness on a voluntary basis and to hold some kind of bridge between themselves and the Jewish world overseas. This observation is of course made possible only by the vantage point of time. At the turn of the century, myriad immediate causes led to the establishment of a rich organizational network.[36]

Several studies made during the 1960s indicate that American Jews living in suburbia continued to associate primarily among themselves, even though their religious ties were weaker than those held by Catholics and Protestants.[37] What holds Jews together when the thrust of modernity is toward atomization, individuation, and fragmentation is something of a mystery. If the answer were known, much of the mystery of Jewish survival through the ages would be revealed. The historian Bernard Lewis, instead of targeting organization or religion as a primary factor in Jewish cohesiveness, signals out a factor called "corporate historical memory."[38] It is ostensibly from that memory, a thing of the spirit to be sure, that the concrete manifestations of the Jewish people, congregations, secular organizations, and thousands of simple social circles come to be.

It is no surprise that Jewish organizations have something to do with Jewishness; but that they should be based on a memory of once having been one people and on a longing to build again a bridge to the remnant of that people is difficult to substantiate. Yet, such may be the case. The *Landsmannschaften,* which dotted the Jewish social landscape at the turn of the century, fit into such a classification, as do fraternal orders like B'nai B'rith and B'rith Abraham. Formal establishment of the New York Kehillah in 1908 and the American Jewish Congress in 1918 are, from one point of view, attempts at some kind of reincorporation or perhaps simply communalization.

To be sure, the Kehillah was a local organization; but its implications were clearly national because it tried to bring order to the heart of American Jewry. The name Kehillah was chosen to conjure up the image of former corporateness,[39] which had its dual roots in the organization of society into separate but interdependent corporations during the Middle Ages and in the Jewish religious culture, which emphasized collectivity and group response. The memory of such corporateness was reinforced by the manner of Jewish organization in eastern Europe. There, communal organization permitted Jews to exercise a high degree of autonomy and self-government between the sixteenth and seventeenth centuries, when it reached its zenith.[40] A residuum of that cohesiveness remained in the *shtetlach* they had left. In their concentration in the Pale, they formed in effect, a separate nation with its own culture, language, religion, and even territory. The only thing that was missing was power.

In theory, the American Jewish Congress was organized to bring "democracy" to Jewish life, which was dominated and mismanaged by "uptown" patricians who knew little of *yiddishkeit* and simply saw their Jewishness in denominational terms. The idea that more democracy can cure the ills of a community is a Progressive reform notion that led to such new instruments as the initiative, the referendum and recall, and party primaries. But we should note that the idea of applying it to Jews presupposed that there was a living Jewish community that required a better form of governance. Members of the "illustrious obscure" like Bernard Richards and Gedaliah Bublik, the Orthodox editor of the *Tageblatt,* in their fetish for community-wide elections, seemed never to have heard of the "melting pot" idea. Elections to determine who would govern the community, even when there was no longer any sanction to make Jews obey, seemed natural.

Similarly, the idea behind the founding of the Kehillah was based on a nostalgia for the order that apparently once ruled Jewish life. It was the chaos and lack of governance that made the Jewish enterprise vulnerable to charges of criminality like those by Police Commissioner Theodor Bingham. The Jewish community would take care of its own without the help of outsiders. Behind the arguments for the establishment of both the Kehillah and the congress was the assumption that such a thing as a Jewish community existed and required protection if Judaism was to survive in America. If the idea of community was abandoned, as had been done by the Reform movement, if peoplehood was to be replaced by denominationalism in order to fit into the American scheme, the Jewish presence was bound to disappear. A separate Jewish people required organization. Indeed, "organization was in the air"; and never far beneath it was the notion of Jewish peoplehood.[41]

If the establishment of the Kehillah and the American Jewish Congress were secular reflections of corporate peoplehood, then the revitalization of the Conservative movement by Solomon Shechter, with its support of cultural Zionism and the notion of "catholic Israel," was its spiritual reflection. But something more was required, something to dress the ideological nakedness of Jewish separateness so that it could be rationalized for both Americans and Jews.

That ideological rational that pointed to a separate tradition with its own claims was articulated in its clearest form by Mordecai Kaplan, who taught at the Jewish Theological Seminary of America for fifty years and founded the Reconstructionist movement in 1921. Perhaps the only theologian to be produced by American Jewry, Kaplan was unique because his theology, if one could call it that, addressed itself not to mediating between God and His people, the normal task of a Jewish theology, but rather mediating between the Jewish people and the secular society. Kaplan maintained that Judaism was a separate, evolving, religious civilization "whose common denominator is neither belief, nor tenet, nor practice, but rather the continuous life of the Jewish people."[42] Here was an open acknowledgment of Jewish exceptionalism. To be a Jew did not merely require adherence to a certain faith, although that could be part of it, nor did it mean belonging to a certain ethnic or hyphenate group. It meant belonging to a separate religious civilization, receiving separate cultural cues, and possessing a separate identity that could never fit entirely into another culture. For Kaplan, it seemed as if, instinctively and without knowing it, American Jews had been Reconstructionists all along.

Such an avowal of separateness and unmeltability was not without risks in turn-of-the-century America and was positively foolhardy in the America of the 1920s. Doubts about the assimilation potential of the "new" immigrants had become common currency. The Progessives, largely of native stock, were particularly disturbed by developments in the American city. They agreed with British historian Lord James Bryce that it was the worst governed unit in Christendom. "Bosses" managed corrupt political machines. Their power was based on being able to lead immigrants to the polls like so many head of cattle. Loyalty was the least that could be expected, but with a Jewish avowal of separatedness, even that was doubtful.[43] The Progressives were tolerant about the need to Americanize. That goal would be achieved gradually through the school curriculum, the church, and the settlement house. But after World War I, an intense mood of nativism and xenophobia demanded something more, a cultural *Gleichschaltung*, in which Jewish separatism and radicalism would find little social space.[44]

It fell to Horace Kallen to propound a philosophy that would create such space. Cultural pluralism, he maintained, was the natural and desirable state of a democratic society that should permit and even encourage dual and multiple loyalties. He saw American society as an "orchestration of cultures" that permitted a minimum of "injustice, suppression, [and] frustration" of one culture by another.[45] Kallen was not addressing himself directly to the Jewish condition in America; but few could fail to see that the concept of cultural pluralism, if accepted, would make allowances for the peculiar way American

Jews sought to accommodate to American society without forgetting their own.

The idea of a Jewish lump in the melting pot gained only gradual acceptance, and in some quarters it remained anathema. But ultimately, a relationship that, in an earlier time would have been rejected on the grounds that it demanded dual loyalty, was accepted by the host culture. It is precisely the relationship that American Jewry has with America today.[46] Yet strangely enough during the twenties, when the idea of physically re-creating some form of Jewish corporateness was active, the Kehillah and the American Jewish Congress withered on the vine. It would be the weak and fledgling Zionist movement that would carry the idea of Jewish peoplehood forward and eventually anchor it in a living symbol of a national Jewish homeland.

But what has won such seemingly easy acceptance from American society today was once the source of great apprehension in the Zionist movement. The contribution of Louis Brandeis to American Zionism occurred precisely because of the way in which he handled the vexing question of dual loyalties. He muted the nationalist-separatist component in favor of philanthropic operationalism without abandoning the idea that such an entity as a separate Jewish people and culture did in fact exist. He legitimized philanthropic operationalism by insisting that to be a good American one had to be a good Jew, and to be a good Jew one had to be a good Zionist.[47]

Once that idea became acceptable, a new Americanized Zionism, devoid of the strong separatist component that characterized it in eastern Europe, but retaining a strong implication of the feeling of peoplehood, was able to play a mediating role between Jews and their Judaism as well as Jews and Americanism. Zionism became a crucial element in a new kind of civil religion for American Jews when the purely religious modality was no longer tenable. By the late 1930s, it would be the peoplehood element in Zionism that was most reminiscent of the Jewish corporateness of long ago. It would be that spiritual sense of belonging, not the physical efforts represented by the Kehillah and the American Jewish Congress that would hold sway. Today, whether it is called Israelism or Zionism, it is the cement that holds Jews to its corporate memory.

There remains one area that deserves brief mention because the duality of the American Jewish posture is so clearly reflected in it. It is that overriding concern that American Jews display for their brethren in other lands, which is manifested in their interest in American foreign policy. That interest became apparent early in the century when four major Jewish organizational efforts were triggered by the problems Jews were facing in foreign lands.[48] The American Jewish Committee (1906) was organized as a result of the Russian depredations, especially the Kishinev pogrom (1903); the American Jewish Joint Distribution Committee (1914) was primarily concerned with the physical nurturing of Jewish communities abroad; the Federation of American Zionists (including Hadassah and Mizrachi) concerned itself with the development of the *Yishuv* in Palestine (its name was changed to the Zionist Organization of America in 1918); the American Jewish Congress (1918) was primarily concerned with an American Jewish contribution to the forthcoming peace conference. Today, that interest is part of all Jewish organizations—fraternal, religious, professional, and philanthropic. It is reflected in their budgets, their travel and educational programs, and the cultural activities that they sponsor. It is natural that it should be so because the tie to Israel is what helps to define them as Jewish.

Historians of American foreign relations long ago discovered the externalization phenomenon in American Jewish political culture.[49] Jews are more interested in American foreign policy than other subgroups, and that interest is more sustained and more apt to result in efforts to project pressure on decision makers.

Students of other disciplines will undoubtedly be able to point out many reasons for such an interest that do not impinge on the Jewish condition in the world. People with a high level of formal education, such as that held by American Jews, are typically less parochial and more concerned with world events. Moreover, Jewish interest in domestic affairs is also higher than that of many other groups.[50] As a highly urbanized, cosmopolitan group, Jews are simply more engaged and more aware that their own interest impinges on what happens abroad. Although all these factors affect Jewish interest in foreign affairs, much of their interest and concern lie with the plight of beleaguered Jews somewhere in the world. So as to help needy Jews wherever they may be, Jewish Americans have learned to pressure the American government, whose benevolent intercession is sought to ensure the well-being of such communities.

Such Jewish interest is most apparent in U.S. policy in the Middle East, but not exclusively. Jews were much concerned about immigration policy in the early decades of this century and toward Nazi

Germany during the 1930s. It is natural that it should be so because it reflects the continual attempt by American Jewry to find an accommodation between the pulls and seductions of a benevolent American culture and the demands of an age-old Jewish civilization from which it continues to draw spiritual nourishment. The turning of at least one eye outward to see what is happening in that Jewish world is necessary and predictable. All of which is to say that the overriding interest that Jews exhibit in the foreign affairs of the nation is like their mobility, the founding of a separate labor movement, and their unique organizational life—yet another manifestation of the duality that appears to be at the center of Jewish life in America and that defines what is Jewish about it.

Ultimately, the historian viewing the American Jewish experience realizes that at its most crucial interstices is the connection with *K'lal Yisrael*, the historic tie that binds Jews together the world over. This connection can take many different forms—the receiving of messengers during the colonial period, the arrangement between American Jewish bankers with Jewish banking houses in Europe, or perhaps merely a socialist Jewish labor leader citing scripture to wring better treatment for Jewish workers from Jewish employers. It is at the heart of American Jewish exceptionalism, what has made Jews come to different terms with the American culture.

Finally, I wish to risk a word on the implications of Jewish corporateness as it affects Jewish continuance in America. I say *risk* because historians are on dangerous ground when they add to the problematics of explaining the past, the role of prophet. But because the vision presented by other disciplines in the social sciences is one of such unreleaved gloom, it might be argued that one ought to do so if only to give balance to the general prognosis. Sociologists and social psychologists studying Jewish identity in America have concluded that it is weakening. A recent demographic projection informs us with utter certainty that, given present trends, American Jewry will have virtually vanished in a century.[51] Others, who nervously take the pulse of American Jewry, repeatedly note failing life signs— the population is aging; the birthrate is ominously low; attrition by intermarriage and other factors is high; the ramshakle Jewish education system is a dismal failure. These realities are ignored only at great peril.

Yet, historians might well wonder if that picture is complete and balanced. They recall that, at any given juncture throughout Jewish history, the prospect of survival was open to question. Jewish enterprise has always appeared fragile; disappearance has always seemed imminent. Indeed, concern over survival is perhaps as old as Jewish history itself. One might note that, had the projections of demographers really been applicable to the Jewish condition, Jewish civilization should have vanished a long time ago. That it did not and does not may also be part of Jewish exceptionalism. It may well be that Judaism is governed by different rules. And as for American Jewry, the signs of an attachment to *K'lal Yisrael*, which again has come to define what is Jewish about it; an overriding commitment to Israel's survival; a watchful eye on Jewry in the former Soviet Union; and a growing interest in the Holocaust—these interests are perhaps stronger today than ever before. At the same time, the Americanization and secularization processes go forward relentlessly. What appears to be happening is that the American Jewish life equation itself has grown larger on both sides of the equal sign. Jews are a subgroup in this dynamic society; but they are also more Jewish, as measured by the concern for Jewish people throughout the world. The American solvent remakes them, but somehow they remain a definable separate presence in American society. That America permits them to be so is a measure of its greatness; and that Jews continue to cherish that unique duality that marks them as different is a measure of their vitality.

3

Jewish Refugeeism

WHEN HISTORIANS SPEAK of myths, they are referring to the stories every people employs to rationalize an event or an experience. Myths have nothing to do with truth or falsity; and if human beings were not thinking animals, myths would not be necessary. The myths surrounding the immigration and acculturation experience are especially powerful, perhaps because a particularly potent rationale was needed to get people to uproot themselves. This essay probes the changes implied in the myths surrounding the Jewish immigration and acculturation experience and suggests that the demythologizing of that original experience is an important ingredient for Jewish survival in America. By speaking of *refugeeism* and *K'lal Yisrael*, a new history can restore the delicate balance between the Jewish and American elements of that identity.

The Melting Pot

Now that celebration of the centennial year of Jewish immigration has come and gone, a great debate concerning models of acculturation is once again occurring among historians. Is American society, as suggested by George Santayana, such a "powerful solvent" that the "melting pot," an image popularized by Israel Zangwill in 1908, is inevitable? If that is so, then the current enthusiasm for things ethnic is merely a "last hurrah" before the "unmeltable ethnic" melts.

This essay was delivered originally on November 13, 1981, as an address before the 50th General Assembly of the Council of Jewish Federations in St. Louis, under the title "The Jewish Immigrant Experience in North America: The Myth of Accommodation and the Myth of Survival."

Or do we live in a society so secure that it encourages diversity as its operating principle? Is a third model discernible? We begin with cultural pluralism, reinforced by cultural and biological supplementation from Jewish communities abroad, but end with the melting pot. Most crucial, if total acculturation is the fate that awaits all subcultures in America, is there is anything in the history of the American Jewish experience that allows survivalists to hope for exemption.

Clearly, the notion of cultural pluralism on which Jewish survivalists staked so much does not appear as viable today as it once did. American society still allows space for group particularity, but it does not assure that there will be something left to plant in that space. It is possible that the concept was chimerical when it was introduced in 1915 by Horace Kallen in an article in the *Nation* entitled "Democracy and the Melting Pot." Writing in the definitive *Harvard Encyclopedia of American Ethnic Groups,* Philip Gleason finds a "racialist dimension" in Kallen's approach to the pluralism idea and suggests that the number of Jewish thinkers attracted to the notion—Franz Boas, Mordecai Kaplan, Kurt Lewin, and others—has the earmarks of a Jewish intellectual conspiracy to create space for a Jewish culture.

There may be some truth in that idea. Even today, it is possible to read Mordecai Kaplan's *Judaism as a Civilization* as a theory and strategy for creating a Jewish lump in the melting pot. Anxiety regarding the possibility of survival in America's benevolently absorbent culture was not confined to intellectuals. It has also been reflected in the several vain attempts to establish institutional barriers so that Jewish corporateness might be preserved. That is the meaning of Judah Magnes's valiant effort to organize a Kehillah in New York in 1908. It is clearer still in the Congress movement, which organized a massive internal election in which hundreds of thousands cast their ballots to determine who would represent the community at Versailles. Finally, we see it in the startling growth of American Zionism, which contained the concept of Jewish peoplehood that was first heard in the Congress movement. The legitimacy of Zionism could not have been established without the ideological rationale put forward by the cultural pluralists.

Cultural Pluralism

From the outset, Jewish survivaliss understood the implications of the melting pot model of acculturation and resisted its blandishments. They sensed that it meant that immigrant Jews had to become something other than what they were in order to be successful. All the separate movements in Jewish organizational life, from the Kehillah to the Jewish labor movement to the various organizational expressions of American Zionism, were attempts to fortify American Jewry against total melting.

Yet from today's vantage, one cannot say with assurance that these organizations were successful. Increasingly, the latest version of ethnic pluralism, now called multiculturalism, is challenged. Similarly, the nationwide program for bilingual education that began in the 1980s has had little success; and *The Tarnished Golden Door*, the 1980 report of the Commission of Immigration and Refugee Policy, takes note of a popular anxiety concerning the unity of the nation and its loose control of its borders that might still apply. Finally, even the most optimistic observer today cannot help but recognize that the signs of cohesiveness and commitment to group particularity are declining among American Jews. A burgeoning intermarriage rate, weakened kinship ties, and diminishing religious passion are manifest. The replacement of a specific or even an eccentric religious credo by a bland interchangeable civil religion tends to weaken Jewish ethnicity. Few students of the Jewish condition in America would conclude that cultural pluralism has carried the day.

From a contemporary perspective, Kallen's notion seems far more prescriptive than descriptive. In fact, Jews could not be ordered to retain their cultural particularity. (It remains to be seen if they can be convinced that it is worthwhile having.) Most used their new-found freedom to rid themselves of the confining fetters of their ancient religious culture. That concept is so apparent that Stephen Steinberg suggests that the melting-pot model of acculturation can no longer be dismissed as "apocalyptic nonsense." American society, he maintains, never furnished the historic and institutional foundations for a genuinely pluralistic society. The evidence is in the "culturally thin" ethnicity that clutters some parts of the American scene.[1]

The myths that accompanied the immigration and acculturation process had to be powerful if they were to fulfill their objective: easing the travail that accompanies all human transplantation and re-rooting. Their power was derived by linking them to the familiar biblical exodus and redemption story. Jews were moving from the slavery of their life in czarist Russia and other areas of eastern Europe to the *Goldeneh medinah* (promised land), which was America. The bitterness of life in eastern Europe at times may have been overstated;

and the notion that there would be social space to retain Jewish culture—the concept of cultural pluralism—may also have been a simplification of what would really happen in America.

The Flow of New Immigrants

But why did not survivalists in the early decades of the century notice that acculturation was actually continuing apace? The answer is that many, especially Orthodox Jews and later Zionists, did warn of the *tref medinah* (unpious society). But in the 1920s, the elaborate organizational structure that had been set in place in the previous two decades and the still relatively strong religious commitment made it seem as if American Jewry would find something distinctive to plant in the space provided. Most important, the continuous flow of new immigrants gave American Jewry a glow of vitality that proved to be a false appearance of good health.

The Sephardic Jewish culture would not have been able to sustain itself without the timely arrival of the rustic, vigorous "Bayern" in the 1820s. But the comparative smallness of the German Jewish migration, perhaps 250,000 in all, and the scattered character of its settlement, compounded by its vulnerability to the siren call of a society willing to fulfill its side of the emancipation transaction, meant that it, too, would soon require supplementation from abroad. The necessary reinforcement came with the Jewish immigration from eastern Europe that began in earnest in 1881 but that, in fact, had started well before that year. The arrival of this group furnished American Jewry with the critical mass to generate a distinctive and conspicuous Jewish culture in America. Without their timely arrival, it is doubtful that a Jewish cultural enterprise in America could long have been sustained.

More that one hundred years after that immigration, we see that the cyclical pattern of diminution that marked the earlier periods of American Jewish history is being repeated. We can also see that American Jewry is reverting to the inconspicuous minority it was during the colonial and national periods. But there no longer exists a Jewish community with sufficient biological surplus and cultural energy to play the traditional role of revitalizer for American Jewry. That demographic hole was caused at first by the effects of the restrictive immigration laws of the 1920s and later by the Holocaust. There is, in fact, a ghoulish tandem between those restrictive immigration laws and Hitler's Final Solution. The former contained a portent of the latter in basing the quota system on the principle of "Nordic supremacy," which meant that quotas were more favorable for potential immigrants from northern and western Europe. It was the same principal that would come to be know as racial Aryanism in the Nazi Reich and ultimately became the theoretical underpinning for the Final Solution. Jews were extruded from Germany and murdered for the same reason that they were not acceptable in America.

Vying for Jewish Humanity

A look at perennial Jewish migration reveals that the relation of that process to Jewish survival is not merely that periodically hard-pressed Jewish communities require a new haven but also that Jewish communities who have accepted modernity, with its acculturation and diminishing birth rate, require outside supplementation to assure their survival. That truism throws a new light on the perennial tension between Israel and American Jewry. Viewed through a demographic prism, one sees that even before its establishment, the State of Israel and American Jewry have needed and vied for the same scarce group of Jews. This ongoing competition colors every facet of their relationship.

A dispute also continues among researchers concerning the wartime Zionists' refusal to separate the Jewish commonwealth from the rescue objective. Could more Jews have been rescued if the Zionist establishment had abandoned the futile struggle to get the British White Paper of May 1939 (which limited Jewish immigration to Palestine) revoked and had thrown its zeal and considerable experience into temporarily settling Jews any place where they might be out of danger? Could more Jews have been saved if temporary havens like the one in Sosua, Santo Domingo, and at Fort Ontario in Oswego, New York, had received fuller support? Peter Bergson (Hillel Kook), who headed a group of Palestinians who advocated these policies, was roundly condemned by Zionist leaders who did not view with favor the settlement of Jews anywhere but in the Jewish homeland.

The tension created by the problem of displaced persons (DPs) has a similar resonance. Zionist leaders were not overjoyed when President Harry Truman offered to accept 400,000 refugees in 1947. The remnants of the Holocaust in the DP camps were earmarked to become the population stock of a new Jewish state. More recently, the acrimony over *Neshira* (the disposition of those Soviet Jews who, upon reaching Vienna, chose not to settle in Israel) shows the familiar characteristics. Two Jewish communities are in competition for the same people. The estimated 6 percent of American Jewry now composed of *Yordim* (Israeli immigrants) is more ticklish still because it indicates that American Jewry is drawing its supplement from Israel, which most survivalists see as the crucial anchor needed for Jewish continuity. It develops that both Israel and American Jewry are dependent for renewal on immigration. The American Jewish need has until now remained concealed, but it is nevertheless there. Once that dependence is understood, the perennial Israeli quest for *Aliyah* from America can be viewed as the paradox it really is. Should it ever materialize, Israel's gain will merely be the reverse side of the other's loss, much the way *Yerida* (Israeli Jewish immigration to America) is Israel's loss and American Jewry's gain. Looked at from the broader perspective of *K'lal Yisrael,* no one really gains from such population transfers.

A Pluralist Community Within a Pluralist Society

There has always been a *Kulturkampf* (a struggle for religious and cultural dominance), rooted in the sequential waves of immigration within American Jewry. Like American society generally, the Jewish community was fashioned out of several separate national cultures whose residual influence continued to color behavior patterns and styles. German Jews appeared to outdo the Germans in their desire to be carriers of German culture, and Russian Jews were quintessentially Russian. The great irony of the often overstated uptown-downtown conflict is that it was fueled by the very national cultures that had rejected these Jewish communities. It was a Jewish version of the conflict between Teuton and Slav.

Such conflicts were not unprecedented in the American Jewish experience. There was a similar disjuncture between the proud, cosmopolitan Sephardic Jews and the rustic, energetic peddlers from Bavaria. The melancholy fact was that it was a conflict exacerbated by the residual influence of their original cultures and itself a certain sign that acculturation within these communities often outweighed a common base in Judaism.

Yet, there is a danger of overstating these divisions, especially if one considers them over a period of time. From the beginnning,the logic of American Jewish development was to become one people. The Sephardic founders eventually merged with the more numerous Jews from central Europe, who, in turn, lost their distinctive identity when they joined the general body of American Jewry, composed primarily of the descendants of the eastern European immigrants.

The pattern was continued by the second-generation Jews of that immigration. First, the distinctive regional variations within that immigration dissipated, and a composite eastern European Jewish type emerged. Forgotten by many students of the American Jewish experience is that, only in America, could the composite eastern European Jew be found reading the Yiddish press or attending the Yiddish theater. Jews from Kiev, Riga, Warsaw, Krakow, and everywhere in between sat together in that audience as they never did in their separate regional locales in Europe. It seemed like the absorbent new American society was determined finally to unify the Jews before totally dissolving their distinctive culture. The conflict between "Bayer" and "Pollack," "Litwak" and "Galitzianer" first became subjects for Jewish humor and finally for memories. The American-born generations afterward could not make sense of the once dearly held distinctions. Instead, there began to develop a common denominator of historical experience, values, and language on which a community might be built.

Jewish Identity Waning

But after World War II, when these requisite building blocks were in place, a strong sense of Jewish identity began to wane. Ultimately, survivalists may conclude that the greatest irony in the American Jewish experience was that the acculturation process that finally created the commonalities upon which a community might be built also contained the seeds for the dissolution of group identity. Today, it is readily apparent that the process of dissolving the distinctive elements of American Jewry is well advanced. There seems to be no way of halting it, except by consciously convincing American Jews that there is something in their cultural heritage worth preserving.

Can American Jews be convinced? At least part of the answer lies in how well history can be retrieved so that a "usable past" that will support the value of a separate Jewish culture can be created. The renowned historian Bernard Lewis calls such a knowledge of the past the "corporate historical memory" of the Jewish people. In the absence of a territory as a binder for much of the Jewish past, memory and ideas have served to bind the Jewish people together. It is the experiential, not the physical, that generates Jewish group identity.

The portrait painted of the immigrant and the acculturation experience has been idealized into a morality tale that begins sadly but ends well. Jews were cruelly persecuted but overcame their tribulations and became fantastically successful in the *goldeneh medinah*. But not only does that story ignore the price exacted, it also tends to tilt the delicate balance between the Jewish and American components of that identity toward the American. The process of demythologizing the immigration saga, which began before World War II, allows us to view the American Jewish experience from the broader perspective of Jewish history, where we learn that Jewish communities ensconced in benevolent host cultures are not unprecedented. Such Jewish subcultures have never been as precisely primed for remolding as those whose identities were derived from space rather than an idea. Moreover, it becomes clear from such a perspective that the major organizational, ideological, and commercial developments of American Jewish history receive their signals and often their character from the broad stream of Jewish history as well as from the specific experience in America. Lastly, a far fuller picture of the immigration and acculturation experience can be gleaned when it is merged with the growing popular story of Jewish refugeeism. When the process is completed, American Jewry will finally have a usable past to buttress its separate group identity.

Demythologizing American Jewish History

The demythologizing process, which links American Jewish history to the major problem now facing it, survival, is well underway. Not surprisingly, seeing the immigration experience from the vantage of the "wretched refuse," those uprooted and displaced peasants who experienced it, was first done by a Jewish historian, Oscar Handlin, in his classic book *The Uprooted*. His lead has since been followed by many others. It has been discovered that religious persecution, even its physical manifestations of pogroms, rarely furnished sufficient impetus for Jews to uproot themselves. Moreover, it cannot account for the thousands of Jews who chose to leave areas relatively free of religious persecution and the millions of non-Jewish refugees who also chose to undergo the travail of emigration. That travail had some specific components that are present at the very outset of the process in the "trauma of steerage" to the processing procedure in the ports where they debarked.

There were serious disturbances among Jewish immigrants processed on Wards Island in 1882, as there were riots in Rishon L'Zion

(Palestine) in 1887. Ellis Island, dubbed *Trern Insel* (isle of tears), did not enjoy a good reputation among Jewish immigrants, its proximity to the Statue of Liberty notwithstanding. Historians have taken a closer look at the early acculturation process and have discovered that the highly touted ability of the Jewish family to withstand the stresses of transplantation have been overstated. New studies on Jewish vice and criminality and the discovery of a relatively high divorce and desertion rate among immigrant Jews present a picture of a community paying a dear price for establishing itself.

For decades, historians have assumed that the recidivism rate was lower among Jewish immigrants compared to other immigrant groups. Jews came with their families and came to stay. For some historians, that fact served as evidence that Jews were more patriotic and more aware of the promise of America. But Jonathan Sarna, in an interesting piece of revisionist speculation, seriously questions whether it is possible to assume that fewer Jews returned to their old homes.[2] The exceptionally rapid mobility, first attested by Stephan Thernstrom (the dean of the new historical quantifiers) and substantiated by dozens of studies since World War II, is being considerably refined. Mobility there was; but according to Irving Howe and other researchers, it was slower and less uniform than generally believed.[3]

The exaggeration of the American Jewish success concealed the existence of the Jewish poor. Today, the almost equally rapid mobility of Asian Americans takes some of the sheen off the extraordinary Jewish mobility. Much of Jewish economic success was supposedly linked to the ability Jews displayed to use formal education as a conduit. But now the oft-repeated love of the "people of the book" for education has been questioned and found wanting. For the first- and second-generation Jews, the school drop-out rate was in fact quite high. It was small business instead of formal education that may have been the more certain path to economic success.[4]

Finally, the Holocaust years have cast considerable doubt on whether subgroup particularity, within the framework of a pluralistic society, yields real political power. Anglo conformity, to use the words of Milton Gordon, a noted sociologist, did not yield anything more than ornamental cultural activities: theater, and an ethnic press. But at the zenith of their political influence, American Jewry could not convince decision makers in the Roosevelt administration to mount a more active rescue effort to save their brethren in Europe. That failure has had a profound effect in the reevaluation of cultural pluralism as offering a survival strategy. One by one, the myths of accommodation give way to the myths of survival.

The Wandering Jew

If the first part of the century projected the image of a courageous immigrant facing a brave new world, then the final decades of that century show a refugee who belongs nowhere and has no claim to any part of that world. The last thirty years have been filled with pictures of crowded DP camps, Hungarian refugees escaping across narrow bridges, terror-filled Vietnamese boat-people, Cubans, Cambodians, Haitian bodies rotting on Florida's beaches, Palestinian refugees training to reclaim their homeland and, of course, the Noshrim. Each passing year brings yet another group of refugees to the fore. The refugee phenomenon does much to puncture the myths surrounding the immigration story, although it furnishes a key to Jewish identity formation in the Diaspora.

It is not so much that American Jewry traces its origins to a group of twenty-three Sephardic Jewish refugees who sailed into the harbor of New Amsterdam in September 1654. Probably most Jewish communities in the long history of the Jews were founded and nourished by Jewish refugees from elsewhere. The rooting and rerooting process is, after all, the *sine qua non* of Jewish history and at the very heart of their identity as a people. The modern persona of the refugee is in one sense merely the latest version of the "wandering Jew" who can be found everywhere but belongs nowhere. The increasing number of refugees is in some paradoxical way additional evidence that the world is becoming Jewish, or at least that the Jewish condition is becoming the human codition.

Refugeeism, as used here then, pertains to this special condition. A refugee, according to the United Nations High Commission for Refugees, is "someone outside his country of origin owing to well-founded fear of being persecuted for reasons of race, religion, nationality or public opinion." But this definition does not encompass the complete reality for Jewish refugees because, even after centuries of inhabitation and after the full rights of citizenship have been granted, we have witnessed the possibility of extrusion and even murder. The mysterious force of anti-Semitism cannot be divorced from the special relationship refugeeism has to Jewish history. In some countries of eastern Europe, Jews feel themselves in danger of becoming refugees at any moment. More than most groups, they have experienced the loss of legal identity linked to being stateless. The refugee lives outside the nation-state system into which human beings have organized themselves. That was the position of the Jews during the years of the Holocaust.

Yet even today, when Israel's Law of Return has eliminated the need for such statelessness from the Jewish experience, we find that Soviet Jews voluntarily assume that condition. Jewish refugeeism reflects the continued anomaly of Jews in society. They are often "in" it but rarely precisely "of" it. That seems to hold true even when it is their own society. That may be the true meaning of *Yerida* and *Neshira*.

In modern times, Jews have been refugees *par excellence;* the compulsion to move to another place seems never far beneath the surface. Even within America, they are among the most peripatetic of its citizens. That continuous movement, voluntary or involuntary, the need to accommodate to a new place and to force it to yield its secrets, has an impact on the identity formation of Jews. The refugee needs to know how life is lived in the new place, and that knowledge requires special skills and insight. Predictably, it is the creative writer rather than the social scientist who first discovers the new agonies aborning. Saul Bellow was among the first to test his mettle against the refugee theme in *Mr. Sammler's Planet.* He was followed by I. B. Singer, himself a refugee, whose early short stories, written in America and now collected in *Lost in America,* frequently depict the refugee condition.

There is, of course, no method of measuring the precise impact refugeeism has had on Jewish behavior patterns. The frequency with which Jewish achievers in all areas have experienced the refugee condition has been noted. It may well be that the "outsider's" position, inherent in the condition of the refugee, offers the necessary marginality to make "value free" judgments about the workings of society. The Jewish refugee really has that alienated vantage fed from two sources. It may be that which accounts for the disproportionate number of Jews traditionally involved in those academic disciplines that study the workings of society and community. It may help explain the disproportionate number of people from Jewish backgrounds who are political dissenters or radicals.

Refugeeism and Achievement

On a more mundane level. refugeeism may contain a clue to the remarkable Jewish economic achievement in America and elsewhere.

We have seen the process of extraordinary achievement by refugees repeated again and again, first by the German Jews of the 1930s, then by the Jewish postwar displaced persons, the Cuban Jews, and most recently the *Yordim*. Within a few short years, these groups often surpass in income comparable indigenous groups of similar age, education, and background. Although there are no statistics, one suspects that a disproportionate number of top achievers in the arts and sciences emanate from these new arrivals. It is as if forcible transplantation, by creating an imperative need to master the new system, releases heretofore untapped energies and talents. Survival requires that the refugees/immigrants learn the flow of power, what is up and who is down. They must learn where life is more secure, what skills have the highest market value, and generally where life is lived with the least degree of stress and despair. They know from their refugee experience the price paid when there is no security in life. Surely, the mastery of such information and the ability to pass it on to one's children has some bearing on the remarkable achievement of refugees in the New World.

Refugeeism and Bureaucracy

Clearly, although Jews are the archetypical refugees, that is also the condition of millions of other uprooted people. Moreover, refugee travail need no longer entail actual physical uprooting. The refugee is a new kind of "dangling man," this time hanging from a bureaucratic string. I. B. Singer pictures him as contending with that faceless bureaucracy for that validating piece of paper that allows him to remain in his disconnected state. If he neglects the contest, he becomes an illegal man compelled to live completely outside the system. He is detached, haunted, and often near madness. He suffers from *Einzamkeit*, which Singer would tell us translates into something more than mere loneliness. He is alone, completely separate and outside, no longer certain whether he has the right to live. Uncertain even if he has the psychic stamina to negotiate for place with the losers of the host culture who occupy its lowest ranks.

That portrait of refugee sensibility is coincidentally a metaphor for the contemporary human condition of an increasing number in our society who feel such estrangement, although they are never physically uprooted by force. They are internal refugees unable to find a place for themselves in society. Estranged and finding little nurture, they have no sense that they are living in a community to which they belong. To the degree that such a sensibility can increasingly be found in a complex urban society, one could say the world has become Jewish. In 1968, when Cohn-Bendit, the French Jewish radical, declaimed, "We are all German Jews," he may after all have been on to something.

Certainly, the refugee aspect of the immigration experience has a central role in retrieving a usable American Jewish past. If that sensibility is being universalized so that the sense of disconnectedness associated with refugeeism can be found everywhere in the society, then one needs to raise the question, "Acculturation to what?" Jews are going "there," but there is no "there" there. The new and better shape, the new alloy to substitute for the old, which is the basic assumption behind the melting-pot model of acculturation, turns out to be chimerical. Even the indigenous population experiences growing difficulty in locating the vital center that holds this society together.

The sense of separateness and in-betweenness of the Jewish refugee can serve to extricate American Jewry from the ardent embrace of a society that may smother or totally absorb and homogenize a distinctive Jewish culture. Is it possible to resist that embrace by first detaching onself and then finding the perennial connection with a separate, preexisting Jewish civilization that has nurtured prior Diasporas in Jewish history? Is it possible by a sheer act of group will to exempt oneself from the fate all subcultures share in American society?

Differentiating the Jewish Experience

There is something in the American Jewish experience and in the way its group identity was shaped that differentiates it from other subgroups that clutter the American social landscape. If the energy remains to will exemption, Jewish exceptionalism can be mobilized to furnish a *raison d'être* for Jewish survival in America without breaking the rules that hold a pluralistic society together. American Jewish exceptionalism does not refer to the remarkable Jewish economic achievement for which it can easily be mistaken. Nor is claiming uniqueness or exceptionality anomolous because it is, after all, the rationale for retaining a separate group identity. If all subgroups in America were interchangeable, there would be no need or demand to belong to them. If Irish Americans can point to their mastery of the "game" of American politics and Oriental Americans can tout their rapid mobility, Jewish Americans have in their arsenal the existence of a separate millennial historical civilization from which they get many of their signals and which is central to their identity formation. The distinctions claimed by other subgroups are related to success in American society and are themselves partly the result of successful acculturation and often the accelerators of that process. Jewish exceptionalism, on the other hand, is related to its separateness linked to claims of *K'lal Yisrael*, the mysterious bonds and relations that bind Jews everywhere together.

The possibility of exemption from the completion of the acculturation process is linked to a preexisting Jewish religious civilization with its own history. American Jewry especially has expressed its Jewishness by its relationship to other Jewish communities. It was especially generous to "messengers" from other Jewish communities during the colonial and national periods. It has consistently petitioned the American government for redress for its brethren—from the Damascus blood libel through the Mortara kidnapping, the Dreyfus affair through the depredations in czarist Russia, Romania, and other areas. That concern was most recently in evidence in its role in protecting Soviet Jewry.

That persistent link to Jewish communities abroad is unique. The typical American immigrant group retains religious ties and strong sentiment for the "old country" that can persist for generations. But for such groups, the act of emigration entails a stepping out of both the cultural and the physical space of the old society. Without such territorial anchors, such subcultures eventually wither, losing their drawing power and meaning in the new land. Jews who were frequently despised by the societies from which they emigrated do not possess such a special sense of belonging. Instead, their identity is ideational and based on historical ties with a religious civilization that cannot be stepped out of. One can step out of space but not out of time.

The persistence of that tie can be noted today in almost all areas of American Jewish endeavor. Its agenda and the flow of the philanthropic dollar give the highest priority to the welfare of Israel, which is more than a friendly foreign sovereignty for American Jews. Not far behind is a parallel concern for Soviet Jewry and other beleaguered Jewish communities. One can note that many of the major turning points of its historical experience are related to things happening elsewhere on the Jewish historical canvas. That is as true for the religious triangulation of Judaism into Reform, Conservative, and Orthodox wings as it is for the establishment of the distinctive American Jewish labor movement. All echo and frequently receive their ideological cues from parallel developments in other Jewish communities. Often these signals are carried to America in the cultural baggage of the immigrants.

American Jewish Melting

From one point of view, American Jewry is simply another diasporic community in a history full of Diasporas. From another, it is part of a benevolent culture whose fate it voluntarily chooses to share. Each world has its own claims that each generation of American Jews must balance. Within the last generation, the balance has begun to tip precariously toward the American side. For many, this is evidence that it has been the melting-pot model that seems to be coming to pass. The promise of cultural pluralism, which was in large part a Jewish conceptualization and wish, continues to be held out by the American society. But that conception never promised that the subgroups who wish to maintain their separate identity would have something distinctive and relevant to plant in the social space provided.

Jews are free in this society, and increasingly they use this freedom to rid themselves of their remaining ethnic and religious ties. The fact that the process of acculturation continued apace was concealed by the waves of immigration that for a time, generated new cultural energy. Today, hope of such biological and cultural infusion is no longer possible. The lid is on the pot, and the contents are simmering. What hope exists for American Jewry to remain a separate ingredient in an otherwise undifferentiated stew?

The most mysterious aspect of the millennial Jewish survival has been its unnaturalness. It occurs against all odds. On one end of the spectrum is the danger of absorption into a benevolent society; on the other is the possibility of physical destruction. At the risk of sounding Herzlian, it seems like both dangers require a conscious will to overcome. That may in fact be the secret to Jewish survival. It does not occur naturally but requires strenuous effort, planning, and consciousness of what is at stake.

Does such a will to survive exist in American Jewry or has the melting extended so far that all that remains is a sentimental echo of a once-strong song? The inspiration achievements of American Jewry that are partly connected to a strong sustaining Judaism are lost to the blandishments of a particularly benevolent and seductive host culture. Jews no longer seem able to duplicate the totalistic culture that, in former times, made them turn instinctively three times daily to the

east. They are uncertain whether the Jewish religioculture offers suffi-
cient nourishment.

It is history that traditionally plays a crucial role in preserving
Jewish identity everywhere in the Diaspora. That history is today be-
ing retrieved and made usable by historians. The powerful myths sur-
rounding the immigration story that tended to tip Jewish identity
toward its American component are gradually being discarded. In its
place is an interest in refugeeism that is related to the age-old image
of the "wandering Jew," just as the former myth was related to the
biblical story of the exodus and redemption. By definition, the refu-
gees are not so immersed within the host society that they cannot see
the dangers it poses for their survival. From that vantage, too, histo-
rians are more able to see and weigh the crucial role the link to a
millennial Jewish religious civilization has played in the American
Jewish past and in American Jewry's identity as a people. The human
material,the periodization of its history, its culture, its myths, and a
good part of its identity stem from that alternate preexisting commu-
nity. Replacement of the myths of accommodation with the myths of
survival indicates that the struggle for Jewish continuance in America
has reached the arena of history. Its outcome may well be crucial to
American Jewish survival.

PART TWO

Anti-Semitism

4

Studying the Problem

IT IS POSSIBLE to have different perceptions on the nature of the threat to Jewish survival in America. Some may think that American Jewry is threatened by a raging anti-Semitism, and others see it threatened by a society anxious to absorb it. Under ordinary circumstances, history could help clarify the picture. Instead, it presents a muddled story that adds to the confusion.

Speaking from a Zionist vantage that assumes that the existence of anti-Semitism in any society is axiomatic, Ben Halpern predictably does not believe that America has been immune from the oldest social malignancy known.[1] Jonathan D. Sarna and Michael Dobkowski conclude that the prevalence of anti-Semitism in nineteenth-century America has been underestimated.[2] Similarly, Naomi Cohen concludes from her research that pluralism has not neutralized the Christian wellsprings of anti-Semitism, so that the American Jew "remains the quintessential outsider in a Christian, albeit secular society."[3] Yet when we turn to Jewish and non-Jewish Americanists, a different story emerges. The existence of anti-Semitism is not denied, but its historical importance is questioned. Thus, Oscar Handlin, in finding that turn-of-the-century caricatures often "involved no hostility, no negative judgment," is comparatively sanguine about the dangers it poses.[4] Edward H. Flannery, although not ignoring its potential for becoming something more, views it ultimately as a "minor chapter in American Jewish history."[5] John Higham, the highly regarded student of American nativism, points out that "no decisive event, no deep

This essay appeared originally in *Jewish Social Studies* 47, nos. 3–4 (Summer–Fall 1985).

crisis, no powerful social movement, no great individual is associated primarily or significant chiefly because of antisemitism." In the mid-1960s, he concluded that anti-Semitism was "a thing of the past."[6] In between, there are numerous historians who fall back on the word *ambivalence* or on *radical ambiguity* to describe the attitude of the host culture toward Jews.[7]

The problem stems partly from the fact that the term *anti-Semitism*, especially in its American setting, is so inclusive and therefore imprecise that the student can classify under it almost anything that involves conflict with Jews, from the perennial contretemps over Christmas creches to the question of alternate side parking on Jewish holidays. Halpern's observation that "we are left with a highly confused, emotionally loaded term from which serious, mutually opposed consequences are drawn not only by polemical antagonists but by purportedly disinterested analysts," is unavoidable.[8]

In this brief discussion, I try to discover the reasons why a phenomenon so readily discernible on the larger canvas of Jewish history should pose such problems in the American Jewish corner of it. It suggests that the necessary taxonomy of anti-Semitic incidents based on their historical valence becomes partly possible only when the anti-Semite gains and holds power. It concretizes latent, often deeply submerged, attitudes in America that otherwise leave few historic traces and pose only an indirect threat to the Jewish enterprise. That anti-Semitism is confined to the private imagination and largely to the private sector, however, does not mean that it is unimportant. The nature of American society is such that crucial decisions occur first in the private sector. A cataclysmic event could catapult a Jewish question into a political one. The unresolved racial problem that ticks like a time bomb just beneath the surface of American society may provide one such contingency. If it succeeds in pushing the question of what Jews should and should not rightfully have and do in America onto the political agenda, then the latent anti-Semitism that persists in American society could find its way to the surface and overtly threaten all that Jews have achieved.

It may be reductive to propose that American anti-Semitism is different because "America is different." After all, every social grouping lays claim to being different. This difference is the reason why humankind forms into separate groupings in the first place. Yet in political organization, America varies considerably even from the

North Atlantic communities from which it originally derived its political culture. Its *pais legal* (state) is a rational contrivance unbuttressed by a single organic human stock welded together by baking in the same historical oven for centuries. The heterogenous pluralistic society that emerged in America not only stemmed from historical circumstances but was also inherent in the dominant Protestant ethos. Before Horace Kallen discovered cultural pluralism at Harvard, historians of religion had already identified American Protestant pluralism.[9] Fragmented along religious and ethnic lines, the new society seemed to lack cohesiveness. Compared to the long-established European nations, it had an inherent problem of national identity. That may account for the stridency of its patriotism or the chicaneries of the once powerful House Un-American Activities Committee (HUAC). The parliamentary assemblies of Europe require no such committees because everyone knows instinctively who belongs to the national community. The Jews, they determine, may be citizens of the state; but no law can make them members of the *pais real* (folk). From the beginning, such a distinction did not work in America. When Peter Stuyvesant characterized the first Jewish arrivals as "blasphemers of the name of Christ," it was no match for the impact of the ledger, the shortage of population, and there already being other "blasphemers" in the colony. The membrane that bound America was destined to be porous and loose. When Will Herberg later noted that Jews were assigned a share of the American religious enterprise out of all proportion to their numbers, he was actually observing the tail end of a long historical process that, officially at least, did not exclude Jews.[10]

With all its familiar imagery, anti-Semitism did find a place in the attitudes of Americans; but its concrete manifestations were sporadic, and there seemed to be little propensity for accretion and development. It did not become a palpable continuing fact that interfered with the headlong thrust of American Jewry for wealth and station.[11] That much historians deduce from the three separate modernizing elites produced by American Jewry at different stages of their development and from the comparative affluence of American Jewry today. What Leo Pinsker and others noted about the Jews of other nations, that they formed such "a distinct element" that they could not be "readily digested," seemed not to be part of the American reality.[12] Instead, a centripetal force seemed to be at work in American society that acted to draw inward all subcultures not based on race. At the same time, a pervasive ahistoricism may account for the normal rule for exclusion of Jews' often being forgotten in practice. It was, in any case, difficult to apply such a rule for fear of unraveling the delicate thread that held the disparate American social experiment together. On the contrary, the tie was strengthened by the Hebraism American society shared in common with Jews. Some Evangelical Protestants hoped that Jewish group cohesiveness would eventually dissolve and that they would accept the light that had first shone at Calvary. Although European societies soon developed opposition to granting Jews full civil and political rights, such rejection is almost completely absent from the American experience, which occurred almost totally in a post-Emancipation setting. In some measure, the Jewish presence at the creation of the republic was the norm and could not be easily removed.

American pluralism posed problems of target-centering Jews for a potentially organized anti-Semitic movement. From the outset, there were other groups whose aberrance was more strident and visible. There were cults who quaked, who shook, who prepared for Armageddon, who felt commanded to practice bigamy or, contrariwise, celibacy. The historic hatred of Jews in the Christian world, if not totally deflected, was at least shared by other religious subcultures, who in some respects were more threatening than the inconspicuous Jewish community. To be sure, Stuyvesant and others ranted about Jews; but they despised and also attempted to remove Quakers, Congregationalists, and Catholics. Ultimately, such religious conflicts were muted lest the fragile polity be divided between "ins" and "outs." The subsequent development of a comparatively broad religious tolerance was based as much on the practical needs created by a heterogenous citizenry as it was on the principles of the Enlightenment. Protestant pluralism helped hold a direct assault on Jews in check. Two examples illustrate the point. The missionary activity among Jews in nineteenth-century America that so concerned leaders like Isaac Leeser was ultimately brought to a virtual standstill by strong opposition from within Protestanism by those who considered that it was a waste of money and energy. Similarly, in opposition to the Sunday closing laws, the Jews were often joined by Protestant Sabbatarians, who were also affected by the laws.[13]

For Americans, pervasive pluralism creates a problem of drawing a distinction between normal intergroup antagonism that will be found in any heterogenous society and the ancient malignancy of anti-Semitism. The search is obfuscated by background noise because all American subcultures are keenly aware of slights suffered and have discovered that there is an income to be earned from touting their victimization. At a meeting of Jewish and Mexican American leaders, sponsored by the American Jewish Committee, all Hispanic speakers, including the Bishop of San Antonio, prefaced their remarks with such tales of woe as to make the Jewish experience pale in comparison. The case for American anti-Semitism becomes literally subsumed beneath a sorrowful tale of general ethnic suffering, and the historian is faced with the additional problem of explaining the special case of anti-Semitism deeply embedded in all Western civilization.

For example, American Catholics can make a good case that, in the 1850s, they experienced a more intense prejudice than the Jews because the animus against Catholics was translated into a political one by the Know Nothing Party.[14] In 1882, Chinese Americans were the first to be excluded, and in 1885, they were massacred in Rock Springs, Wyoming. American anti-Semitism reached a high point during World War I, but so did hostility against German Americans.[15] And Jews certainly did not experience anything like the anti-Japanese feeling that culminated in their internment in 1942. Traditionally in American society, not only has hostility been directed against ethnic minorities but a great deal of tension has also occurred between various ethnic groups. When such hostilities are directed against Jews, they assume an anti-Semitic coloration because, even in America, no alternate metaphor to oppose the Jewish group interest has developed. That makes it difficult for the historian to distinguish normal intergroup conflict from the ancient disease of anti-Semitism. The historian John Appel, who specializes in the study of anti-Semitic and antiethnic caricatures, concludes that "Jews were not the only and not always the first group to feel the sting of exclusion, discrimination and ridicule," and "antisemitism never fused into a major political movement or a significant wave of violence."[16]

Pluralism poses a twofold problem for the student of anti-Semitism. Judgments on its prevalence are made difficult because the touting of group victimization has become a veritable sport in American politics. It has spilled over into the writing of ethnic history, in which the whole gruesome picture of ethnic oppression comes to more than the sum of its parts. Secondly, the media highlight real and imagined inequities in sound and color, so that the contemporary researcher has difficulty in drawing a balanced picture. Thus, oppression has become a matter of opinion, and those who have not experienced it are told that they cannot really know about it.

The student of anti-Semitism also encounters problems in differentiating pluralistic societies. Was the opposition to the admission of

Jewish refugees during the 1930s an example of anti-Semitism, or was the severity of the depression the reason that many Americans, who were not anti-Semitic, thought that the time for opening the gates was inappropriate? Both attitudes are evident in the historical record.[17] How can one account for the fact that, until 1937, American Jews themselves did not favor admission of their fellow Jews?[18]

Moreover, Jews form a pluralistic community within a pluralistic society, so that the term *anti-Semitism* is overflowing with meaning.[19] Those various meanings cause a confusing targeting problem for anti-Semites. Should they aim their slings and arrows at Judaism, the religious denomination, or simply the ethnic Jewishness borne by the Jewish people? Both are increasingly less visible. Should they confine their animus to the imagined grasping merchant or creditor and forget about the admiral who single-handedly modernized the submarine fleet or the comedienne who has a special talent for exposing life's travail in modern urban America? Both are in the picture, and they are projected against a background that is equally contradictory for historians. Although they discover evidence of exclusion and slander, they also become aware of a high intermarriage rate and remarkable achievement. How do they make sense of such a conflicted experience?

Researchers have often been befuddled by pluralism. In the pathbreaking study of authoritarian personality commissioned by the American Jewish Committee in 1944, the anti-Semitic personality was discovered to be abnormal.[20] Yet in the rush to classify such a person as other than normal, the fact remains that the authoritarian person could have found a target for pathological hatred in any one of the despised groups this society produces. It did not have to be the Jews and certainly not only the Jews.

Because its exceptionality takes us far beyond the befuddlement inherent in studying complex pluralistic societies, we need to take special note of anti-Semitism among African Americans, as highlighted by the 1981 Yankelovich study.[21] We learn that anti-Semitism among African Americans, especially among their leadership and their youth, is resistant to that great inhibitor, formal education. Might this strain of anti-Semitism be something on the American scene that could yield new insights to social scientists?

Most historians of the American experience would agree with John Higham that "the Negro revolution has overshadowed the remnants of anti-Semitism in America and that it is no longer easy to regard the latter as the representative type of prejudice."[22] If any group has had reason to feel that it is despised and persecuted, it is the African Americans. In the context of pluralism, the conventional wisdom among Jews has long since concluded that the animosity toward African Americans has served as a major deflector of hatred against themselves. Thus, a group that has inadvertently served as a shield for American Jewry is generating what may ultimately be identified as the most indigenous form of American anti-Semitism. From the historians' vantage, the crucial fact regarding the emergence of anti-Semitism among African Americans is that, with all the "scientific" tools in their possession, social scientists did not foresee its stridency or its sustained impact within the black community. It is the outgroup *par excellence*, not the majority society, which produces a palpable, sustained strain of anti-Semitism. Unlike the European variety, it grows right out of the characteristic group conflicts of American society.

I classify it as indigenous because, measured in terms of time, African Americans are more indigenous than either the "old" or the "new" immigrants. More important in the generation, reflection, and refraction of what passes for popular culture in America, African Americans occupy a special position. In some disproportionate measure, American culture is black culture. In the words of Gunnar Myrdal, an African American is an "exaggerated American."[23] Anti-Semitism is indigenous in another respect. The conflict that occurred in Ocean Hill–Brownsville in 1968 and that resulted in arguments over quotas and affirmative action is rooted in something very American. It is a conflict over a legitimate kind of "spoils"; it relates to the "who gets what" question that has been at the very heart of American politics since the Jacksonian period. The conflict between Jews and African Americans features all the familiar characteristics that form part of the anti-Semitic syndrome; it has not only an element of intergroup conflict but also a peculiar fixation on Jews; it has borrowed images and rhetoric from abroad, especially from the Third World; it has an element of religious tension, which stems from the presence of religious exotica among African Americans; it has envy of the Jewish position and an exaggerated notion of their power, which is standard in the anti-Semitic imagination. Above all, it is inchoate and lacks ideological coherence, which is also typical of the American scene. An understanding of the dynamics of American anti-Semitism might well be found in studying its presence among African Americans.

Yet, even such a study would offer few answers to another vexing problem encountered by historians. How can attitudes, ideologies, and rationales be linked to verifiable anti-Semitic acts? As John Higham observes, "a prejudice that is primarily latent rather than overtly mobilized—surely the case with antisemitism in America— seems more important to the psychologist than to the historian because the psychologist is far better equipped to deal with the phenomena."[24] From a historical perspective, the collective punishment of Jews under Grant's General Order Number 11 or the brutal lynching of Leo Frank has a far higher valence than an anti-Semitic slur by a prominent American. The former is an overt act that has an immediate and direct impact on Jews; the latter betrays an attitude that will remain latent, if it is not matched by power.

For historians, the dilemma posed by determining the historical weight of each separate incident or pronouncement does not stop there because it is difficult to measure the importance of overt anti-Semitic acts or even whether they can be classified as anti-Semitic. Should historians, for example, view the Supreme Court decision to permit a Christmas creche to be constructed on public property in Pawtucket, Rhode Island, as a case of overt anti-Semitism? It reflects a Christian hegemonism that generates apprehension in Jewish communities the world over; but it does not directly impinge on the Jewish condition in Pawtucket, nor has access to Jews been denied. Conceivably, the Court decision may permit Jew to display a Hanukah menorah in the same area. Is the State Department's refusal to locate the American embassy in Jerusalem an example of anti-Semitism? It has a negative impact on the Jewish interest, but one can argue that it serves the American national interest.

Similar difficulties are encountered in examining the attitudinal category of anti-Semitism. Where does one place images and rhetoric that are in fact ambivalent or philo-Semitic? The perception of images is itself culture-bound and evokes different feelings in different cultures. The caricatures of the grasping Jewish black-marketeer or the swashbuckling Israeli soldier, which had such a prominent place in Soviet anti-Semitic propaganda, may have been effective in anticommercial societies in the Soviet orbit or in the preindustrial nations of the Third World. In societies that hold entrepreneurial energy in high regard and admire military efficiency, however, the impact was minimal or even the reverse of what was intended.

How such images are transmuted into attitudes depends on the preexisting mental set of the viewer. Moreover, attitudes can demonstrate enormous fluctuations. The Poles, surely not a people known for their love of Jews, silently applaud the same swashbuckling soldier that the controlled press held in such contempt. Morton Keller, viewing over one hundred surveys in Stember's *Jews in the Mind of America* reached the optimistic conclusion that anti-Semitism was a "disappearing problem in the United States.[25] Yet merely three years later, two researchers analyzing the findings of the Survey Research Center of the University of California at Berkeley concluded that anti-Jewish attitudes and stereotypes persist in large sections of the population and that the projection of a demise of anti-Semitism was premature.[26] Indeed by 1981, pollsters were finding that education and race were crucial variables in their measurements.[27] With such contrasting conclusions, it is small wonder that the notion that anti-Semitic attitudes were measurable was questioned. Polling results could be radically altered by changing the wording of questions. The increasing sophistication of the public permits respondents to present acceptable answers to the pollsters without betraying their true feelings, which they may sense are unacceptable.[28]

The Holocaust, an event of high historical valence, compounds the problem of distinguishing between latent and overt anti-Semitism. It confused the former, which is present in the history of all diasporic communities, with processed murder, which is not.[29] In a perverse way, it gave "normal" anti-Semitism a bad name. Even though there is a certain logic in viewing the Final Solution as the ultimate anti-Semitic act, it is no simple task to find the direct link between it and the "normative" anti-Semitism that existed in pre-Nazi Germany.[30] One can wonder if there would have been a Holocaust without the presence of the demonic figure of Adolf Hitler.[31] Does his personal pathology imposed by means of a totalitarian conduit on a people, admittedly made ready by its history to receive and implement his will, demonstrate a simple causal relationship between anti-Semitism and the Final Solution? After years of delving into the German archives, especially the files relating to the crimes of *Rassenschande* and *Judenfreunde*, Sarah Gordon, an American researcher, concludes that few German voters were attracted to the Nazi Party because of its anti-Semitism and that for both party members and the general public, the solution of the so-called Jewish question stopped well short of the Final Solution.[32] Similarly, Michael Marrus reminds us of the difficulties Nazi officials experienced in communicating their anti-Semitic obsession in Germany and the occupying areas.[33] That was one reason for keeping it secret instead of touting it. Thus, the intent to murder was confined to a handful.

More perplexing is what research reveals about the individual anti-Semite. Readers of the transcripts of Adolf Eichmann's pretrial interrogation and the works of Gideon Hausner and Hannah Arendt may dismiss Eichmann's repeated insistence that he was not an anti-Semite as self-serving attempts to garner the sympathy of the court.[34] A work, however, based on seventy hours of interviews with Franz Stangl, the former commandant of Treblinka, reveals a quotient of anti-Semitism not appreciably greater than others of his cultural and class background. Stangl did not become a mass killer of Jews because of an obsessional hatred. He came to his position by a series of bureaucratic decisions made for him and imposed on him, sometimes against his own desire.[35] But an obsessive anti-Semite like publisher Julius Streicher, whose *Der Stürmer* articulated the murderous intent of the Nazis, was never directly involved in the implementation of the Final Solution. Many with the *Einsatzgruppen*, the special SS killer units that operated behind German lines in Russia, display a life pattern far more like that of Stangl than Streicher. Clearly, historical caprice and loss of personal autonomy had more bearing on who became a mass murderer of Jews than an anti-Semitic attitude. In 1992, that finding was verified by Christopher Browning's research of a reserve police battalion, a military unit directly involved in mass murder in the East.[36]

The fact that American anti-Semitism remains attitudinal and does not harden into ideology poses additional problems for historians. Such an ideology has three identifying characteristics: it is conceived by an accredited intellectual; it contains an analysis of a "Jewish question" that is, it attempts to present an emotional attitude with a coherent rationale; and it has a "praxis" element that proposes a course of action to solve the problem. America has had thinkers like Brooks and Henry Adams, who were anti-Semites, but none like Ernest Renan, Joseph Gobineau, or Houston Stewart Chamberlain, who devoted themselves to fashioning a worldview based on the Jewish problem. Although American anti-Semites might have borrowed heavily from European thinkers, they rarely possessed credentials as intellectuals. They remained agitators. The threat they posed stemmed from their ability to feed the latent anti-Semitism that we must assume is present in the minds of the general public.

Strangely, however, a coherent ideology of anti-Semitism, with its standard "conspiracy theory" component, is not present in American history. Anti-Semitism is the progenitor of all such conspiracy theories, and it is evident on both the Right and the Left of the political spectrum. On the Right, it is usually associated with the pan-movements and the integral nationalism of the nineteenth century.[37] On the Left, it was first propounded by such utopian socialists as Charles Fourier and Pierre-Joseph Proudhon, who found Jews loathsome because they were the "incarnation of commerce." It was picked up by Bruno Bauer and his disciple Karl Marx and finally fed into the anti-Semitism of Joseph Stalin. Thus, Bebel's cry that anti-Semitism was "the Socialism of Fools" flies in the face of its legitimate socialist lineage. It accounts for the existence of "useless" or "unproductive" or "parasitic" classes. The first such "parasitic" group was imagined to be the Jews. In that sense, socialism contained the seeds to develop into anti-Semitism of the intellectuals of the Left.[38] It is mentioned here because the very conception that some classes were "parasitic" or "unproductive" and would best be tossed on the "dustbin of history" served as the warrant for Nazi genocide. From the vantage of national socialism, the Final Solution is more comparable to the liquidation of the kulaks than it is to the Turkish murder of the Armenians. Marxist ideology also contains the germ for the contemporary form of anti-Semitism that takes the shape of anti-Zionism. It was first conceived to be a reactionary bourgeois nationalist throwback and then a phenomenon related to the final imperialist stage of capitalism. Lenin, whose thinking on imperialism leans heavily on the work of John A. Hobson, also incorporated his view that Zionism was a "Jewish conspiracy."[39] The link between anti-Zionism and anti-Semitism, which is so fashionable today, can be traced back at least to the beginning of the century.

Some of the socialist elements of anti-Semitism are discernible in American thought. The Populist fixation with the "money conspiracy" and its anti-Semitic spin-off exemplifies it best. Yet generally, American soil has proved to be unreceptive to an ideology of anti-Semitism rooted in Marxist concepts. In contrast to Europe, America did not grant intellectuals elevated status. More important, the Marxist-Socialist concept that gained considerable influence among a sizable portion of the European intellectual strata made little headway in America. Whatever the answer to the hardy perennial question "Why is there no Socialism in the United States?", socialism's limited influence meant that the seeds of an anti-Semitic ideology contained in its anticommercial aspects also could not sprout roots. One can detect such splutterings in the Populist rhetoric of the 1890s and in contemporary African American anti-Semitism, but it is not given coherence by a systemic ideology. The same absence of ideological coherence is perceptible in another ideological source of Nazi anti-Semitism, social

Darwinism. In the American version, social Darwinism was primarily a justification for the free-wheeling business economy at home and for the dominance over lesser races and "backward" areas abroad. When it came to anti-Semitism, however, Populist writers like Ignatius Donnelly attributed Jewish nobility and talent to centuries of struggle for survival against anti-Semitic persecution.[40]

Strangely, the most certain evidence of the nonideological character of American anti-Semitism can be noted in the character of American Zionism. More than anything else, Zionism is the Jewish ideological response that is based on the assumption that anti-Semitism is inherent in the Diaspora. It can be used to measure the Jewish perception of anti-Semitism. The Zionist movement was a slow-starting affair among American Jews. It did not fully establish itself until the years of the Holocaust; and from the beginning, its character, like that of the anti-Semitism it reacts to, is nonideological. It is based on philanthropy and refugeeism and speaks rarely of reshaping the Jewish people. It is nonnationalistic and eschews resettlement in Israel, a recourse more suitable for Jews who live in areas where anti-Semitism poses physical danger.[41]

In summary, measuring the extent of anti-Semitism in America poses some especially difficult problems for historians. The pluralist character of American society makes it difficult to differentiate anti-Semitism from intergroup tensions normally at play in such societies and may allow less "popular" groups to deflect an animus directed against Jews in a more homogenous society. More vexing is the fact that American anti-Semitism is largely attitudinal and displays little ideological coherence. It is invisible in the sense that attitudes do not leave a tell-tale fingerprint on the historical canvas. That occurs only when attitudes are transmuted into concrete actions. When historians mix together such visible incidents with rhetoric and other evidence of the prevalence of anti-Semitic sentiment, the resulting portrait lacks historical meaning. Attitudes and incidents have entirely different historical valences. Grouping them together poses the danger of creating a new historical datum in which there may be little evidence of anti-Semitism.

A complex society whose code of civil behavior discourages candid expressions of anti-Semitism has produced a complex anti-Semitism that requires a taxonomy to classify each incident and make sense of it collectively. That would permit us to understand the difference between a Populist spokesman, who everywhere sees the Jewish "cash nexus" but in fact has never seen a Jew, and a Georgian mob, influenced by years of being exposed to anti-Jewish images and rhetoric, who at a particular juncture in history spontaneously converts an internalized attitude into overt action and lynches Leo Frank.[42] It would permit us to calibrate the difference between New York Police Commissioner Theodor Bingham's publicly proclaiming his feeling, unsupported by facts, that Jews generate a disproportionate amount of crime in the city and Senator Henry Cabot Lodge's quietly and slyly acting out his anti-Semitic proclivities by attempting to sneak a literacy requirement into the immigration law to limit the number of Jews entering the country. Although publicly proclaimed, Commissioner Bingham's belief remains in the realm of attitudes. It may slander Jews, but it does not deny them access or limit their freedom; and it can be and was fought and challenged. Senator Lodge's silent attempt to use his political power to limit Jewish immigration has a potentially far more direct impact. It is power that sorts things out by separating the ephemeral from the real and the latent from the concrete. It acts like sunlight on the growth of vegetation.

In retrospect, one can see that it was the National Socialist's assumption of power that transformed the situation in the Reich. It endowed what was merely sentiment with the possibility of becoming public policy. That "officialization" swept the millions, whose anti-Semitic sentiment may have been latent or conceivably nonexistent, into the vortex. It became acceptable, even profitable, to become anti-Semitic. Yet, it was state power instead of popular will that established the norm. That fact accounts for the remarkable reversion to the latent form of anti-Semitism the moment the Nazi regime lost power. The anti-Semitism that had been central to the Third Reich's ideology left remarkably few historical echoes in its wake, and so students of contemporary German culture are hard pressed to locate even a trace of the passionate sentiment that caused the death of millions.[43] With the vanishing of authorized state power, popular anti-Semitism seems to have been pushed back into the closet. It has again become merely latent.

America has had its share of vigorous anti-Semitic orators and organizations, but generally they have lacked official power, even on the local level. There has been no Jewish question on the American political agenda, which indicates a continued unwillingness to deal with a central question of all organized anti-Semitic programs: the insistence that Jews have too much wealth and power, which ought to be taken from them. It is true that some minority groups declaim that they have not received their fair share of what America has to offer. Yet, the effort to correct such inequities has not led to a consideration through politics and governance of the question of what Jews, or any other group in the society, should have. It does not seem likely that the question of how wealth and power are distributed in America can ever become part of the formal political power transactions that are a basic part of the political process. To impose them politically against one group, whether the Jews or the Episcopalians, would threaten the very foundations of the ethos of achievement that is the driving force of the American economy. Not only is America unready to recognize the existence of a Jewish question but the transference of the management of such a question to the public arena is also impossible to imagine. The anti-Semitic grievance seems destined to be confined, as it has always been, to the private sector and the private imagination.

Of course, this does not mean that it is a neutral force that poses no danger. Most important things that happen in America, including the decisions regarding allocation of resources, happen privately. It also does not mean that some cataclysmic event could not catapult a Jewish question into the political process. There was a period during the depression of the 1930s in which anti-Semitism had become so strident that it seemed as though it would enter into the political dialogue. Yet thereafter, during the periods of great social stress—the McCarthy hysteria, the lost war in Southeast Asia, the oil boycott, the loss of American marines in Lebanon—when the circumstance for a surfacing of anti-Semitism seemed present, no great proclivity to bring a Jewish question into American politics occurred. Without such official amplification, American anti-Semitism has remained too inchoate to deny Jews those spiritual and material benefits that all Americans have come to respect as rightfully theirs.

Yet, the perception of inordinate power in Jewish hands, a mainstay of the anti-Semitic imagination, poses a special problem. It matters not that it is a flawed perception shared by some Jews. The establishment of a Jewish state that has been compelled to use power more frequently than most nation-states has given the anti-Semites new fuel for their fantasies and a tangible target for their animosity. At the same time, Israel's inordinate security needs have caused a gradual alteration of American Jewish political culture. American Jewry, acting partly as an advocate before the American seat of power, has been compelled to become more active and therefore more conspicuous in the political process. The Jewish reentry into history with the establishment of Israel has predictably carried American Jewry along with it. The nurturing of Israel has become a crucial part of its political agenda. To see to Israel's needs, a direct deployment of political influnce has often been necessary. The conspicuousness of American Jewry in the political process is attributable to other factors aside from the needs of Israel, but the total effect is the same. It has become a tempting target for anti-Semites, who see in the "Zioniza-tion" of American Jewry substantiation for their central fantasy, that there exists an international Jewish conspiracy. Because "Israelism" is an important tenet in the civil religion to which most American Jews adhere, by attacking it and the founding ideology of Zionism in which the Jewish state is rooted, anti-Semites can easily get at the center of contemporary American Jewish sensibility and concern.[44] That is what anti-Semites need to do.

Therefore, it is power that differentiates anti-Semitic attitudes from anti-Semitic acts and allows historians to determine the relative importance of each discrete anti-Semitic incident. Power is not the only measuring rod, of course. It is conceivable that, in a democracy, an intensification of anti-Semitic attitudes to create a near consensus can create an attitudinal change. Yet, such a change also requires a kind of power. No group has better reason to understand the impor-tance of ideas and public attitudes in history than the Jews. They have been submitting "civilizing" ideas to the world for millennia. Their recent history, however, also demonstrates that, unmatched by power, civilizing ideas offer precious little protection. Latent attitudi-nal anti-Semitism, which is denied access to officializing power, as it is in America, poses only a remote danger. Jewish defense agencies expend ample resources in monitoring such attitudinal changes and fighting them in the public-opinion arena. But from a historical per-spective, the struggle for the minds of the American public is only a preliminary skirmish. The real problem is to deny omnipresent anti-Semitic constituencies access to power that can make a private atti-tude official policy. The best way to avoid such action is for American Jewry to continue to generate and amplify its own political power.

In these postwar decades, few will argue that anti-Semitism poses no danger. That the force of anti-Semitism has shifted its focus to Zionism and Israel and continues to demonstrate an unerring in-stinct for what lies at the center of Jewish sensibility indicates that it is a dynamic force. What is argued here is the need for a better method for weighing the importance of each anti-Semitic incident so that the danger it poses can be better assessed. The possibility of an outburst of anti-Semitism triggered perhaps by a domestic or foreign crisis or a sustained, unresolved racial crisis can furnish the circumstances for that outburst to occur. Still, that does not mean that every incident, whether it concerns a slander by a candidate for the presidency or the claim by a fundamentalist spokesman that God does not hear the prayers of Jews, is a signal that a pogrom is about to happen. From a survivalist point of view, the problem with reading every untoward anti-Semitic incident as part of the accumulation of evidence that it is happening here in America is that it tends to conceal a reality that has seemed historically to exist in tandem with American anti-Semitism. Jewish survival has been, and is today, as much threatened by the desire to accept and absorb American Jewry as it is by hatred of Jews, probably more. If that is true, then it is more important than ever to make a sound historical judgment of the role anti-Semitism has played in American Jewish history. This brief examination is presented in that light.

5

The Struggle for Middle-Class
Status and Acceptance at Harvard

A NEW GROUP of Jewish aspirants to the American middle class ar-
rived during the prosperous 1920s. They were the sons and daughters
of the eastern European immigrants. Unlike the earlier German Jew-
ish arrivistes, their struggle to establish themselves occurred in an
economy that had become more consolidated and offered fewer op-
portunities for those who were largely bereft of capital. Unfortunately,
these new immigrants came into a climate of ugly xenophobia that
sought to restrict immigration and to stigmatize the immigrant com-
munity. Predictably, because they were easily identifiable by their dis-
tinct culture, language, and urban location, these Jews became targets
of a special animosity. The German Jewish merchant and peddler of
the nineteenth century had felt the sting of anti-Semitism in caricature
and slander and talk of a satanic plot to control the world economy.
Thanks to Henry Ford's *Dearborn Independent*, that rhetoric reached a
crescendo during the early twenties. It culminated in an anti-Semi-
tism that sought complete exclusion and thus threatened the mobility
of second-generation Jews.

When Jewish entrepreneurs had established small businesses or
had pioneered in establishing new industries, such as the fur trade
during the colonial period or the film industry during the twenties,
there was little that the poorly organized anti-Semitic groups could
do to restrict them. After all, courageous enterprising was a cherished
quality of a free market economy.[1] Comparatively few members of the
preceding Sephardic and German Jewish communities had chosen
higher education as a path to achieve middle-class status.[2] But in the

twenties, Jewish families began a new strategy and invested in their own human capital. They sought formal education and professional training.

That strategy led directly to the "invasion," the enrollment of Jewish students in all kinds of institutions of higher learning.[3] University officials located near Jewish population centers in eastern cities spoke of the "invasion" in alarmed tones. But it was the startling increase in Jewish enrollment at Harvard, the nation's premier university, that brought the conflict between Jewish aspirations and the established university culture to a head. The intellectual culture generated by Jewish students was viewed as a threat to the established conventions of American higher education that sought to mold character as much as to develop minds.

Had Harvard's decision to limit enrollment been allowed to stand, Jewish social advancement through university certification would have been hampered. Thus despite the small number of students involved, some Jewish leaders decided to challenge Harvard's enrollment policy.

In this essay, I examine the shadowy area in which the Jewish drive to achieve middle-class status, first through the instrument of small business and then through formal education and certification, was confronted by those who wished to restrict Jews during the 1920s. Whether in the immigration law or in Harvard's enrollment policy, the anti-Semitism of quotas went beyond the rhetoric of the anti-Semitism exemplified by Henry Ford. This new anti-Semitism posed a direct threat to the aspirations of the children of the eastern European immigrants, who were determined to make a better life for themselves. It also serves as a window through which to view the underlying American Jewish condition in the twenties.

The decade betweem 1919 and 1929 did not begin auspiciously for American Jewry. There was reason to suspect that, although the new immigration laws of 1921 and 1924 did not specifically mention Jews, the authors of the laws were convinced that the nation was about to be flooded by penniless Jews fleeing their war-devastated communities in eastern Europe. Nor did Jews find solace in the decision of the newly reorganized Ku Klux Klan to add Catholics as well as Jews to its familiar Negrophobia. Jews understood that Henry Ford's publication of *The Protocols of the Elders of Zion* went beyond the denial of hotel accommodations at Saratoga Springs and even beyond the lynching of Leo Frank. Ford had, after all, become an American folk hero beloved by millions of ordinary Americans, and he possessed enormous financial resources to promote anti-Semitism.

Nevertheless, that Jews established themselves economically during the twenties, despite such signs of hostility, is not as paradoxical as it might seem. Adversity, which in this period was coupled with opportunity, may have fueled the immigrant Jews' need for economic security. The decade of the 1920s possessed both. It was a prosperous period marked by the development of a new multiplier industry, the automobile, to replace the railroads and by an increase in productivity from newly developed electric power.[4] The result was a 40 percent increase in labor productivity and a consequent 11 percent rise in real income. There would be more leisure time to spend such income as the work week declined by almost two hours. Some, looking at the 5,174 bank failures between 1921 and 1929 and the peersistent malaise in the agricultural sector, would note later that it was a false prosperity, but that concept hardly concerned those who were prospering at the time.[5]

What was distinctive about the economic situation of American Jewry in the 1920s was not its great wealth or power but its configuration, "the curious . . . distribution in particular squares of the checkerboard.[6] Jews tended to congregate in nonpreempted areas of the economy or to pioneer in new ones like the film industry. They were frequently found, according to a *Fortune Magazine* study, where manufacturing and merchandising converged or in areas like the clothing business, where a Jewish presence had already been established.[7] Other such distinctly Jewish business areas were wholesale and retail merchandising of tobacco products, the distillation and merchandising of liquor, and auxiliaries of the clothing trade: hatmaking, furs, button retailing, and belts.

Jewish entrepreneurs were of course not exempt from the adverse effects of a rapidly changing economy, especially if they were an established part of the preexisting economic order. There was, for example, a reduction in Jewish banking, which rapidly lost its Jewish character after the death of Jacob Schiff in 1921. Jews no longer fulfilled their management and capital needs from within the family and "crowd." With the possible exception of Goldman-Sachs, Jewish investment bankers made a good transition to the more complex, regulated investment market of the 1930s after the Glass-Steagal law was passed. But as early as 1911, Kuhn Loeb had taken on a non-Jewish partner, and Goldman-Sachs had followed suit in 1915. And by 1924, Lehman Brothers was no longer exclusively a family concern.

There was actually a moderate decline of prominent Jews in the top rungs of the economy. Of the 449 names listed in Henry Klein's *Dynamic America and Those Who Own It*, a popular survey published in 1921, only 33 of the 449 names were Jewish.[8] The Guggenheims were still listed among America's four richest families , but they no longer actively managed their mines. Well known Jewish names like Straus, Schiff, Lewisohn, and Rosenwald, however, remained conspicuous in the second tier of fortunes of $20 million and less.[9]

The de-Judaizing of the German Jewish banking nexus did not occasion a matching de-Christianizing of non-Jewish banking houses. In 1936, the *Fortune* study reported that "there are practically no Jewish employees of any kind in the largest commercial banks."[10] August Belmont and Company was dissolved in 1930, and Seligman Company almost completely curtailed direct investments in June 1939. Others, like Kuhn Loeb and Lehman Brothers, also curtailed their business during the depression. Although in the early twenties much of the German Jewish business establishment was still intact, it had not kept pace with the expanding economy. By the thirties, private investment banking, which had been a major economic asset of the preceding German Jewish community, was no longer in the Jewish arena. There was also some loss in an area where we would least expect it, large-scale retailing. Few of the new chains were Jewish owned, and many small Jewish retailers faced a challenge to remain in business.[11] Even the largest Jewish-owned retailing establishment, Sears Roebuck, fell upon bad times during the recession of 1921 and was only salvaged by the timely action of Julius Rosenwald, who invested a portion of his personal fortune to save the business.[12]

Anti-Semitic restriction sometimes played a role in shaping the Jewish economic profile. Jewish entrepreneurs displayed an uncanny ability to convert a handicap into an advantage. Few Jews were to be found on the boards of directors or in top management of America's major corporations. Yet, Jews were not totally unfamiliar with the manufacturing end of the automobile business.[13] The new industry followed the pattern of American basic industry and employed only three Jews in managerial positions and almost none on the boards of directors. But by 1927, Jews were already prominent in the automobile equipment market—tires, mirrors, headlights, et cetera—and became conspicuous in the thriving used car market.[14] The business career of John D. Hertz is typical. A Czech Jew who had settled in Chicago, he founded the Yellow Cab Company in 1915, which went on to become number one in public transportation and car rentals.[15] Similarly, there were almost no Jews to be found in the steel industry, with the exception of Inland Steel, which had some Jewish managers. But, according to the *Fortune* study, the scrap metal business, which by 1924 capitalized at over $300 million, was 90 percent Jewish owned.[16]

In secondary industries and merchandising, Jews were represented beyond their proportion of the population. They were making a name for themselves in industries such as real estate development, housing construction, printing, show manufacturing, kosher foods (based on a specific Jewish market), textile manufacturing, hotel keeping, the new film industry, and general entertainment.[17] As early users of the newly popular credit buying, Jewish merchants continued to establish large and small department stores, especially in middle-sized cities. Such stores capitalized on the established Jewish merchandising grid, which had first developed during the colonial period. In the twenties it was a phenomenon still largely confined to the east: Marshall Fields of Chicago and Prince, Scott and Company were not Jewish, nor were the big chain stores, such as Woolworth and Kress.

The breadth of Jewish *embourgeoisement*, especially through merchandising, surpassed other groups. Jewish department store ownership, for example, was merely the most visible part of a merchandising interest that reached into virtually every town in America. In many cases, Jewish merchants preceded the development of the town or hamlet, which was organized around them. During the twenties, it was often a successful small business that strengthened the back and shored up the pride of many second-generation American Jews.[18]

Predictably, when a new industry developed whose product consisted of words and images, such as advertising, publishing, radio, and film, the Jewish influence was more prevalent. The use of language and images is after all culturally close to home for Jews. The Jewish impact on the development of commercial radio is an especially interesting example because, together with Jewish influence in the film industry, it became the bugaboo of the anti-Semitic imagination. After the federal government lifted the ban on privately owned radio sets in 1919, the radio industry developed rapidly. By 1922, large-scale manufacture of radio sets began; and by 1929, 40 percent of American families owned radios. The first nationwide network,

The National Broadcasting Corporation, was organized by the Radio Corporation of America in 1926. The Columbia Broadcasting System followed suit in 1927. In both cases, Jews played a prominent entrepreneurial role. But they did not supply the capital to build these networks, and the local stations (562 by 1924) that bought their programs were characterized by a conspicuous absence of Jews.[19] The same was true of the printed media.

Jews were prominently represented in newspapers, as in ownership of the influential *Washington Post* and *New York Times;* but the large newspaper chains were overwhelmingly non-Jewish.[20] Similarly in the burgeoning advertising business, six of the largest 200 agencies were owned by Jews, but few Jews were to be found in non-Jewish agencies and none in the lucrative position of accounts manager. Advertising was resistant to hiring Jews. Agency owners placed a high priority on looking and acting "American." Some Jews did of course "pass," which led to a favorite joke regarding such employees: "He used to be Jewish, but he's all right now."[21] In publishing, there were virtually no large Jewish firms before 1915; but by 1925, there were seven small, quality Jewish houses.[22] Clearly, when "mind" industries, such as radio and film, had a need for intellectual and entrepreneurial verve, Jews found their way to these new areas of the economy. Thus, the film industry, a once marginal storefront business largely in the hands of Jewish nickelodeon owners, became a major business enterprise.[23] But even here it is difficult to detect a Jewish strategy to influence national perception or even a distinct Jewish sensibility, which can sometimes be noted after World War II. Despite the apprehension of anti-Semites, it was the lure of profit instead of the desire to influence public opinion that drew Jews to these industries.

Most observers would agree with Nathan Glazer's conclusion that the two decades between 1920 and 1940 served as a "great fulcrum," transforming American Jewry from a proletarianized immigrant group to a middle-class one.[24] There is less agreement on whether the primary instrument for this transformation was intense education or small business. By the twenties, both were being used simultaneously.[25] In many cases, sons of immigrant workers were moving directly to higher education and the professions; but as often as not, the 70,000 new immigrants who arrived between 1921 and 1927 were compelled to start at the bottom of the economic ladder.

We move next to a closer examination of the factors that made up the process out of which grew the third commercial elite in the

American Jewish experience. During the colonial and early national periods, Sephardic Jewry had produced a commercial elite based on ocean commerce, industrial secrets, and enterprises in undeveloped sections of the economy.[26] Similarly, the German Jews of the nineteenth century had produced a commercial elite that evolved primarily from merchandising and eventually culminated in a Jewish commercial banking nexus popularly known as "our crowd." By the 1920s, the American economy had undergone considerable change from the openness of the pre–World War I decades. It was more consolidated and mature and broader in scope. To achieve place, the second generation of eastern European Jews had to employ a more varied strategy. This cohort was also numerically larger and more conspicuous than the former and required a broader spectrum of opportunities. Both external and internal factors were involved in its choice of education and certification to achieve middle-class rank, eventually affecting thousands of Jewish families.

They climbed from the proletarian immigrant generation to a modern, educated, urban middle class in barely three decades, one of which was marked by a severe economic depression, and they did so far earlier than other groups of the "new immigration."[27] Often, they hardly had time to accustom themselves to their new position. They continued to speak with accents and use the hand gestures with which they were familiar. I mention this fact because we must be aware of the juxtaposition of accelerated mobility with only minimal acculturation to understand the adverse reaction in such institutions as Harvard. By the 1940s, many second-generation Jews bore, in their economic if not social and cultural characteristics, a greater resemblance to the established Protestant groups than they did to their fellow immigrants. The intensive use of formal education and certification allowed them to bypass the roadblocks to which Jews were heir. This was the first group in American Jewish history to use a combination of professional training and traditional business enterprise.

To state that Jews were undergoing professionalization in the 1920s is to oversimplify. During the twenties, the classification *professional* was not a precisely defined category because certification had not developed to the extent that we know it today.[28] Comparatively few Jews actually became professional, and it was not really a new phenomenon. Higher training had been occurring all along, even in the first generation. It may be more accurate to observe that, in the twenties, Jews enhanced their skills through formal education and training and that their attainment of professional status represented merely their most obvious achievement.

How extensive was this movement? One 1934 survey based on thirty-six middle- and small-sized cities points out that the first phase of the movement between 1920 and 1950 was relatively slow, so that the number of Jews in the professional category varied from 7.4 to 12 percent.[29] Those figures are not far different from those for the Jews of Berlin or Vienna or other areas of large Jewish populations. American Jewry was following a typical postemancipation urban pattern in its occupational distribution.

Because such enhancement involves intense education, figures on Jewish school attendance reveal a remarkable record. Although Jews were less than 3.4 percent of the general population in 1934, they supplied 10 percent of the national student population and a far higher percentage in Jewish population centers. Moreover, the higher the educational level, the more disproportionate the Jewish presence compared to other ethnic groups.[30] Jews simply attended school longer and were more likely to graduate. In some cases, the depression actually reinforced the stay-in-school phenomenon. In 1935, Jews supplied almost three times as many students as their proportion of the population.

When the welfare state program of the New Deal created a much-expanded federal bureaucracy, newly minted Jewish professionals—lawyers, social workers, and economists—were able to find their first positions with the government. Later, when the economy was placed on a war footing, they were again in an ideal position to use their elevated skills.[31] Unemployment in the Jewish community during the depression did not vary much from that for non-Jews, but it might have been greater given the persistence of restrictive hiring practices and the fact that marginal small businesses, especially in the luxury fur and jewelry trades where Jews concentrated, were severely affected by the depression. Employees with higher levels of education were in some measure more quickly reemployed and were considered to have better potential for retraining.[32] Education also carried monetary rewards. According to Barry R. Chiswick, second-generation Jews had a 16 percent higher earning capacity.[33] Small wonder that they grasped any opportunity for formal higher education.

Thus, the Jewish investment in education proved to be a highly profitable one. Chiswick states that education and certification had a 20 percent higher rate of economic return even after controlling the data for occupation, region, and time.[34] Most interesting for those Jews who argued so passionately about the real and imagined difference between Romanian and Russian Jews or between Galizianer and

Litvak is the fact that the Jewish rise in station was across the board. Chiswick states that there were "no systemic differences among Jews by parent's country of birth."[35]

The Harvard problem began formally during the summer of 1922, when rumors circulated that Harvard intended to follow the practice of limiting Jewish enrollment that was already established at Columbia, Syracuse, Princeton, Rutgers, and other major eastern universities. These universities had experienced an amazing rise in the registration of Jewish students.[36] By 1920, former bastions of Protestants like Hunter and City College in New York City had student populations that were 80 percent to 90 percent Jewish. By being located in the city with the largest Jewish population and with no tuition, they stood little chance of resisting the flood of Jewish students. Indeed, CCNY would soon become known as "the College of the Circumcised Citizens of New York." According to Morris Raphael Cohen, its best known Jewish professor, its atmosphere had little of the gentility associated with American colleges. America had never seen anything like it. "The obvious crudeness of our youth, whose fine idealism had not yet been tempered by hard and cold realities, struck some of my colleagues as the chief evil that the colleges of the country needed to convert," observed Cohen.[37] But the officials of Harvard did not consider it their mission to convert raw Jewish students to civility.

The Jewish "inundation" of Harvard, although less marked, was no less keenly felt. In 1920, its Jewish enrollment was a mere 10 percent; but one year later it had risen to 15 percent, and by 1922 it stood at 20 percent. The imminence of quotas at Harvard was known well before President Abbott Lawrence Lowell, unlike the heads of other universities, decided to go public with his scheme to limit the admission of Jewish students. He was doing so, he proclaimed, not only for the protection of Harvard's integrity and character but to prevent the growth of anti-Semitism within the student body. "If their number should become 40 percent of the student body," he explained in a letter to Alfred Benesch, a prominent Jewish alumnus from Cleveland, "the race feeling would become intense. When on the other hand, the number of Jews was small, the race antagonism was also small."[38] Like Henry Ford, he was surprised at the uproar in the Jewish community. After all, he had not used the subterfuges employed at other large universities faced with a similar problem. Surely, the

Jews could see the necessity of the new policy.[39] As will be revealed later, some of them actually did see it Lowell's way.

I need not detail the development of the imbroglio that compelled Lowell to hand the case over to a special committee after the faculty refused to empower the admissions committee charged with implementing the new policy. Three of the faculty members on the committee were Jewish, and they and Julian Mack, the only Jewish member of Harvard's Board of Overseers, thwarted the scheme, at least temporarily. But here we are primarily interested in discovering the reason for American Jewry's intense reaction when in fact Harvard was among the last of the elite universities to try to implement such a policy.

It was not Jewish students per se but a new kind of Jewish student who triggered the decision to implement quotas. Harvard experienced little difficulty in absorbing Jewish students before the turn of the century, when the Jewish applicants were primarily from established German Jewish families who in manners, dress, and estate were hardly distinguishable from the non-Jewish majority. "But at the turn of the century," observes Samuel Eliot Morison, the historian of Harvard, "the bright Russian Jewish lads from the Boston public schools began to arrive. There were enough of them in 1906 to form the Menorah Society, and in another fifteen years Harvard had her 'Jewish problem.'"[40] Many of them were "tram" students who lived at home. Those who lived on campus were segregated in two dorms, one of which, Walter Hastings Hall, was soon dubbed "little Jerusalem." They arrived with a different purpose from what Thorstein Veblen called the "cultivation of gentility" and the mastery of the "canons of genteel intercourse" preferred by the Protestant establishment.[41] They brought with them a distinctive eastern European Jewish style that took ideas seriously and gave high priority to what observant Jews call "lernen," a close study and mastery of text. When transmuted to modern secular values, this style came to mean a celebration of scholarship as reflected in academic performance. When a Jewish youth earned the highest marks on a standard battery of tests to measure character and psychic soundness given to entering freshmen, it was sufficient to rate the headline "Jewish Youth Attains Highest Rating in Psychological Tests in Colleges" in the *American Hebrew,* which regularly published scores of the New York State Regents scholarship examination and listed the percentage of Jewish winners.[42]

Lest we overdraw the image of a community drawn exclusively

to what contemporary student culture contemptuously calls "nerd-ism," I hasten to add that such was hardly the case. American Jewish culture gave a high priority to academic achievement but it also es-teemed athletics. At least part of the complaint against Jewish stu-dents related to their supposed unwillingness to enter into the social life of the campus, most of which was dominated by national frater-nities. But only some of that social isolation could fairly be attributed to a different set of values. They were as much excluded by others as self-excluded. Most fraternities did not welcome Jews and certainly not Jewish students who returned home or, worse, held jobs after classes.[43] Jewish students did form their own fraternities, but they never became the rage among the children of immigrants. When Harry B. Chambers, New York's commissioner of the Board of Educa-tion, advocated the reinstatement of fraternities in the high schools in the spring of 1922, it created a considerable stir in the Jewish commu-nity. The *American Hebrew* opposed it because it interfered with the socialization of Jewish students and "led to self-complacent snob-bery," recommending instead organizations like Arista, founded by William Felter, the Jewish principal of Girls High School in Brooklyn. Arista was "a society open to all who measured up to a high standard of character and scholarship. . . . The one is open, while the other is dark," Felter observed.[44]

Academic achievement was highly rated, but it never stood alone in the emerging Jewish constellation of values. When Vienna's champion Jewish soccer team visited the United States in 1927, a veri-table craze of enthusiasm swept the Lower East Side; and when the baseball team of the almost all-Jewish Seward Park High School won the city championship, despite the fact that the team had no field on which to practice, the *American Hebrew* and the Yiddish dailies played the story to the hilt.[45] The names of Jewish students who had earned a letter for athletic performance as well as the records of Jewish boxers and stars in baseball and football were regularly published in the An-glo-Jewish press.

Scholarship also meant more than simply earning good grades, although that was its most obvious manifestation. At Columbia, where one-fifth of the students were Jewish, nearly half the students elected to Phi Beta Kappa in 1922 were Jews. Their preference for mental work was, however, not limited to study. The *Columbia Specta-tor* became one of the best college newspapers in the country when Jewish students took over its editorship; and although the football team may have attracted few Jewish students for scrimmage, acting in a varsity play did. The cultural atmosphere of the university took on a tone of high excitement. Jewish students could generate a full student culture where athletics played merely one part and scholastic achievement was given high priority.[46] Meyer Shapiro, who would become the nation's most distinguished art historian, was a member of the class of 1924; Lionel Trilling, perhaps its most noteworthy literary critic, graduated a year later; and Sidney Hook received his doctorate there in 1927. They were only the beginning.[47]

Predictably, emphasis on academic achievements did little to endear Jewish students to most of their Christian fellow students, who placed great value on learning the social graces, which they believed were necessary for the positions they aspired to in business and society. One often notes in the reaction by Harvard students that, whether they admired Jews or despised them, they inevitably were aware of the change of emphasis a Jewish presence on campus caused. At times, the reaction was a familiar anti-Semitism, reflected in this ditty that was popular at Harvard in 1910:

> Oh, Harvard's run by millionaires
> And Yale is run by booze,
> Cornell is run by farmers' sons
> Columbia's by Jews.
>
> So give a cheer for Baxter Street
> Another one for Pell
> And when the little sheenies die,
> Their souls will go to hell.[48]

At other times, non-Jews felt a direct sense of proprietary loss, as reflected in this reaction of a Harvard undergraduate at the time of the crisis: "The Jews tend to overrun the College, to spoil it for the native born Anglo-Saxon young persons for whom it was built and whom it really wants."[49] Some thought that, whether one chose to excel in scholarship or athletics was a matter of choice, and neither preference deserved condemnation. "If the Jews have a complex on athletics," noted Professor Richard Cabot, who taught philosophy and ethics at Harvard, "our boys have one on the Phi Beta Kappa Society."[50] There could be no mistaking who he thought "our boys" were. Nor did all agree with Cabot's placement of academic achievement on a par with athletics. Morris R. Cohen quotes a military training instructor at CCNY addressing his captive student audience: "If you want to be a he-man, go in for football, if you want to be a nut like Einstein, stick to the books."[51]

In the classroom, the change of atmosphere was palpable. Jews broke the students' solidarity against their professors. Now the moment the professor posed a question, there was no longer a stony resisting silence; instead, all the Jewish hands shot up, anxious to respond.[52] Unknowingly, such students violated the taboo against showy scholarship. The response was predictable. "History is full of examples where one race has displaced another by underliving and overworking," observed one student.[53] Another at Columbia School of Medicine noted that he now had to work much harder: "The Jews set the pace. They keep the scholastic standards high and make the rest of us work harder than we have ever worked before in order to keep up with them. Somehow or other they have an emotional intensity which drives them to study longer and harder than the average Christian."[54] Most preferred to attribute the superior performance of Jewish students to overzealousness.

According to the well-known drama critic Walter P. Eaton, the problem was not based on the resentment of academic competition but "an instinct for self preservation. . . . In the last few years . . . a class of Jew has grown up, who by his innate cleverness and ambition and will-to-power, has reached our universities, but brings with him little or no cultural background, unpleasantly aggressive manners, and in general, an atmosphere disturbingly at variance with the spirit of the place he enters." Like many others, Eaton did not fear what he called Jewish cleverness. He observed that their mental equipment was actually modest. What he resented was their "rudeness of manners, lack of courtsey . . . and general vulgarity."[55] They did not accommodate to the rules of the college community; instead, they tried to change them, Jewish students were accused of wanting only to take from the university and to give little to it. The Harvard Semitic Museum, donated by Jacob Schiff in 1902, and the generosity of Jewish alumni, did not dissuade the opinion of non-Jewish students.[56] They perceived the presence of an alien culture.

The Jewish perspective on the limitation policy was of course far different. They simply could not agree that it was their coarseness and insufficient standards of personal hygiene that had brought on the problem. Even if there was some truth in such complaints, they could hardly serve as the criteria a liberal college like Harvard were bound to follow. Generally, Jews viewed scholastic merit as the most important criterion in university life, a belief in which many non-Jews concurred. That was the view expressed by a columnist in the *Harvard Graduates' Magazine*. "If some one racial group does gather to itself the virtues and excellences, mental and moral, so abundantly as to acquire of right a dominating representation in Harvard University, that right must be accorded it."[57] But most undoubtedly believed that, if the possessions of such virtues were applied as standards of admission, Jewish representation would not be dominant, merely present.

Clearly, something else was involved that was based on fear and resentment. Harry Starr, president of the Menorah Society and deeply involved in the limitations case, began by believing that the problem stemmed from the dislike of only certain Jews. But he soon learned differently. "We learned that it was *numbers* that mattered; bad or good, *too many* Jews were not liked. Rich or poor, brilliant or dull, polished or crude—*too many Jews*." He concluded that the policy had to be fought, and that it was up to Jews to remind Harvard of its tradition of complete equality and openness.[58]

That was the position taken by most Jews, who refused to accept Lowell's contention that he was favoring limitation to prevent the rise of anti-Semitism at Harvard. They recalled that Lowell had opposed the appointment of Louis Brandeis to the Supreme Court in 1916 and that his advocacy of restrictionism at Harvard had been accompanied by a strong restrictionist position on immigration. But a small minority of "uptown" Jews did see merit in it. "One of the saddest features of the whole matter," wrote Louis Marshall to his brother-in-law Judah Magnes, "lies in the fact that some of our Jewish snobs are openly favoring a limitation which would exclude a large percentage of the Russian Jews who are seeking to get an education at Harvard and other institutions of like rank."[59] Often, they were scions of the nineteenth-century German Jewish immigration who shared the notion that Jews were pushing too hard and sending their children to universities fully one generation ahead of the other groups who made up the "new immigration." The result was, according to one Harvard savant, that "there were in fact more dirty Jews and tactless Jews in college than dirty and tactless Italians, Armenians, or Slovaks."[60] A sermon at Temple Emanu-El in New York on September 22, 1922, sought to attribute the onerous characteristics of eagerness for money and material success to European rather than Jewish culture. The alleged "boisterousness and loudness" of Jews only seemed that way in contrast to the English and Americans of native stock, "who are generally cold and undemonstrative."[61] But Walter Lippmann, writing in the *American Hebrew*, was less inclined to make excuses:

The rich and vulgar and pretentious Jews of our big American cities are perhaps the greatest misfortune that has ever befallen the Jewish people. . . . They undermine the natural liberalism of the American people. . . . I worry about upper Broadway on a Sunday afternoon where everything that is feverish and unventilated in the congestion of a city rises up as a warning that you can not build up a decent civilization among people who have lost their ancient piety and acquired no new convictions, among people who, when they are at last, after centuries of denial, free to go to the land and cleanse their bodies, now huddle together in a steam heated slum.[62]

For Lippmann, himself a Harvard graduate and the son of an established German Jewish family, it was all the fault of the Jews who seemed incapable of "moderate, clean and generous living." But on one point, "the loss of ancient piety," another Harvard alumnus, Maurice Stern, agreed. "It is not the Jew who practices his Judaism who stirs up anti-Semitism, but the Jew who neglects it, besmirches and disgraces it."[63] Professor A. A. Goldenwasser, of the New School for Social Research, thought that Lowell was wrong but at least sincere. That was more than he could say for Nicholas Butler of Columbia and the other presidents of major universities who used subterfuge and concealment to impose such barriers. "Harvard," Goldenwasser insisted, was still the "most open minded," and "President Lowell is the least prejudiced of the heads of great American Universities."[64] Even Alfred Benesch, who was among the first Jewish alumni to confront Lowell, admitted in his letter that "Harvard probably has a problem with some of its Jewish students." But he attributed it not to their religion or race but to their poverty, their need to work, and the fact that they simply could not afford to live in the dorms.[65] Although Julian Morgenstern, president of Hebrew Union College, agreed that "noisy and assertive" Jews without an interest in athletics who thought only of earning a diploma were a problem, it was not a Jewish problem but a problem of the unacculturated foreign born. Jews were entering the university prematurely. He was convinced that quotas were not directed against Scandinavian or Italian Americans because their children were not yet knocking at the university door. It was not a case of anti-Semitism but the problem of "the foreign born, unAmerican, or not-yet American Jew."[66]

The *American Hebrew*, conscious of the fact that Jewish enrollment in the universities reached well beyond the Jewish proportion of the population and that the universities, after all was said and done,

were private institutions that voluntarily assumed a public respon-
sibility, called for building up public colleges as a solution: "The na-
tion . . . must provide the means to offer higher education to all her
children who seek it. . . . The day of the state college and city univer-
sity is dawning. State institutions will become the great depositories
of American democracy." It was a prophetic city.[67]

In fact, Jews like Lippmann were the exception rather than the
rule. Jews confronted the Harvard limitations case with remarkable
confidence. Marshall, the outspoken leader of the American Jewish
Committee, identified Lowell as an "advocate of the higher anti-Semi-
tism" and counseled against allowing him to put the burden on the
Jews. "He has created the issue. He has insulted the intelligence of the
American people. He has played with fire. . . . He has made his bed.
Let him lie in it. We, as Jews, will not admit the soundness of his
premises. We must insist upon the equality of right of treatment."[68]
Horace Kallen, who learned of pluralism as an undergraduate at Har-
vard, also perceived that the *numerus clausus* did not stem from a
failure of Jewish students but the sense of vulnerability felt by non-
Jews when faced with the phenomenon of an ambitious minority anx-
ious for place. He wrote to a friend, "It is not the failure of the Jews
to be assimilated into undergraduate society which troubles them."
They do not want Jews to be assimilated. . . . What troubles them
is the completeness with which Jews want to be and have been assim-
ilated."[69]

Kallen may have gone too far. Student life at City College, where
Jewish students were the majority in the twenties, as described by
Morris Cohen and others, was distinctively different. It was charac-
terized by a rough give-and-take at odds with the genteel intercourse
of the Ivy League colleges. Even today, discourse among the New
York intellectuals, now three and four generations removed, is known
for its passionate no-quarter-given quality.[70]

The Harvard case was special because of what it symbolized.
That is why Jews made such a fuss about it while ignoring the impo-
sition of quotas at other universities. It was not only that arriviste
Jewish students had a penchant for scholarship. From an immigrant
Jewish perspective, the intellectual atmosphere at Harvard may have
appeared strange and cold; it was certainly a far cry from the exciting
give-and-take that characterized Jewish intellectual discourse. Har-
vard aspired to being more than merely a finishing school for the
wellborn; its goal was to train an aristocracy based on ability, and that
idea endeared it to Jews. If Harvard closed its doors, that action

would serve as a signal for other American educational institutions to limit Jewish access. Had that occurred, the Jews' rapid climb out of the working and lower middle class of their immigrant parents would have become more difficult. "Harvard is injecting into American College life an insidious poison which may not be eliminated in decades," cried the *American Hebrew*.[71] Yet, it had not raised a similar alarm over NYU's or Columbia's quotas because, as respected as these institutions were, they did not establish the norms for other institutions to follow. The second generation, concerned about establishing itself, understood that accessibility had something to do with keeping Harvard's doors open. They saw it in American terms. Limitation would be nothing less than "treason to America" because access to talent "is the American Ideal! . . . That has been a beacon of light to the Jews and the oppressed of all lands."[72] The victory, observed an *American Hebrew* editorial, "will carry its influence far beyond Cambridge. Like the shot first heard at Concord bridge it will be heard round the world."[73]

The solution imposed on Lowell was paradoxical. When the faculty committee reported back ten months later, it rejected the idea of quotas as running counter to Harvard's tradition of "equal opportunity for all regardless of race and religion." It fully supported the Jewish view that merit and academic achievement were the crucial criteria for admission to the university. It even ruled out "any novel process of screening which could be construed as a covert device" to limit enrollment of qualified students.[74] One the surface, that decision meant that Jews had won their battle. Harvard would remain in the ranks of the liberal universities. But the report also recommended that Harvard seek "a wider regional representation" through the "highest seventh" plan, which would encourage preparatory schools located west of the Mississippi to send capable students to Harvard.[75] At the same time, the number of available spaces in the freshman class was limited to one thousand. That restriction proved sufficient to reduce the Jewish student population to 10 percent by 1931.[76] In a sense, those favoring limitation had won after all. But nine years later, President James Conant redefined Harvard's mission along the lines of academic merit that had been insisted upon by Jews all along. The proportion of Jews then rose to 25 percent.

From a Jewish perspective, the 1920s served as the staging period for the remarkable achievement of contemporary American

Jewry, which began in earnest after the interruption of the depression and World War II. The extraordinary economic mobility of Jews has drawn the interest of historians. The decade of the twenties contains clues to the strategy Jews employed to achieve place. I have suggested here that it was achieved through a linkage of traditional small-business activity and the enhancement of the skills of a portion of the second-generation cohort. At the pinnacle of that enhancement was professionalization. In the post–World War II period, the linkage of "shoe string capitalism" with skill enhancement produced American Jewry's third commercial elite, the one Nathan Glazer and Daniel Moynihan have called "egghead millionaires."[77] These were Jews who made their fortunes by the use of a professional or academic skill in combination with the traditional penchant for small business. In a word, rather that clothing or scrap metal, they sold their enhanced skill on the free market.

From a Jewish perspective, what was different about the twenties was that Jews began to invest in themselves, in their human capital. Increased education and skills gave them better access to an increasingly complex economy that required such skills. Although few Jews could be found in managerial positions in basic industries like transportation, mining, or steel during the twenties, their presence increased in the newly established research laboratories and legal departments of major American corporations.[78] By the 1930s, Jews could also be found in the creative departments of the full-service advertising agencies as the experts in marketing surveys, motivational research, and the psychology of consumption. In the film industry, Jewish movie moguls, who ultimately had to turn to Wall Street for financing, turned to Jews for screenwriting, adaptation of story lines, and sometimes for stars, too. Jews could be increasingly found in the research and development departments of industry. Possession of some special skill—writing, script editing, accounting, design, research, engineering, or legal knowledge—was becoming the ticket to finding place in industry, the expanding government bureaucracy, and the not-for-profit sector of the economy. Such skills were taught in professional and graduate schools and required certification or licensing, hence, the movement by Jewish young people to enroll in such schools.

When Harvard, a major university recognized by all as playing a principal role in establishing the conventions of American society, threatened to curtail that development by limiting the enrollment of Jewish students, they resisted. Why there was such concern regarding

Harvard's admission policy when other major universities subject to the "invasion" had earlier followed the same policy in more drastic and insidious form and aroused little outcry should not be a source of puzzlement. One major factor was the realization that Harvard's policy would serve as a signal to other universities that limitation of Jews was acceptable. We can also observe that the distaste for Jewish students focused on the ambitious sons of the eastern immigrants who, like all arrivistes, were more concerned with goals than with learning the social mores of the children of the well-to-do, including occasional descendants of established "uptown" Jewish families. The conflict was not only over the number of Jewish students at Harvard. Far more Jews were attending CCNY and NYU. It was about what the public announcement of such a policy meant. That is why the resolution of the Harvard case is remarkable. Publicly, the policy of limitation was rejected; but the enrollment of Jews was nevertheless limited by other, less public means. That tactic, for the moment, served the needs of both sides.

In a sense, the Harvard case marks the last stand of a social order that held that the right to station should be determined not by merit but by behavior and birth. Had it prevailed, the impact would ultimately have been felt beyond the American Jewish community. It would have hampered the development of those crucial elites without which no modern complex society can function. During the twenties, a generation of Jews, arguing the virtues of the merit system, was preparing itself to become part of those elites. There was of course an element of group self-interest in advocating open access based on academic merit. It would facilitate their climb to the highest rungs of the economic ladder. Eventually, aspiring Jews were victorious in their battle for professional training and acceptance at Harvard. The struggle against quotas at Harvard may prove to be one of those rare instances in history where doing good and doing well coincided.

PART THREE

Political Culture

6

Sources of Jewish Liberalism

THERE WAS A TIME, not so long ago, when a historian called upon to
discuss a Jewish contribution to any facet of American life would
have approached his task with some trepidation. Such inquiries,
bound as they are to produce illusionary identities with the host cul-
ture and long lists of heroes, are reminiscent of the apologetics end-
lessly generated by spokesmen of the immigrant generation to justify
their presence in America. But today, a more acculturated, securer
Jewry is better prepared than formerly to take candid measure of its
impact on American society. There is greater readiness to acknowl-
edge its distinctiveness; but paradoxically, it is more difficult to find
examples. If it exists at all, where is its locus and what is specifically
Jewish about it?

The problem is nowhere better illustrated than in finding a spe-
cific Jewish impact on American politics. Jews were present at the
creation of the republic and played a role in fashioning the religious
tolerance linked to an overwhelmingly secular society. There were
personalities like the Sheftalls of Georgia, Benjamin Nones, Mordecai
Noah, and Judah Benjamin, who earned some measure of prominence
in the politics of the period. But they were individual voices who
made their weight felt on all sides of the political spectrum. The Ger-
man Jewish stewards, anxious above all to enter the mainstream of
American life, spent much energy in denying the existence of a spe-
cific Jewish political interest. In one sense, they were not far wrong.
During the German Jewish hegemony and during the later domi-

This essay appeared originally in *Judaism* 25, no. 3 (Summer 1967) under the title
"The Jewish Contribution to American Politics."

nance of the eastern European Jews, group priorities were clearly aimed at establishing an economic base. American Jews maintained a relatively low political profile. "We hear of the Irish vote, the German vote, but who ever hears of a Jewish vote?," noted the *Northern Monthly* in 1858. That was the "way things should be," according to the *American Israelite*. "In regard to public and political questions there is no union among us." Despite men like August Bondi and the outspokenness of some abolitionist rabbis, most Jews, to the dismay of the abolitionists, took their cues on the crucial slavery question from the German Americans in whose communities they frequently resided.

To some degree, eastern European Jews adhered to a similar pattern. At times, it appeared as if the radicals among them co-opted the political voice of the community. It frightened patricians like Jacob Schiff and Louis Marshall, who only dimly perceived that, for most of the new arrivals, the emigration and transplantation experience was revolution enough for one life-time and that they wanted nothing so much as to make their independent way in the new environment. Eastern Jews were actually loath to take part in the earthy quid pro quos that characterized local politics. "Der Ate," the predominantly Jewish eighth district in New York City, had a relatively low voter turnout at the turn of the century. Unlike the Irish, who had, in any case, virtually preempted the local political machine, Jews could not conceive of politics as merely another form of group aggrandizement. Having taken almost no part in politics in the "old country," they came to American politics with austerely moral assumptions of what the political process was supposed to be. "I was pained by the ease with which corrupt politicians were able to persuade our uneducated Jews to sell their votes," Abraham Cahan relates sadly in his diary. "There were no elections in the country from which we had fled. The ballot box and all it represents was the sacred hope for which many of our socialist comrades in Russia had martyred their lives." It would take years before Jews entered fully into the political process. "The Jews were regarded as so completely taken up with their economic adjustment to the new country that their frequently mentioned absence from the political machinery was accepted as entirely explainable," noted one observer. Small wonder that the city with the largest Jewish population in the world did not elect a Jewish mayor until Abe Beame was elected and then only when the great metropolis was in decline.

Had the Jewish impact on politics been stronger, identifying its specific Jewish content might pose less of a problem. To be sure, there has always been intense interest in political ideology among American Jews; but for various reasons that include the absence of a binding historical experience, American Jewry's political voice has often lacked coherence and focus. The separate internal political life of the Jewish community, which claimed much political energy, had more than its share of fragmentation and strife. Each political segment— anarchist, socialist, Zionist, and their numerous subdivisions—had its own particular interest and its own insistent claims for loyalty that took precedence over the whole. Jews, especially the Jews of eastern Europe, were an ideologically hot people who, coincidentally, were forced to operate in the ideologically cool atmosphere of an Anglo-Saxon culture. The Kehillah, a remarkable attempt to reestablish the corporateness of New York Jewry on a voluntary basis, succumbed instead to the centrifugal ideological pulls within the community. So it would be with virtually all attempts at achieving unity within American Jewry. It was particularly evident in secular politics. The Jewish voter was a maverick who did not take leadership from above. Because followers did not follow, leaders could not lead. The Jewish vote was not so much delivered as it was granted independently by each Jewish voter. Yet, there was a definable Jewish political thrust because Jews appeared to come independently to a similar political position.

Not until the post–World War II period did American Jewry achieve some modicum of unity. The strong association with the Democratic Party is actually of relatively recent vintage. The switch from the Republican Party occurred in earnest in the election of 1928; and once in the Democratic fold, Jews quickly assumed key positions in the liberal-urban-ethnic coalition that buttressed the New Deal. It was the Roosevelt administration that taught Jews about the political rewards for loyalty, and few subgroups were more loyal to Roosevelt than American Jewry. Although other hyphenates veered away from the New Deal after the election of 1936, Jews increased their support. Not only were they rewarded with some entrée into Roosevelt's charmed inner circle but they also shared in federal office patronage. So intense was the identity of Jews and the New Deal that the pejorative, "Jew Deal," was sometimes used by Roosevelt's many haters. To this day, American Jews wear the mantle of New Deal welfare state liberalism, even when they are, in fact, something more and less than that. Thus, it was the New Deal that gave American Jewry a taste of the sweet fruits of political participation, and Jews did not readily forget the lesson in the postwar decades. During these years, their voice was amplified further by a gradual muting of the uptown-downtown divisions as a result of continued secularization and *embourgeoisement*. It was the many facets of that class, religiocultural gap that had kept American Jewry divided during the early decades of the century. In addition, the impact of the Holocaust, which carried with it a lesson on the price of disunity, and the creation of the state of Israel finally furnished American Jewry with the common seminal historical experiences around which it could coalesce.

The period of comparative unity and identity building was destined to last less than two decades. By the mid-1960s, there were portents of the impending dissolution of the liberal-urban coalition, with which Jews had cast their political lot. In the election of 1972, over 35 percent of the American Jewish vote was cast in the Republican column. It could be reasoned that this shift in Jewish voter sentiment was a momentary aberration. In any case, it was not as great a swing to the Right as that of many other subgroups in that election. But there were additional disturbing signs that the Jewish voice on major issues not affecting Israel was once again fragmented. Less mobile and less affluent ethnic Jews seem to have departed from the universalistic, liberal ideology to cast their ballots simply on what they sense to be the Jewish group interest. They perceive a political reality in which everyone votes his or her own interest and reason that Jews make themselves vulnerable by not doing so. On the other hand, more Americanized, affluent, and educated Jews continue, in some measure, to uphold universalist humanist principles. Thus, the new internal split in American Jewry seems at once to be reminiscent and a reversal of the old uptown-downtown division.

Even such an attenuated examination of the historical background of American Jewish political behavior is sufficient to raise a major problem. Aside from the fact that it is Jews who are casting their ballots in a certain way, is there anything distinctively Jewish about the political patterns and preferences of American Jewry? Wherein lies its Jewish component? For example, one might assume that what is distinctive about Jewish political behavior is ultimately rooted in the Jewishness of the Jews rather than in a contemporary condition or some other factor. Unquestionably, historians can make much of the civic virtue of American Jewry for Jews are particularly good human material for making democracy work. Studies show that they are consistently better informed on the issues and more involved in the political process, that they and their organizations are more likely to take positions that transcend their parochial interest, that their voting volume ranks above other groups, and that they have become an important source of campaign financing. That is all true enough, but what is uniquely Jewish about such behavior?

Politically and otherwise, however, American Jews depart from the norm. They *are* different, but that difference is caused more by their specific historical experience than by the memory of the ancient religious and prophetic precepts that originally served to make them a people apart. Few in the largely secularized American Jewish community are knowledgeable about the roots of their idealism in their religious culture; and undoubtedly, a close scrutiny of sources would inform us that almost any reasonable modern political ideology can find some justification in Scripture. The Jewish political posture in America, as elsewhere, is an external sign, a fingerprint, to deeply rooted historical assumptions regarding the kind of domestic and world order that best assures Jewish continuance. With the exception of the extreme Left, the *sine qua non* of Jewish political behavior is survival, and the associations with modern secular ideologies like liberalism[1] or socialism or some other form of humanistic universalism are adhered to if they offer appropriate survival strategies. (In that sense, much of the political dialogue within the Jewish community really concerns itself with a conflict over what is more crucial for Jewish survival—the survival of Jews or of Judaism. That differentiation emerges most clearly in Isaac Deutcher's essay *The Non-Jewish Jew,* in which he argues that he would give up Judaism in return for the 6 million victims of the Holocaust. Such a transaction was, of course, never in the offing.) Classifying American Jewish political proclivities as liberal, a standard practice among observers of Jewish political behavior, is inadequate because it neither transmits the changing meaning of the term in American politics nor informs us regarding the deeper underlying motivations of Jewish political behavior.

Once the historically conditioned and special Jewish sensitivity to survival is understood, many of the puzzling aspects of Jewish political behavior fall into place. There is, for example, the sensitivity that American Jewry has demonstrated in confronting the root problems of American society. American Jews were among the first to fathom the centrality of the problem of race in American society and contributed notably to the political mobilization of the African American community. At the turn of the century, many Jews, no less than Progressive reformers and their earlier Republican mugwump precursors, were aroused by the mismanagement of American cities, the abuses of the trusts, and the gross inequities left in the wake of the leap from a rural-based, agricultural economy to a complex, urban-based, industrial one. Jews were staunch supporters of the notion that government had a role to play in managing the economy to assure a minimum living standard for all. Welfare statism became an important part of the Jewish political agenda; and it was Roosevelt's hesitant movement in that direction, not his foreign policy, that won the hearts of Jewish voters in the 1930s. An urban-based group, they were among the first to recognize the significance of the deterioration of American cities and to propose programs to reverse the trend.

In the area of foreign affairs, the Jewish antennae appear to be even more sensitive. For obvious reasons, American Jewry was among the earliest advocates of using American power to stop Hitler when it might have been possible to do so. They were ardent supporters of strategies for international order, as embodied in the concept of the League of Nations and the United Nations. Similarly, the staunchest advocate of protecting minorities in the newly formed nations after World War I, through legal clauses imposed on them and written into their constitutions, was Louis Marshall, the leader of the American Jewish Committee. In the same vein, one of the conceivers of the idea of imposing on war the stigma of illegality, as embodied in 1928 in the somewhat visionary Kellogg-Briand Pact, was Salmon O. Levinson, a Jewish lawyer form Chicago. Poor human material for cold war hysteria, American Jewry, by and large, concluded relatively early that the Vietnam intervention was a blunder from which America had somehow to extricate itself. In a word, in both domestic and foreign affairs, American Jewry has acted as a kind of barometer for sensing the crucial problems confronting the nation.

Liberalism, which has been used to identify the Jewish political gestalt in America, is only an outer and perhaps temporary masking. Behind it lies a well-honed survival wisdom that recognizes that there must be ordered change in both the domestic and the international arena lest everything worthwhile be swept away by events whose dynamism is such that they cannot be curtailed. It is almost as if Jews had instinctively come to understand that deep-seated inequities in the social order, when mobilized by groups seeking change, can spell insecurity and danger for their own group interest. Paradoxically, although Jews are inevitably labeled as liberal, there is a deep-seated conservatism in their political complexion because, more than most groups, they recognize that, in the long run, there must be room for change in the social order if the system that nurtures them is to survive. That is the reason why they demonstrate sustained concern for the underdog; that is why they do not vote their class interest; and that is why they reject ethnic particularism.

We turn finally to the question of the Jewish contribution to American politics. If American Jewry were a normal subgroup, we might simply take the measure of how it stood on the crucial issues of the day and draw appropriate conclusions. But, like Jewish communities throughout history, American Jewry cannot claim the dubious distinction of being normal. It is not merely another ethnic or religious or hyphenate community in a nation composed of such groups. Its precise status continues to defy classification. It is, to be sure, shaped by the American society with which it has cast its lot; but it also has, as part of its Jewish connection, a long, separate history of its own that shapes its vision. It lives delicately suspended between two cultural pulls, the Jewish and the American. It is that connection to *K'lal Yisrael*, the mysterious tie that binds Jews everywhere together, and that also determines its unique political character. It is the lessons of Jewish history that have furnished American Jewry with its sensitive antennae and its basic assumptions regarding the social order. It is also that connection that compels American Jewry to exert a special effort to influence the U.S. government for help in its mission to nurture the perpetually beleaguered Jewish communities abroad. It is for that reason that U.S. foreign policy contains the most discernible signs of a specific Jewish influence.

Throughout American Jewish history, much of American Jewry's financial and organizational resources have been earmarked, not for influencing domestic politics, but to give direct aid and to enlist the influence of the American government for the benefit of coreligionists abroad. Even those major Jewish secular organizations that were originally organized to fulfill a fraternal function, such as B'nai B'rith, the Workmen's Circle, and the Jewish War Veterans, ultimately found that much of their work involved improving the condition of Jews elsewhere.

Yet even in the area of foreign affairs, where American Jewry has traditionally been compelled to make the most concerted effort to project its influence, the actual impact on official policy is difficult to discern. There are those like John Snetsinger and Stephen Isaacs who assign considerable ability to the community to work its will on decision makers. But their conclusions remain controversial.[3]

Before 1945, the Jewish voice in American foreign affairs lacked focus and coherence. Rarely could Jews agree on what ought to be done and how best to do it. In the eighteenth and nineteenth centuries, the Jewish question rarely received priority in American policy. The moment that a special plea was presented, it triggered countervailing pressure from other ethnic and special interests. Even in the example of the most conspicuous victory—the successful abrogation of the commercial treaty with Russia in 1911—Louis Marshall worked through Congress rather than with the policy-making executive branch. More typical of the Jewish impact was its failure to move the Roosevelt administration during the Holocaust. One ought not be chagrined or guilty regarding the minimal Jewish impact on policy. The actual parameters of such influence are constricted. Irish Americans and German Americans, whose communities have larger numbers and whose foreign-policy goals in the early decades of the century had a clear and specific focus, were no more successful than were Jews in working their will among powerful government officials. Concealed in the paroxysm of guilt that flooded American Jewry after the Holocaust is a group hubris that encourages Jews to believe that they actually possess a significant secret power to change major policy behind the scenes. Nothing could be further from the truth.

That reality brings us to the final point regarding the impact of American Jewry on politics. There is a tendency, common to both Jews and their detractors, to assign to the community a power that it does not possess. In a sense, both are locked into an illusion of centrality that makes too much of Jewish influence. In the case of American Jewry, it leads to shouldering responsibilities that Jews do not have the power to meet; and in the case of the anti-Semitic imagination, it leads to the fantasy of a secret Jewish conspiracy that is able to manipulate power holders for its own nefarious objectives. Of course, reality is otherwise. The Jewish impact on American domestic and foreign policy, in the rare instances in which it can be identified, is peripheral. In the last analysis, it is almost impossible to imagine that American politics would have been startlingly different in its basic outlines had American Jewry not found an alternative Zion in America.

7

The Changing Liberalism
of American Jewry

ALTHOUGH THE QUALITIES that once distinguished Jews from other Americans have all but vanished, their special political culture remains. They continue to be liberal, but they are no longer the most liberal group in the electorate. And even though liberalism is a dynamic, constantly evolving phenomenon, today's brand of Jewish liberalism would hardly have been recognizable to the immigrant generation. Survey research, the most popular method for determining trends among groups, reveals little about how Jewish liberalism evolved to become what it now is. Both the persistence and the shape of Jewish liberalism require historical explanation.

So disparate are the principles of liberalism that finding their logical base can be daunting. Obviously, liberalism is rooted in the relationship between citizens and the secular state that grew out of the Enlightenment, as encompassed in the well-known slogan of the French Revolution, "Liberty, equality, fraternity." Thus, citizens are free to pursue happiness as the boundaries of community allow. Whether their pursuit leads them to some form of self-realization or to the accumulation of estate does not matter. What matters is that, at least before the law, all citizens are equal. In its simplest form, fraternity is related to the right of citizens to associate in religious, social, and political institutions so as to form a civil society that mediates between the state and its citizenry.

A different version of the essay appeared originally in *The Americanization of the Jews,* ed. Robert Seltzer and Norman Cohen (New York Univ. Press, 1995), under the title "From Equality to Liberty: The Changing Political Culture of American Jews."

In our country, these rights are embodied in the Constitution and especially in its Bill of Rights. Liberty is also assured by what John Adams called "political architecture," which keeps the legislative, judicial, and executive functions separated and checking each other. It is designed, as Woodrow Wilson once noted, to handcuff government. That was no accident because it was believed that a government that was prevented from governing assured the citizenry its sphere of liberty. "That government governs best which governs least." The form that liberalism took in the early national period was thus more libertarian than egalitarian.[1]

The perceptive reader will by now have noted what Marxist dialecticians like to call an "internal contradiction." Left to its own devices, will liberty, which allows free rein for our unequal talents, not make a shambles of equality? That is what Tocqueville foresaw. The society of free and equal individuals envisaged by the French Revolution could exist only in theory. In reality, a polis composed of free, private, individuated citizens had nothing to hold it together.[2] The disparities in wealth and station inevitable in the free society would surely erode the bonds of fraternity as well. How can justice prevail in such a society? A government that is so empowered might regulate such inequities; but in order to secure liberty, we have by design underpowered government. How then can such a system work?

The answer might well be that it has worked more by dint of the ever-increasing size of the gross national product than by the internal logic of its founding principles. The defenders of the libertarian variety of liberalism, which today substitutes for a conservative politics in America, argue that this is no accident. Liberty in the economic sphere has released such enormous new productive energies that we have become the first society in history in which insufficiency of goods and services is not a perpetual plague. That makes the grinding problem of how to distribute wealth equitably far less stressful. If the economic pie is ever growing, less energy can be expended on the question of "who gets what."

From a historical point of view, all American politics is played out in the arena of liberalism. The American political dialogue has liberty at one end of its axis and quality at the other. As the Enlightenment's favorite child, with very little of a feudal past, America could not legitimately produce a conservative ideology. Rather, in the liberal context, conservatives are those who try to get the government off the backs of the citizenry so that it can get on with the serious business of producing wealth. Conservatism in American politics is the tendency that, in the name of liberty, opposes expanding the government sector to furnish social welfare or even to regulate business. In contrast, the egalitarian-minded left wing of the Democratic Party, to which most Jewish voters adhere, wants the wealth produced by private enterprise to be shared with those who have little to sustain themselves—the homeless, the unemployed, the handicapped, single parents, victims of AIDS, or whatever new group of unequals they can find. Predictably, liberals conceive of the government's taxing power as an instrument for the fairer distribution of wealth.

What liberalism does is what the Left has always done in parliamentary democracies. It seeks out the regnant inequity and places it on the political agenda. During the national period, it sought to remove the remnants of feudalism, the payment of quitrent, and property qualifications for the franchise. During the Jacksonian period, the franchise was further liberalized and the United States Bank was attacked as a citadel of privilege that ought not to be strengthened by government authority.[3] During the 1850s and the Civil War, liberalism sought to extend freedom and citizenship to the slaves. That goal was achieved through the civil rights amendments, especially the Fourteenth Amendment. The Progressives sensed that the trusts needed to be regulated because their power was not only corrupting the political process but also threatening to curtail liberty. It was a case of checking private power to the degree that government power was checked.

The New Deal is noteworthy because it tilted liberalism away from its libertarian pole toward its egalitarian-statist one. That was not precisely a new trend. There had been deep government instrusions during the Civil War and the Progressive period. For example, the Freedmen's Bureau, specifically designed for the rehabilitation of the former slaves, set a precedent for government-sponsored social engineering in the nineteenth century. But it was the Great Depression with its foreboding of revolution that set the stage for a broader, more sustained effort at restructuring through the agency of government.

During the depression, a much larger sector of the public required government nurturing. Not only would the freewheeling capitalism that characterized post–Civil War industrial development have to be controlled but the citizenry would also have to be assured some kind of security from the vagaries of the business cycle: Social Security to protect the unemployed and the aged, the Civilian Conservation Corps (CCC) to protect the resource of youth, and even an attempt at conservation on a regional basis to protect human and natural resources with the Tennesse Valley Authority (TVA). Government became a permanent fifth wheel in the economy. The legislation of the first New Deal marked the deepest government intrusion yet into the economy and through it into the lives of the citizenry. With it came a tilt to the egalitarian side of liberalism.

But the recurrence of economic collapse in 1937 cast serious doubts on the efficacy of a welfare program paid for through deficit financing rather than through wealth produced by the economy. There was a retreat from structural reform toward the more limited policy of providing a stable economic environment in which capitalism might thrive. By the second New Deal, we note a steady retreat from the government intrusion and social engineering that characterized the early years of the New Deal. Aware that the early program was not producing desired results, Roosevelt abandoned the notion of working with "big business" (his National Recovery Administration [NRA] had in any case been declared unconstitutional) in favor of business regulation. The government would now attempt to stabilize the economy indirectly through its fiscal policy, including new banking laws and a strengthening of the existing Federal Reserve System. Under Thurmond Arnold, the antitrust division of the Justice Department was reactivated. The problems posed by the depression were never fully resolved. World War II started the economic machine pumping again. It pumped so well that, by the end of the war, managers were speaking of the "miracle of production" without which the Allied victory would not have been possible. The triumph of libertarianism, at least in the eocnmic sphere, which can be seen in the "supply side" economics of the Reagan and Bush administrations, also grows out of the New Deal experience, especially the second New Deal and the wartime industrial mobilization.

Jewish liberals welcomed the New Deal's welfare state program, especially its positive attitude toward organized labor. The "trickle up" twist of its eocnomic policy, which pumped millions of dollars into the economy through "make work," placed the New Deal within ideological striking distance of traditional Jewish political proclivities, which emphasized the just society in which the "forgotten man" would receive his due. (Rabbi Stephen Wise, the quintessential Jewish liberal of the first half of the twentieth century, took credit for the "forgotten man" phrase.) Jews, seeing the state as an instrument to help achieve a just society, were persistent in demanding that government do more. That tendency was buttressed by socialist ideology, which reinforced the statist aspect of Jewish political culture. American Jewry historically looked to government intercession for its brethren in the foreign-policy arena. Now, second- and third-generation Jews abandoned the pledge given to Peter Stuyvesant that they would always take care of their own. In 1933, hardpressed Jewish social-work agencies removed Jewish dependent families from their rolls so that they might qualify for government relief. For Jews, power is granted to government but its leaders are assigned a matching responsibility to "repair the world." Communalism is based on shared responsibility.[4]

That penchant for the egalitarian aspects of liberalism was not yet fully present in American Jewish political culture in the eighteenth and nineteenth centuries. Before the arrival of the eastern European Jews, the Jewish political profile was kept low. The exposed position Jews assumed when they supported the Whigs in the American Revolution was exceptional, although considering the liberal bias of the Revolution and the relationship of its principles to the Enlightenment, the support it received in the small Jewish community seemed natural. Less easily explained is their support of the physiocrat, anti-urban Jefferson over Alexander Hamilton, whose financial program was designed to buttress the very commerical sector of the economy with which Jews had cast their lot. Apparently even during the national period, Jews did not vote their pocketbooks. In the liberal context, such altruism is not so strange. "It is an ironic fact," observes George Will, "that we are a nation of people who talk like Jefferson, yet we live like Hamiltonians."[5]

Jews did not notably join in the struggle to abolish slavery, and with the exception of Louis Brandeis, who had not yet found his Jewish constituency but who was instrumental in creating the 1914 Clayton Anti-Trust Act, there was little interest in an ameliorative solution to the trust problem.[6] Socialist-oriented Jews preferred the totalistic solutions of socialism. The trust problem would be solved when government assumed ownership of the "means of production." Only a handful of acculturated Jews involved themselves with Progressive reform, especially its advocacy of municipal restructuring. But eastern European Jews, who are unfamiliar with the reform process, sought a total solution in the just society that socialism would bring.

Most first-generation eastern European Jews were not yet fully ready to enter the American political arena. In 1900, the number of Jewish voters in New York City was low; and socialist candidates ran poorly in Jewish districts, where Republican candidates were usually preferred.[7] Jews sought to solve their social, cultural, and economic problems by employing traditional instruments of communal organization that they believed could be re-created in the free environment of America. That was the thrust of the New York Kehillah, the American Jewish Committee, the Congress and the American Jewish Federation movements, all of which were established in the first two decades of the century.

Jewish liberalism became fully fashioned during the prosperous twenties and the depression thirties. As the second generation became more involved with the problem of living in America, some of the European cast to the Jewish political culture was abandoned. During the prewar period, the thrust and energy of left-wing Jewish political culture was anchored in socialist ideology with its strong statist component. It was disseminated through the Jewish labor movement, a network of Yiddish schools and neighborhood social and fraternal clubs—the *Landsmannschaften*—and, above all, through the Yiddish press. These ideas persisted in the 1920s but would grow weaker as the Yiddish-speaking culture declined.

The immigrant political culture was not alone in its concern for social justice. The Reform branch of Judaism had a strong social-action component that was active in everything from municipal reform to antilynching legislation.[8] Stephen Wise, a Reform rabbi, served as a bridge to the secular liberals who found their home in the reconstituted American Jewish Congress, which he led. It also had a social-action commission.[9] Other Reform rabbis like Judah Magnes and Abba Hillel Silver were no less avid than Wise in their pursuit of liberal causes.

During the twenties, the Jewish electorate shifted its allegiance to the Democratic Party, which would become the home of egalitarian liberalism. In the Sixty-sixth Congress (1919–1921), there were five Jewish Republican representatives and only one Democrat. By the Seventy-fifth Congress (1937–1939), the situation was reversed. Of the ten Jewish representatives elected, nine were Democrats and only one was a Republican.[10] The number of Jews voting for Socialist candidates like Eugene V. Debs was disproportionately high, about 24 percent in the election of 1920. They also showed a maverick tendency to veer off to third-party candidates like the Progressive Robert M. LaFollette Jr., who received 22 percent of their vote in the election of 1924. But the drawing power of Socialist candidates in Jewish districts declined in the twenties. The Lower East Side district, which had sent

Meyer London to Congress, was gerrymandered out of existence in 1922, and Jewish districts in Williamsburg and Brownsville, which had a sizable Socialist vote, were disrupted by the split in the Socialist Party.[11]

The majority of Jewish voters were attracted to Al Smith, the Democrat reform governor of New York, who although linked to the Tammany machine, displayed considerable political skill in creating the reform wing of the Democratic Party. Smith, moreover, surrounded himself with a group of reform-minded Jewish advisors— Belle and Henry Moskowitz, Joseph Proskauer, Samuel Rosenman, and Robert Moses—who were viewed with pride by Jewish voters. In the election of 1928, Jews gave Smith 72 percent of their vote. The liberal-urban-ethnic coalition, with its prominent role for Jewish advisors, which also would characterize Roosevelt's New Deal, actually found its roots in the Smith administration during his tenure as governor of New York.[12] The 82 percent of their ballots Jews awarded Roosevelt in the election of 1932, which rose to over 90 percent in the three subsequent presidential elections, was based squarely on the new constellation of forces that began in 1924 with second-generation Jewish voters. Even Jewish socialists felt compelled to vote for a highborn, reform-minded patrician, although a third party had to be created so as not to compromise their socialist principles.

From the outset, Jewish liberal political culture possessed both a statist and a libertarian/reformist wing, but the former outweighed the latter, especially when socialist-inclined Jewish voters were added to the scale. The acculturation process itself would, however, act to right the balance. Several developments in the 1920s weakened the socialist thrust and established the bases for a stronger libertarian one. Although there was great concern about the restrictionism embodied in the immigration laws and the Harvard enrollment case and the virulent anti-Semitic rhetoric displayed by Henry Ford in the *Dearborn Independent,* it was clear that these forces were not sufficiently strong to halt the headlong drive by Jews to achieve middle-class status. They succeeded in doing so a generation before other ethnics of the "new immigration." By 1923, they had wrung a satisfactory agreement from Harvard, which, on the surface at least, seemed to establish a precedent to give their children access to the nation's best universities.

By 1927, a humiliating public apology had also been wrung from Henry Ford. The Ku Klux Klan and other nativist groups were much weakened by the end of the decade. Jewish students were flooding into law and medical schools in disproportionate numbers and professionalization was well underway. Jews, it became clear, were not the sons of workers nor would they produce sons who were workers. It seemed that even their sojourn in small business and manufacture would last only one generation. The prosperity of the twenties was fully shared by Jews. Under such circumstances, preaching the imminent collapse of the market economy sounded increasingly hollow and discordant. Not only were a growing number of Jews involved in the small business of the Jewish ethnic economy, which lent it a natural libertarian coloration, but their children were also moving toward the professions through formal education and certification. In the decades after World War II, the education and professional level of Jewish liberals resembled that of the latter-day non-Jewish Progressive reformers.[13] Thousands of second- and third-generation Jews were exposed to the engine of American liberalism, the university. Once enrolled, Jewish students were far more prone to assume that there was a link between being educated and being liberal. Jewish liberalism, like its American counterpart, would be anchored in an educated middle class with pronounced elitist tendencies. A good part of the change in character of Jewish liberalism, its change from egalitarianism to libertarianism between 1920 and 1970, can be attributed to its changed class base.

The move to the center of the liberal spectrum was enhanced further by the collapse of the extreme Left in the Jewish political arena, where the most extreme egalitarianism and statism were anchored. The Russian Revolution had initially earned applause and support in the left wing of the Jewish community. It generated hope that a just society would finally be established in Russia in which Jews would share equally with other subject nationalities. Chaim Zhitlovsky, a well-known Jewish radical voice, for example, suggested that the newly established Communist International (Comintern) was "the only organization that seeks to realize the word of the prophets."[14] But even as the Joint Distribution Committee (JDC) appropriated millions of dollars in partnership with the Soviet government to resettle thousands of impoverished Jews in the Crimea, the benevolent aura cast by the revolution faded. The Soviet policy of reshaping the Russian Jewish class structure and its hostile attitude toward religion and Jewish communalism had led to the exile of thousands of rabbis, Hebrew teachers, and Zionist and Bundist leaders. Many were never heard from again. The Crimean venture, on which so much hope was staked, developed into a social engineering scheme to reshape Russian Jewry into something that might better fit the Communist mold. Clearly, the Soviet government had little use for a separate Jewish ethnic culture, whether religious or secular.[15]

At the same time, the Communist Party of the United States, following a strategy ordered by the Comintern, targeted the Jewish labor movement for penetration. It was viewed as a stepping stone to infiltrate the American labor movement. In 1926, that strategy led to a costly, mismanaged, twenty-six-week strike that virtually destroyed the International Ladies Garment Workers Union (ILGWU). Communist organizers of the strike had not hesitated to use the union's security fund to keep their lost cause afloat.[16] The costly strike taught Jewish labor leaders a bitter lesson regarding the willingness of the Communist Party to exploit the unions for their own grand design. By 1929, the Communist threat had peaked. Jews of the "socialist persuasion," like Lillian Wald, Horace Kallen, and David Dubinsky, distrusted the heirs of Lenin who ruled from the Kremlin. Baruch Vladeck, managing editor of the *Forwards*, and Morris Hillquit, chairman of the national committee of the Socialist Party, adamantly opposed extending diplomatic recognition to the Soviet Union. In 1928, the Communist Party again underwent one of its many splits; and the ILGWU again emerged in the thirties, under the leadership of David Dubinsky, firmly in the social-democratic fold and ready to accept ameliorative measures to improve the conditions of its rank and file. But by the mid-thirties, the composition of the ILGWU, which more than any other Jewish agency pointed the way to the new liberalism, was paradoxically no longer predominantly Jewish.

That trend away from the statism of the totalitarian Left was disrupted by the depression. The collapse of the economy after the crash of 1929 gave the failing Communist Party another opportunity to root itself in the Jewish community. Many socialist-minded Jews became convinced that the long-awaited collapse of capitalism predicted by Marx had come to pass. The disaffection was especially strong among Jewish students whose career paths and hopes for attaining professional status had been disrupted. Some estimate that the Jewish membership of the Communist Party may have reached 30 to 40 percent during the thirties.[17] That membership actually represented a minuscule proportion of the Jewish population, but it was sufficient to pin the "radical" label onto American Jewry again. In reality, the purges of the thirties and the signing of the Nazi-Soviet Nonaggression Pact in August 1939 caused a rapid decline of the Communist influence among Jews.

The most powerful influence on American Jewish liberalism was the overwhelming popularity of Roosevelt among average Jewish voters. It was said that Jews had *"drei velten—die velt, yene velt, un Roosevelt"* (three worlds: this world, the next world, and Roosevelt). The aura of the New Deal with its concern for the "forgotten man" and its social welfare legislation fit neatly into Jewish political culture, which viewed government as an instrument to create the conditions for social justice. Indeed, the very term "New Deal" was thought to have been coined by Samuel Untermeyer, a well-known Jewish writer.[18] The reformist, ameliorative New Deal program was within easy striking distance of the social-democratic principles to which many Jews were drawn.

American Jewish liberalism finally found a home and political address in the New Deal, but the first New Deal also reinforced the Jewish penchant for a liberalism with a strong statist component. The direct forging of that connection came through the ILGWU. Its leadership founded the American Labor Party (ALP) in 1935 in New York State. It called itself "the party of the permanent New Deal" and attracted thousands of Jewish voters to its banner. In the election of 1936, 40 percent of New York State's Jewish voters cast their ballots for the ALP ticket. It also broke the hold of the Socialist Party on the Jewish Left. In that year, Norman Thomas, the Socialist Party candidate, received 87,000 Jewish votes, compared with 250,000 cast for the ALP. It served as a bridge for thousands of socialist-oriented Jewish voters to enter the mainstream of American politics. When the ALP was penetrated by the still-vigorous Community Party in 1938, it changed its name to the Liberal Party, the only party in American political history actually to carry the term *liberal* into the political arena.

The fate of American liberalism in the postwar era need not occupy us very long. With the exception of the Eisenhower years (1952–1960), liberal Democrats—Roosevelt, Truman, Kennedy, and Johnson—occupied the White House between 1932 and 1968. Together with the Carter years (1976–1980), these Democratic administrations will probably go down in history as the liberal period, although Carter was an outsider whose administration may mark the final exhaustion of egalitarian liberalism. The willingness to absorb social democrats like Michael Harrington may have been the wellspring of Johnson's War on Poverty. The new university-educated liberals, who had a proclivity for making public policy but were anticommercial by career choice, may also account for the antibusiness cast of these administrations. Their distaste for the acquisitive ethic led inevitably to the abandonment of the libertarian notion of equality of opportunity in favor of the egalitarian notion of equality of results, the high point of which was the imposition of affirmative action quotas. The new liberalism of the 1960s challenged fundamental libertarian values like competition, equal opportunity, and free enterprise, values that the American electorate was not ready to give up. Prone to view itself as the protector of the oppressed, this "new class" was typical of intellectual elites in the West in its preference for public policy devoted to reshaping society. It was the inclination to social engineering manifest in the civil rights movement that took liberalism out of the mainstream of American politics.[19]

The counterthrust of the Reagan years was predictable. On the economic side, we have already noted that the retreat from statism began during the second New Deal. During the prosperity of the postwar decades, the swing to liberalism's libertarian pole was accelerated. Although there was much hand wringing about government cost and the high taxes required to fund welfare programs (today called entitlement programs), there was little inclination among Republican libertarian liberals to remove the cushions that the New Deal had installed in the economy. Libertarians now talked of a social-service net that would let no one starve. Nevertheless, antigovernment bias persisted.

The libertarian-liberal victory of the Reagan years was played out on a world stage. The cold war was fought against a totalitarian power and tended to bring statism into more disrepute, even as its exigencies caused a growth in government power and expenditures at home. Ultimately, the collapse of the world Communist movement gave a powerful impetus to the idea of a market economy and privatization. These economic resonances of libertarian liberalism were bandied about in Eastern Europe with the same fervor that "class struggle" had once been. At home, it was thought that even the public education system, once the stronghold of egalitarianism but now failing to develop the skilled work force requisite for an advanced industrial economy, would be improved by allowing the free market represented by the voucher system to work its wonders.

Once the war was over and prosperity seemed assured, those hitherto neglected problems concerning race and social inequalities would be brought to the fore by liberalism playing its traditional role, a point unforeseen by libertarians. As it turned out, whether such problems dealt with race or the destruction of the environment, they inevitably entailed increased government expenditures. Willy-nilly, American liberal politics became budget politics.

Unlike Europe, where the problem of class was uppermost, in America according to the 1968 Kerner Report, it was the unresolved problem of race that threatened to split the nation into two contending parts. By the 1960s, the race problem had gained the highest priority on the liberal agenda. Accompanying the race question was a whole series of new problems: gender inequality, rights for the handicapped, gay rights, infants' rights, animal rights, and problems concerning the physical environment. Looming over all is the contentious question of abortion rights, which places the conundrum of how far human liberty can safely be extended in an entirely new context. It is a particularly vexing problem for conservatives, whose libertarian brand of liberalism would logically dictate a proabortion position. What greater liberty can there be than control over one's own body?

Now the best-informed and most activist constituency in the American electorate, Jews played an important role in the sundry "movements" that characterized the 1970s, and 1980s. Survey research continued to find Jews "more liberal" than other groups.[20] But sociologists, who seemed most preoccupied with the problem, did not often understand that liberalism itself was an ever-changing phenomenon. Their surveys failed to reveal that on issues like affirmative action quotas, Jewish opinion had changed to the point that Jews were now outside the liberal consensus. This change did not fully register because on other issues, such as support of welfare programs, the Jewish responses remained predictably liberal.

At the heart of the change was the long-range impact of the Holocaust on the Jewish *mentalité*. The Holocaust undermined a basic tenet of liberalism, that there exists a "humanitarian spirit" or a "spirit of civilization" in both the nation-state and the international order that could be mobilized to fill an ethical need. Most states had done little to rescue European Jewry during the Holocaust. Moreover, World War II and the postwar years contained some terrible lessons regarding the Soviet Union, a totalitarian state addicted to egalitarianism. For some, it provided sufficient evidence that the American founding fathers had after all not been so far off the mark in their suspicion of state power. In both Nazi Germany and the Soviet

Union, Jews had been subject to a special animus. Yet, the idea that the state itself might be malignant did not prevent most Jews from supporting the idea of a Jewish state. American Jews had come to believe that a state was a necessary step without which Jews would remain vulnerable. But there were some, like Hannah Arendt and Martin Buber and to some extent Judah Magnes, who saw even a Jewish state as retrogressive.

A second factor in transforming Jewish liberalism relates directly to the founding of Israel in 1948. As early as 1940, the Zionist consensus had begun to change American Jewish political culture. After 1948, the care and support of the State of Israel became a major component of American Jewish identity. But support, as Brandeis had foreseen, did not mean that American Jews would have to settle there to build the new society. Rather, for American Zionists it meant political advocacy, the representation of Israel's case before the American seat of power. That, in turn, often required a partial abandoning of the universalism lying at the heart of Jewish liberalism. Increasingly, Jewish liberals had to make difficult choices between the interests of Israel, the tenuous security of which required direct, sometimes preemptive use of military power, and such cherished universalist principles as the right of national self-determination, especially for Palestinians. The way Israel exercised power over its Palestinian population was particularly disturbing to those Jewish liberals who had come to view civil rights as the central principle of liberalism.[21]

Zionism sectarianized American Jewish political culture. It did something else as well. If, with the creation of Israel, Jewry reentered history, as Zionists were wont to claim, it seemed willy-nilly to draw American Jewry with it. American Jews came out from the behind-the-scenes role they traditionally played in politics as pundits, campaign managers, poll takers, the professionals, to become office holders and lobbyists. During the 1930s, the number of Jews in Congress hovered around ten. The election of 1990 sent eight senators and thirty-three representatives to Congress. Today, there are more Political Action Committees (PACs) concerned with Israel and general Jewish causes than with the concerns of any other ethnic group. The result is a split in the Jewish electorate that is partly generational. Older committed Jews give the security of Israel the greatest priority and view the fulfillment of their liberal aspirations in terms of the welfare of the Jewish state. The younger group, strongly influenced by the war in Vietnam, is more concerned about traditional liberal values. Nurtured in America, many of these young liberals did not directly experience the bitter consequences that followed when Jews found themselves bereft of sovereign political power. Also, they were on a collision course with Israeli political culture, which has been shaped by the power it exercises over an occupied people and by the need to assure its survival in a hostile region, where it is often called upon to use its military power. Similarly, the separation of church and state, so central to the American Jewish sensibility, is emphasized less in Israel, where a Jewish state assures observant Jews the protected environment to live a religious life.

Another factor that altered the shape of Jewish liberalism in the 1960s was the African American thrust finally to enter the mainstream of American life. The partnership between blacks and Jews on the civil rights issue had been well established before World War II. Jews had been instrumental in supporting black defense organizations like the NAACP, furnishing leadership training and legal resources, and supporting African American colleges. During the twenties, Louis Marshall, president of the American Jewish Committee, sponsored antilynching and anti-Ku Klux Klan legislation. Jewish impresarios played a major role in opening American popular culture to black artists. The affinity between blacks and Jews, which may have been based on a common feeling of victimization, was also reflected in their voting behavior. Politically, both groups had found a niche in the left wing of the Democratic party during the New Deal period. They became Roosevelt's staunchest supporters.

If during the thirties there were worrisome signs of disharmony caused by the anti-Semitic oratory of black street-corner preachers and the targeting of Jewish stores for looting during several riots, it was underplayed in the Jewish press. That remained true even when some black spokesmen, including W. E. B. Du Bois, opposed the admission of Jewish refugees, insisting that Germany had a legitimate grievance against Jews. Hasia Dinner has suggested that Jewish support for black causes was a way for Jews to broaden their own rights without becoming conspicuous by advocating their group interest in creating a more open society.[22] Whatever the motive, American Jews played an important role in advocating that equality be fully extended to the nation's African American citizens.

By the 1960s, the black-Jewish linkage had begun to wear thin. A new group of younger black leaders pushed Jews out of leadership positions in the civil rights movement. The Ocean Hill–Brownsville conflict (1968) serves as a historical marker for Jewish splitting off from a liberalism now almost wholly dominated by the civil rights issue. Preoccupied with the seeming intractability of the race problem, the left wing of liberalism advocated special entitlement laws to hasten the goal of black equality. Representative of such laws was affirmative action, which required quotas. Most Jews opposed the abandonment of the merit system that had smoothed their path to achievement of middle-class status in prior decades and protected their access to civil service employment.[23]

By 1990, the Jewish liberal profile showed a marked differentiation on other liberal issues requiring direct government intervention. Blacks replaced Jews as the most intensely liberal-minded group in the electorate, especially on issues concerning government programs to assist minority groups. Jewish liberals often found themselves compelled to choose between the Jewish interest and the liberal position. The polarization was widened by a growing sense that the African American leadership was anti-Semitic. Leaders like the Reverend Jesse Jackson reintroduced anti-Semitic currency, which had been all but ruled out in the political dialogue. Beneath it all was the question of resource allocation. African Americans adopting the posture of an internal Third World nation, argued that monies given and lent to Israel would find better use in rehabilitating the people of the inner city. The argument then turned on the "who gets what," or spoils, question, which has always been central in American politics.

Another reason for the Jewish swing to libertarian liberalism relates to what we may loosely identify as the American Jewish success story. It is no secret that, by the 1960s, Jews had achieved a numerically disproportionate position among the technocratic, cultural, governmental, and managerial elites who administer and shape American society. They are the ethnic group with the nation's highest per-capita income and the highest degree of professionalism. In the 1920s, when the foundations for that achievement were put in place, middle-class status was often achieved by aspiring Jews against considerable resistance and at great sacrifice by families living on the economic margin. There was an investment made in human capital. A son was sent to law school or medical school by the earnings of the entire family. Although there was some "suicidal altruism," that is, Jews who favored a public policy that automatically granted special advantage to victimized minorities as compensation, most Jews opposed policies that, in the name of justice, abandoned merit.[24] Their own achievement stemmed from an individual effort in a free society. They had adhered to the rules, which had now been abandoned. Government-sponsored programs to raise specific groups to a level that Jews had achieved on their own did not sit well. In entrance professions like teaching, long a favorite channel for aspiring young Jews, affirmative action translated into blocked mobility channels, the equivalent of employment discrimination.

Much that was statist and egalitarian was not bound up with the race question. Some Jewish thinkers undoubtedly were aware that it was the Communist Party, following the dictates contained in Stalin's writing on the national question, that advocated a highly separatist policy to solve the race problem. When the party fell further into disrepute among Jews because of its hostility toward Israel and the undeniable evidence of virulent anti-Semitism in the Soviet Union and Poland, its stock declined even more. The capture of the "Negro question" by the extreme Left made it anathema to many Jews.[25]

Reinforcing all these reasons was a historical change that went almost unnoticed by social scientists. The institutions that supplied the motor force of the Jewish liberal enterprise, the Jewish labor movement, the *Forwards*, Workmen's Circle, and the dozens of socialist-minded fraternities and summer camps, had by 1990 virtually vanished from the scene. Once the quintessential liberal agency for secular Jews, the American Jewish Congress is but a bare shadow of its former self and has difficulty staying in business. Pressed by a triumphalist Orthodox branch, the conservative and Reform movements have grown far more concerned with their Jewishness, which, we have seen, acts as a brake on highly universalistic liberal causes. By 1988, the Liberal Party of New York State drew fewer voters than the Conservative Party and was virtually defunct. The agencies that traditionally drew Jews to liberalism are much diminished in influence.

This does not mean that Jewish liberalism has totally lost its distinctive idealism. There is no scarcity of Jews who call on the political process and the state to do more, to seek justice. The need to search out the most pressing current inequity is insufficient to explain why so many young Jews continue to be political activists for causes as widely different as world peace and the welfare of striped bass in the Hudson. They want to instill a humanitarian conscience into the political process. Selfless idealism remains a prized quality in American Jewish political culture.

On the surface, liberal politics is issue-oriented; but beneath is the politics of redemption. It is that characteristic of Jewish liberalism that makes it so difficult to carry forward transactional politics, the kind preferred in the American political process. Dealing with prophets whose politics are based on righteousness is never an easy task.

The issues of peace, the environment, or the homeless continue to draw a disproportionate number of liberal Jews, but they do not easily lend themselves to the politics of the possible. There has developed over the generations a distinctive Jewish political style that places a high premium on commitment, on giving oneself over to the cause. In the first generation it was called *ibergegebnkayt*, which, translated from the Yiddish, means devotedness. This phenomenon also needs to be taken into account in explaining the persistence of Jewish liberalism. Such liberals reject the contemporary solutions that place so much faith in the free market economy, not because they favor socialism, as did an important segment of the first generation. One suspects that the new generation does not understand the difference between a market and a command economy and the relationship this distinction bears to the two kinds of liberalism. They reject the market economy as a mechanism that cares little about those who cannot make it or about what is happening to the environment. For the liberal *mentalité*, life should be more than merely the providing of goods and services. It should have transcendence.

Taking leave from the left wing of the liberal movement did not mean that Jewish liberals became politically homeless. In some sense, the Jewish electorate has moved closer to the American mainstream. The old ethnic and regional constituencies that buttressed the New Deal have gradually been homogenized out of existence. The defeat of McGovern in 1972 may have been the last hurrah of the old liberalism. The program of the statist liberals has been largely rejected by the American electorate. Jewish liberalism today is less committed to government-sponsored social engineering and more comfortable in coming to terms with the Jewish interest when it is in conflict with a universalistic one. But Jews remain well within the liberal camp of the Democratic Party. Fifty percent of the campaign funds of that party is raised by Jews, and 68 percent of its vote in a recent election went to liberal candidate Michael Dukakis in 1988 compared with 46 percent of the general electorate. But that is a far cry from the over 90 percent awarded to Roosevelt in 1940 and 1944. Being Jewish still remains a more powerful determinant of the Jewish vote than being rich. In California, 65 percent of Jewish voters with an annual income of over $75,000 voted for the Democratic candidate Diane Feinstein, compared with 38 percent of non-Jews in the same income bracket. Seventy-three percent identify themselves as liberal, compared with 42.19

percent of non-Jews. Moreover, on liberal issues, wealthy Jews differ hardly at all in their voting preference from less wealthy ones.[26] But Jewish liberalism has changed its orientation from an emphasis on egalitarianism to an emphasis on libertarianism. That has happened because it has undergone two processes since World War II, Judaization and Americanization, that make it different from what it once was.

In historical terms, the Jewish political posture corresponds roughly to the liberalism of the second New Deal, which abandoned social engineering in favor of indirect regulation of the economy. Jews continue to favor an active regulatory role for the state but they want it done through existing instruments, the taxing power, monetary policy, rather than through direct intrusions like affirmative action. It is in the area of taxation and spending that the sharpest differentiation occurs between Jewish liberals and that of the general white liberal voter. Despite their considerable per capita income, Jews are more inclined to favor high taxes to fund entitlement programs. For example, they give much greater support to programs like Aid to Dependent Children, all forms of income maintenance programs, even support for AIDS research and care; but they overwhelmingly reject restructuring the economy to prevent great disparities of wealth, direct intrusion (such as affirmative action quotas, censorship of pornography, and regulation of the gay lifestyle), and they are more than twice as likely as their fellow Americans to support abortions without restriction.[27]

In a word, there has developed an antistatist libertarian component in Jewish liberalism. As Jewish liberals see it, job placement, sexual orientation, family planning, and religion are in the private realm and therefore by right ought to be free of government interference. It is not, however, complete libertarianism. Like other Americans, Jews have come to favor capital punishment, but in lower percentages. Jews, therefore, are no longer so politically deviant, especially if one compares their political profile with that of other highly educated, high-income groups. Their liberalism has been open minded, tolerant, forward looking, peace oriented, and humanitarian, yet also aware of its own group interest. It has lost confidence that a just society can be created by government fiat. It is the universalism of a secular, highly individuated, firmly middle-class yet ethnically conscious community. That should not surprise us. What else could it have been?

8

The Jewish Vision
of American Liberalism

THERE IS A COMICAL ASPECT about the use of the dreaded L-word to beat Michael Dukakis black and blue in the 1988 presidential election. From a historical perspective, Reagan Republicans are as much the inheritors of American liberalism as the Democrats. The conservative position, which they sought to defend by attacking liberalism, has customarily experienced great difficulty maintaining itself in American politics because the basic principles of this nation, which originated with the Enlightenment, are liberal. That is the reason why a liberal presence can be located even in the most conservative recesses of American political culture.

What are those principles? They are the familiar ones inherited from the Enlightenment and embodied in our Declaration of Independence and the Constitution. They can be viewed in abbreviated form in the famous slogan of the French Revolution, "Liberty, equality, fraternity." Those who think about that slogan will note that it contains an internal contradiction, one of several which plagues liberalism. Liberty and equality are incompatible. If there is liberty, we are free to develop our unequal talents. Left to its internal logic, liberty will make shambles of equality and, in extreme cases, will erode the fraternal bonds that make community possible. Our Constitution, whose principles stem from the Scottish Enlightenment, is libertarian; it seeks to preserve the sphere of individual liberty from the tyranny of

Another version of this essay appeared originally in the *Jewish Frontier* 56, no. 3 (May/June 1989), under the title "American Liberalism: The Jewish Wrinkle."

government. It does so by what John Adams called "political architecture." That is what the "checks and balance" system, which has for generations handcuffed our government, is all about. Anyone who has seen the graffiti in the New York City subway, or the violence in our cities, knows that the assumption of the forefathers that the *citoyens* would rein in their rapacious natures (as they imagined they did in the Greek polis) has since been proved too optimistic. Like all liberals, the founding fathers were insufficiently pessimistic about human nature. Liberty has made a shambles of equality and weakened the bonds of community, as it was bound to do.

To make matters more complex, another idea, stemming from the German Enlightenment, has also been grafted on to American liberalism. It is embodied in the notion of *Rechtstaat* and views the purpose of governance as related to the search for justice. Those who recall the biblical admonition, "Justice, justice shall ye seek," will find the concept familiar. Liberalism has Hebraic roots, as does much of Western civilization.

By now the perceptive reader will have located yet another flaw that bedevils American liberalism. How can a government, deliberately underpowered in order to avoid tyranny, possess sufficient power to fulfill its other injunction, to do justice? Now we can better understand the twentieth-century polarization in American politics. The Republican Party of Reagan and Bush opt for libertarian liberalism, the one that says "get the government off our backs." The McGovern/Johnson Democrats opt for a *Rechtstaat* liberalism, which seeks justice by eliminating the great inequalities that liberty has created. They are both principles of American liberalism. American politics revolves on a political axis that has liberty at one end and equality on the other.

How does such an ideology, full of internal contradictions, produce a system that works? There are several answers. It works badly. Ideology is not a strong driving force in modern secular society, where free citizens do not welcome its fetters. Liberalism is not an ideology, in the classic sense, but a set of disparate principles which, according to Arthur Schlesinger Jr., the polity calls into play again and again.

Liberalism is the motor force that pushes American politics forward. It seeks out the regnant tyranny, slavery, war, the abuse of the trusts, racism, sexism, poverty, homelessness, and environmental issues and attaches them to the political agenda. Without liberalism, there would be no political dialogue. What do conservatives, whom we note are merely libertarian liberals, do? They do not say we should eliminate social security, or we should not have civil liberties, or we should not have a clean environment. They say we can do it cheaper and better by doing it through the private sector. America has no authentic conservative position because it never had a corporate feudal past to conserve.

What has all this to do with American Jewry? More than any other subculture, it was American Jewry that helped shape the egalitarian/justice dimension of American liberalism, linked today to the left wing of the Democratic Party. It helped restore "republican virtue" to American society, which by 1890 had been almost destroyed by a rapacious "robber baron" libertarian capitalism that echoed the highly individualistic frontier culture that had held sway in the nineteenth century. It did so by advocating a communal dimension to public policy that it drew from its own distinctive political culture. That Jewish contribution to liberalism ultimately became the heart of the controversy that marked the development of the liberal point of view.

What is that particular point of view? The Jewish concept of freedom, *Herut*, like the idea of the *Rechtstaat*, which stems from it, views freedom as always being linked to responsibility. It is expressed through community, rather than above or against it. It was a principle supported in Jewish religious texts and in their historical experience in the Diaspora that required a limited rather than an absolute freedom. Additional reinforcement was found in the ideology of socialism. Jews are free, to be sure, but only to be better members of the community, better fathers and husbands, and most important, better Jews. The idea of being free to become a "robber baron" or a rapacious sweatshop owner was anathema. That is what Louis Brandeis heard and so admired when he helped negotiate the Protocol of Peace for the garment trade in 1911.

But the full idea of *Rechtstaat* awaited the maturation of the Jewish labor movement. It was there that the programs of the welfare state were incubated: unemployment insurance, old age pensions, medical benefits, cheap housing, paid vacations, college scholarships for the children. Finally, when the American Labor Party was organized in 1936, it for a time considered calling itself "the party of the permanent New Deal." Its successor was the Liberal Party, the only party to actually carry the word *liberal* into the American politic arena. They were both sponsored by the Jewish labor movement, especially the International Ladies Garment Workers Union (ILGWU). Unlike the libertarians of the eighteenth and nineteenth centuries, who feared government tyranny, Jews viewed government as a crucial ingredient in creating an equitable and just social order.

But by the very nature of the things it deals with, liberalism is dynamic and changing. By the 1960s the omnipresent issue of racial justice again began to reconfigure the liberal agenda. It was imagined that, in order to create a more egalitarian inclusive society, the merit system in the public and private sector had to be downgraded through affirmative action that inevitably entailed the use of quotas. For Jews, the merit system was sacred and quotas were anathema. Many Jewish liberals began to rethink the efficacy of government-sponsored social engineering. Jewish liberalism was becoming more libertarian and less government centered—in a word, more American and less recognizably part of the eastern Jewish immigrant culture.

PART FOUR

Secularism

9

The Secular Mind-set

A STARTLING BIT of information stands out in my mind from my graduate school days when studying the Social Gospel movement. As the area below Fourteenth Street in New York City was filling up with new immigrants at the turn of the century, a goodly number of the established churches found themselves with diminished congregations, which compelled them to close their doors. I do not recall if we were presented with matching data showing that fraternal clubs, including saloons, increased in number; but I am convinced that, had researchers bothered to look, they would have found that they did. Modern man's need for fraternity, if not for divine authority, remains irresistible.

Concern about the reason for such an unhappy state of affairs served as the spark that brought the Protestant churches to care about the poor and homeless. That is what the turn-of-the-century Social Gospel movement was all about. Church leaders concluded that the church was no longer relevant to the new constituency. A constituency that was poor, spoke a different language, and experienced all the discomfort that acculturation brings in its wake. Then, as now, being irrelevant was considered the "kiss of death" for a "living" church. But social scientists might just as easily have attributed their decline to more mundane reasons. Newly arrived immigrants may simply have felt uncomfortable in the established middle class environment of such churches. The immigration process often meant being, at least momentarily, declassed. Potential congregants may have

This essay appeared originally in the *Jewish Frontier* 56, no. 1 (Jan./Feb. 1989), under the title "The Secular Mindset: Personal Choice and Personal Strength."

also felt that they could not afford the tithe that membership required. Moreover, a sizable proportion of the inhabitants of the lower east side were Jewish or belonged to other minority religions.

Immigrant Jews also felt uncomfortable in established synagogues. When Stephen Wise established a branch of the Free Synagogue on Clinton Street with "free" seating in 1907, it lasted barely a decade. The same happened when other "uptown" congregations tried to recruit worshippers in the ghetto. Not only did they not attend Temple Emanu-El, then located within walking distance of the ghetto, but many no longer attended any religious services, except on the high holy days. Today, we know that an intense secularization process had begun among Jews even before they arrived in America. Like other ethnics, Jews generated alternate socialization institutions based either on kinship like the *Landsmannschaften* or on association with the Jewish labor movement and various Zionist or socialist ideologies.

But in the first generation, attempts by established synagogues to find roots in the immigrant community seemed destined for failure. By the second generation, the story was different. As Jews became more established, there was a spurt in synagogue building—especially in the Reform and Conservative branches. But bricks and mortar did not mean that something vital was happening within. Aware that a way had to be found to link Judaism to what Jews were actually becoming, Mordecai Kaplan and others founded the Jewish center movement. The centers were soon referred to as a "shul with a school and a pool." They reflected an attempt to keep up with the broader, and incidentally more secularized, horizons of the second generation. The centers did draw Jews, especially in the new areas of second settlement, but the old religious spirit could not be rekindled through architecture and programming. The problem was how to accommodate the new secular attitude, whose development seemed inexorable. Reconstructionism, the movement Kaplan founded, eventually became a twig among the three branches of Judaism.

Shtiblach (room—Orthodox Jews often held services in rooms rather than in fancy buildings) and small chevras of the faithful persisted in the ghetto, much as Pentecostal store-front churches do in the barrio today. They were supplemented, during and after World War II, by the transplantation of the remnants of the Chassidic courts and other forms of Orthodoxy as well as the indigenous development of neo-Orthodoxy. Today, in a period that some have characterized as one of Orthodox triumphalism, such communities are found everywhere. But there are few who see them as reservoirs of great moral and political energy. They seem more interested in furnishing their adherents with a support structure and external controls and are more intent on living and preserving the inward life of the faithful than they are in changing the world. I imagine that the same holds true of pietistic communities in other religions. They are fortresses against the pervasive secularism that Christian fundamentalists have taken to calling secular humanism. In Israel, most Orthodox groupings do not muster strong feeling regarding such issues as disposition of the occupied territories. On the extreme end of the religious secular continuum, they attract a comparatively small number of adherents. The thrust of the times continues to be toward secularism, with most people finding a comfortable niche somewhere between the two poles.

Although cults seem to have attracted a disproportionate number of young Jews, their net impact is also minor whatever their totalistic ideology. They often possess the characteristics of religion and undoubtedly some hope to become just that. Most lack eternality; that is, they are linked to finding a solution for the latest malaise of modernity and therefore represent a temporal response to a problem, whether it is drugs or sex. In a sense, they are postsecular religions that are rooted in pronounced secular sensibilities. My niece who chants some strange words, totally unrelated to her cultural background, tells me not to worry. This thing she does is not a religion but merely a form of crisis management. The words alone smack of a fascinating juxtaposition of the most ancient with the most modern. "What's wrong with that," she argues, it helps her and does not hurt anybody. It is an instrumentalist approach to religion; but if I had informed her that the very problem-solving approach she favors is the certain sign of a secular mind-set, she would not have understood. At the same time postsecular religions retain some familiar elements of the "old time" religion. The other day, I overheard members of a cult community talk about their stringent diet. They consumed only certain foods which, I imagine, they thought brought them closer to immortality. What struck me was that their rules were even more confining than the laws of *kashrut*. I thought of the linkage between food taboos—what is allowed to enter the sacred body—and religion. "The more things change, the more they remain the same."

But the proliferation of such postsecular religious communities is surely not the wave of the future. They tell us something about our time in history—a time marked by a failure of secular assumptions to generate a livable life for a sizable portion of the general population. They may help in crisis management because for such people, life itself has become a protracted crisis. Scientologists claim to keep their adherents off drugs. Communes may fulfill a fraternal function to counteract the aloneness and anomie of modern urban life, which is also part of the secular condition. But most important, they offer the faithful a marked path to follow, a requisite confinement. For most people, that is too confining and too monolithic a strategy to deal with the complex, multileveled reality of modern urban life. Modernity is pluralistic. It cannot be based on a single awe-inspiring truth or even a single version of virtue.

From a distance, one can envy the seeming harmony and stability of such totalistic communities. But that is an illusion, as anyone who has lived in a kibbutz knows. What really happens in such communities is that a stabilization of life in the urban free-fire zone is achieved by limiting freedom and autonomy and concealing the play of other forces. For people who, for whatever reasons, have not internalized controls and suffer because of it, the extrinsic ones offered by the religious community or cult, are more than welcome. They are imperative if some form of life is to go forward. But although communalism fulfills an important need in the postsecular world, the postsecular religions who "sell" it are, in the long run, destined to fail for the same reason that the churches failed below Fourteenth Street.

The fulcrum of modern life, especially in America, is freeness (some call it autonomy). The individuation that results is what secular identity formation is all about. It is about choices. We make decisions for ourselves that the tribe and family used to make. Free secular persons do not take their behavioral cues from the minister or rabbi; they can ignore ideologies that seek to control. They do not accept Judaism's yoke of Torah or Zionism's yoke of *aliyah,* unless they voluntarily choose to do so. Even the decision to continue life is voluntary. That is why so many religious ideologues are upset about the rash of euthanasia cases and suicides. Their premise is that life is sacred and does not belong to the person living it. The modern secular mind-set is based on precisely the reverse assumption. Modern life is lived, not in the name of some larger good, but for oneself. That much the inside traders and other sundry swindlers have accurately perceived.

The result, we have seen, is chaos and the loss of the quality of life. In 1927, the Jewish community of New York experienced its first rash of suicides, and Rabbi Stephen Wise spoke about what was wrong to the United Parents Association. His statement sounds strangely familiar:

> There is this acquisitive passion—the dominance of things, and things, and things. There is too much education and too much psychology fostering the idea that life is self-expression and self-realization until it reaches the newest most tragical and final man-ifestation—the extinction of life itself.

What Wise was describing was the selfness (not selfishness) of modern secular identity formation. Yet, the solution of so much of what passes for religion is to somehow limit the choices that freedom brings in its wake. For some proportion of our urban population, that may be the only way to handle modern urban life. Happy are those who can accept such limitations or who understand that, in the absence of their own internal controls, such external ones allow life to move forward, if only in a prepackaged form. But what of those who have, in some measure, internalized controls and who welcome, indeed require, the "free air" of the city.

I place most of my Jewish social cohort in this category. They prefer to live with perdition, which in Latin has something to do with lostness. Most have an advanced secular education and some professional skill. They are urbane, if not precisely urban. Many possess good Jewish backgrounds and play leadership roles in the Jewish community. Others maintain only a tenuous connection with it. They were not born into a totalistic religious environment and have not learned with their mother's milk what a Jew must do. Neither have they voluntarily accepted such controls somewhere in midlife, nor are they members of cults. They feel discomfort among "frummies" but maintain firm friendships with them on an individual basis and when secular ground rules for behavior are accepted. They are unchurched out of choice even though some belong to the congregation. Often they take from the fabric of observance those things that appeal aesthetically: the lighting of Sabbath candles, the saying of the *kaddish* for a departed one, perhaps even a modified form of *kashrut,* which today is called kosher style—as if there were such a thing. Their secular persona does not permit *Halakha* (Jewish religious law), or Zionism, to dictate basic life decisions. They will not "make" aliyah or involve themselves in the toilers' "struggle," unless they want to. With them, everything from community organizations to ideology must be voluntary because they alone are masters of their fate. Belief in God becomes for them problematic, not only because the quest for rationality makes belief in the supernatural problematic but because they have placed themselves at the center of His universe where they sometimes act like minigods. They have internalized controls and live at the interstices of two cultures, belonging fully to neither. They represent the ultimate development of a new kind of secular identity, autonomous, individuated, a tribe of one.

In the modern period, they are the most productive element in the Jewish community. It is impossible to imagine what Jews or Western history would be like without the scientific and cultural contributions of the Jewish secular elite. It goes beyond Freud, Einstein, Herzl, or Kafka. There developed in the cities of western Europe a disproportionately Jewish elite that generated the modern point of view. This elite is doing much the same thing in urban America. It is shaping the very way we think. Based on some esoteric skill—law, medicine, physics, computers—these intellectuals are wielders of a new kind of power. During the Holocaust, it was they who composed the "Jew Deal," the influential Jews near Roosevelt who had access to the Oval Office. They were disproportionately involved in the Manhattan project, which developed the atomic bomb. Should another crisis arise, it will again be the influence of such Jews that will have to be mobilized. They seem to be able to live without a church and to remain tolerant and experimental in their approach to life. It is not that they have rejected Judaism or any other religion, they are simply once removed from it. Yet although they live outside of the established community, they are good citizens and can play leading roles in it. In some measure, Theodore Herzl, Chaim Weizmann, and Nahum Goldmann are representative of such Jews.

It comes to this. The urban church, by which I mean any all-encompassing ideological fraternity, plays entirely different roles for different segments of the urban population. Its role becomes most problematic, not with people who need something to hold on to, but with individuated secular types who may be just as lost but who function well. For them, a church or synagogue must furnish some form of transcendence or spirituality that they can accept on their own terms. It cannot be hegemonic, and it must be authentic.

That is a far cry from the role a church needs to play for that large segment of our urban population whose internalized controls are not fully developed, so that the linking of freedom, which is available in its purest form in America, and responsibility cannot be achieved. On the contrary, these people use freedom to rid themselves of the "fetters" of tribe, community, and finally, family. That balancing of freedom and necessity is often lost in the American form of secular society, and that condition is nowhere more apparent than in our cities. We live in a society that is committed to ever more freedom, and yet what we produce is increasing chaos and violence. Clearly, what is happening is that, in our expansion of the sphere of freedom, we are also removing the extrinsic controls provided by church, school, family, and professional orders, which people who have not developed internal controls require in order to function.

By their very nature, secular Jews cannot be carriers or agents of Judaic or Jewish culture. Neither can they long be bound by ideological or communal fiat. Perhaps more than religious persons, they are subject to all the vicissitudes and temptations of modernity. Some consider that their individualism and their unwillingness to limit their freedom make them an inherently anticommunal force. An examination of the list of givers to Jewish philanthropy or the roster of those who accept communal leadership roles should convince us that the case is otherwise. It is true that secular persons do not do the humane or just thing under the guidance of the church or synagogue. They are not great believers in ideology or institutional religion. Yet, they often achieve a broad tolerance and sense of fairplay through personal choice and personal strength of character. The freedom of secular Jews can also lead to great moral stature. The idea of pluralism, which serves as the lubricant for heterogenous societies like those of America and Israel and which is requisite for their survival, comes to us from the secular world. It is a basic element in the secular mind-set.

10

Judaism and Jewishness

THE STORY of what happened to Jewry on the way to becoming Americanized is full of strange turns because the national container in which that acculturation process developed was unlike any in the long history of the Jewish Diaspora. America was different, and so too would be its Jews. Over a period of three centuries, its characteristic communalism and the faith and religious law on which it was based were reshaped. In the process, its internal cohesion was weakened, and its religion was made to fit into America's civil religion. The power of the synagogue to determine for the new secular Jews how life should be lived, much less by what rules to live by, was eliminated. American Jews take few of their behavioral cues from their rabbis. These changes were not coerced from a reluctant people. No American subculture has more welcomed the opportunity to free itself from the restrictions of a religious system steeped in laws and regulations to govern behavior during every waking moment. Yet, no community has been more insistent on having social space to develop its distinct culture, though few any longer are certain about the content of that culture, And despite the weakening of its communal bonds, it remains a conspicuous, sometimes noisy presence on the American scene. It is perhaps the most politically engaged group in the nation.

The intense secularity that has left a once pious people ambivalent about its religion stems in considerable measure from influences

This essay was presented at the Forum on Society, State and Religion: The Jewish Experience, Feb. 15, 1988, under the sponsorship of the American Jewish Committee. This is the first time it has been published.

let loose in the host culture by Protestanism. America takes religion more seriously than other western nations but, at the same time, strictly upholds the wall of separation between church and state and continues its intense love affair with all things modern. When there is a conflict between the persistent Christian hegemonism and secularism, whether over school prayers or Sunday closing laws, Jews are usually found on the side of the secularists. They understand instinctively that, given the intense religiosity of America, the separation of church and state preserves their space.

Jews are aware that pervasive secularism promotes an unbridled selfness that undermines the communalism that has historically served as the cornerstone of Jewish continuance. In some measure, the reaction to the larger world of America determines the contours of the American Jewish presence. It is there where individual Jews must live their day-to-day lives. But Jews are different from other subcultures in America because they receive signals from a preexisting/coexisting millenial religious civilization, which also has its claims. When Horace Kallen, one of the major thinkers of American Jewry, proposed the idea of cultural pluralism in 1915, it became part of a strategy to permit more space for the expression of Jewish particularity. It was accepted by American elites because it confirmed what had already developed on the ethnic and religious fronts. Ethnically, America had become a "nation of nations"; and religiously, Protestantism had proliferated into numerous denominations that, when added to Catholicism and Judaism and numerous exotic religious sects, made the religious world appear like a department store where the consumer rather than the deity reigned supreme. Cultural pluralism, which became a buzz word in all discussions regarding American Judaism, clearly worked to its advantage. Some argue that, in its unwavering support of Israel, American Jewry had gone beyond its bounds. If that is true, it is a measure of America's extraordinary tolerance of American Jewry's particularity.

For practical reasons, the American polity was compelled to develop a tolerance for religious diversity that was no easy task for the population of the colonies. They had often emigrated in search of a place where they might worship freely. But like many who take religion seriously, they were not tolerant folk who were prepared to extend that freedom to others. To have an established church would have divided the polity into "ins" and "outs" and made it vulnerable to both external and internal threats. Pluralism served the Jewish community well for other reasons also, for it meant that the community was never alone in its aberrance. There were those who quaked and shook and saw the imminence of Armageddon, and who therefore could deflect the wrath of the majority. Peter Stuyvesant, the seventeenth-century governor of New Amsterdam, may have despised the Jews and counseled the directors of his company to get rid of them at the earliest moment, but he also hated Papists, Congregationalists and Quakers.

The wall created between church and state protected Jews; but beyond that, the formula that was ultimately developed for the organization of the national community generated a centripetal force that sought to gather in all communities, with the distinct exceptions of the Negro and the Native American. It was not consistently applied as the many conversionist efforts of the eighteenth and nineteenth centuries attest. The struggle against Sunday blue laws and other forms of Christian hegemonism persisted well into the twentieth century. Yet from the beginning, the American polity was different. It was an artfully constructed *pays legal*, a rational contrivance, which for practical as well as ideological reasons permitted Jews to join.

What were these ideological reasons? They stemmed from the principles of the Enlightenment. Almost totally devoid of the feudal historic freight that burdened the nation-states of Europe, here the multiple differentiations between citizens never took root. All were to be equal. Political and civil liberty was by right the patrimony of the *citoyen*, which included Jews from the outset. The fact that America's political evolution occurred almost totally in the post-Enlightenment period meant that the tensions between pre-Enlightenment and post-Enlightenment interests did not determine the contours of the emancipation transaction. Jews were "present at the creation," they had become citizens of most of the states before the republic was established. There was little inclination to dispute their right to belong.

Indeed, there was an inclination to welcome them precisely because they were Jews. There were some who thought that Jews especially should be part of the "New Jerusalem." There was an affinity for things Hebraic in colonial America. Steeped in Old Testament lore, the early settlers often saw themselves as the "children of Israel" and the new country as the "promised land." Even today, place names in once Puritan Massachusetts and Mormon Utah as well as other states where Protestantism was strong, read like a biblical atlas. There are Jerusalems (Salems), Babylons, and Hebrons in many states of the union. There was a period in the early eighteenth century when the best Hebraists were not Jews, but Gentiles anxious to familiarize themselves with Scripture in its original language. The Republic, President Coolidge later informed the nation, was held together by an "Hebraic mortar." Although these Bible-drenched Christians often held antagonistic views of actual Jews, it gave Judaism a special parental place. Even if the Jews had gone astray and the Covenant now bound a new people, there was still a special place for Judaism. Perhaps they would one day see the light that first shone at Calvary. Rather than a pariah people, they were a people who dwelt near the source. There was that sense of continuance that later encouraged both Jews and Christians to speak of the Judeo-Christian tradition.

The Hebraism of the colonial settlers warrants our attention because it goes far to explain the special benevolence of the American environment concerning Jews, which, in turn, explains much regarding the development of Judaism and Jewishness in America. In the 1950s, Will Herberg, a sociologist of religion, called attention to the fact that although American Jewry formed only a little over 3 percent of the total population, Judaism, the religion, was treated as though it represented one-third of the total population. As evidenced by such things as the frequency with which rabbis were called upon to deliver religious invocations at civic functions, it was in fact one of the three major religions. Clearly, the Jewish experience in America was marked by such a remarkable confluence between itself and the host culture that it gave Jews extraordinary access to the promise of America and held out the prospect of full integration on equal terms. Anti-Semitism there of course was but this was also a new page in the millenial history of the Jewish Diaspora. No other Jewish community had to conceive of its survival in circumstances of acceptance, not by monarchical flat, but by an openness generated by a genuine pluralism reinforced by the ideology of the Enlightenment.

Disintegration or Transformation

It would be natural to imagine that, given such a benevolent host environment and the sense of at-homeness that it engendered, that American Jewry would have seized the opportunity to elaborate its religious culture, as it had done in Spain. There are some researchers who read the history of American Judaism that way. But the survival anxiety of recent years serves as a signal that this is not the confident posture American Jewry has assumed. Apparently, for some diasporic communities, survival can be as much threatened by benevolence and tolerance as it can by virulent anti-Semitism. Moreover, whether one feels that American Judaism is disintegrating or merely being transformed into something else, the signs of radical alteration are undeniable.

There is a diminution of the religious piety that served to bind Jewry in the premodern period. Freed of the sense of victimization, American Jewry seems to have lost its will to survive. That loss of vitality was not easily discernible in the nineteenth century, although some like Isaac Leeser complained of it even then. It was concealed by the rapid development of institutions, rabbinic academies, synagogues, an elaborate system of organized philanthropy and fund raising, and an organizational infrastructure, which gave American Jewry the appearance of health. Yet today, it is clear that the building of the brick-and-mortar edifice occurred at the juncture when the totalistic environment that turned a Jew toward the east wall thrice daily for prayer, as if by Pavlovian conditioning, could not be reproduced in modern America. Survival would require an act of will. Nor was such a loss of identity and spirit confined to the religious enterprise.

By the 1920s, it was no longer possible for survivalists complacently to believe that, even if religious identity diminished, there was still the safety net of Jewish ethnicity, which could catch assimilating Jews. Survivalists could reason that perhaps religion was not the only way one could express one's belonging in a modern age. But it soon became apparent that the same process that was eroding the religious spirit was also weakening the bonds of ethnicity. Few social scientists today are as certain, as were Horace Kallen and Mordecai Kaplan, that the melting-pot model of acculturation is not really what is happening. Behind all is the process of secularization that continues apace and shapes the mind set and perception even of those who resist its influence. Its massive impact can be seen everywhere in American Jewry; but because it entails a change in perception, few fully fathom how it impacts on American Jewish identity.

The decade of the 1920s serves as the anchorage of many of the changes that are now fully manifest, for it was the period in which second-generation Jews, the sons and daughters of the eastern immigrants, moved into the mainstream of American life. We need not detail here the rise in real income, the professionalization and general occupational enhancement of American Jewry during this period. Many of the changes experienced by the second generation are better understood when viewed in retrospect. For example, on the religious front, data indicate an enormous and expensive expansion of operations. New synagogues, usually of the Conservative and Reform branches, arose in areas of second settlement and attracted thousands of new congregants. Between 1912 and 1922, the Conservative movement grew from 22 to 350 congregations. During the single fiscal year 1921–1922, the Reform movement's Union of American Hebrew Congregations added 26 congregations to the 200 that already belonged. Especially successful were the new Jewish centers, "a shul with a pool and a school," which offered an entire way of life for its members. In 1927, there were 47 such centers with about 100,000 members. The figure had risen to 234 centers with 435,000 members by 1941. Also established were new rabbinic organizations for the Conservatives and the Orthodox, and the Jewish Institute of Religion by Stephen Wise (later absorbed by the Hebrew Union College (HUC) of the Reform movement). The separation between Orthodoxy and Conservatism was not as apparent as it is today. In the spring of 1926, there was talk of unification of the Orthodox branch's Isaac Elchanan Yeshiva with the conservative Jewish Theological Seminary. The negotiations failed; but both institutions continued to thrive, until they were severely hit by the depression. Rabbis were being trained, and an organizational edifice was being built for the operation of a Judaic church in America. On the surface the "striking growth of Judaism," proudly proclaimed by the *American Hebrew* on May 29, 1925, seemed to be borne out by the physical facts.

But closer scrutiny reveals a far gloomier picture. There is, for example, the almost banal incident of the need for sacramental wine to celebrate the *kiddush* (a prayer that ushers in the Sabbath) that occupied the learned minds of the community in the early twenties. It seemed that some "fake" rabbis were getting around the Volstead Act of 1919, which made provisions for enforcing the Eighteenth Amendment, by using its exemption, which allowed fermented wine to be purchased for religious purposes. Did the Halakha require that fermented wine be used? The Orthodox, whose transient congregations were sometimes used for such illegal purpose, argued that it did, although some rabbis must have been fully aware that the thousands of gallons of wine so ordered could not possibly be consumed for the sanctification of the *kiddush* alone. At the same time, there occurred the fierce kosher meat and poultry wars, in which underworld thugs were used by both sides. It was hardly inspiring to the diminishing number who clung to *kashrut* (dietary laws) when they learned that they were paying high prices for meat and poultry, 70 percent of which was in fact *terefa* (unkosher). Most crucial for our understanding, the actual demand for kashrut (kosher food) in New York City had in fact declined by 25 to 30 percent.

More than the integrity of the observant community was involved in the *kashrut* problem. The complaints of the difficulty of rearing children according to Jewish law reached a crescendo during the 1920s. The synagogues were built, but they were frequently empty. Even such attenuated annual attendance was declining. A study in 1935 revealed that 72 percent of Jewish men between the ages of fifteen and twenty-five and 78 percent of women had not attended services at all during the preceding year. By 1929, the 2,948 congregations, one congregation for every 1,386 Jews, had a total budget of 16.5 million dollars. But in New York City, only 3 percent of the Jewish population held synagogue membership. Undoubtedly other "state of the faith" indices—the number of children receiving religious education, the number of mikvehs (ritual baths) built, and the number of sabbath observers—would show a similar decline. That decline in knowledge of the religious culture was as true of the rabbinate as the laity. An indigenous English-speaking rabbinate was being produced. In secular terms, it was increasingly well educated. By 1937, 64 percent had earned the BA degree, 23 percent held an MA, and 12 percent were the proud recipients of the Ph.D.; but unfortunately, those impressive numbers did not transfer over to knowledge in Judaic subjects, where the picture was disappointing. It includes the graduates of HUC, who did not speak Hebrew on one extreme and the appearance of Orthodox "wonder rebbes," who resembled the fraudulent "rainmakers" of the revivalist Protestant denominations, on the other. Moreover, the increase in secular education encouraged a growing number of rabbis, traditionally the most learned member of the Jewish community, to think of themselves as merely professionals, a category that came into its own during the 1920s. Increasingly, such rabbis were more occupied with personal counseling of congregants, administration of large congregations, and being the Jewish representatives to the Christian community.

One could of course argue that this depiction of the malaise is incomplete. After all, the twenties were a decade when institutionalized religion entered a period of disrepute, especially among the opinion-leader elite, who were disheartened by what they believed the 1925 John T. Scopes trial in Tennessee revealed about the ability of organized religion to accommodate to modernity. The impact could not help but be felt by American Judaism. Others may note that the disruption of the chain of generations was not as dire as imagined. The journalist Judd Teller, a keen observer of Jewish life during the twenties, noted that Jewish neighborhoods were considerably darker on Friday nights than on weekday evenings, and one could see the Sabbath candles flickering in many a flat. No matter how secularized a Jew had become, he could still be moved to tears by a rendition of Eli Eli, a favorite cantorial chant. That may of course be true, and it compells us to add that the break from tradition was gradual; it occured in generational increments. Moreover for the secularizing Jews of the twenties, who did not yet make the division between *Yiddishkeit* and Judaism, and who often continued to recognize Orthodoxy as the only valid expression of religious Judaism, such a break was not acknowledged. The visible trappings of religion could be maintained for decades, even though the perception of the role of religion in life had changed. But eventually, such Jews, or more likely their children, lapsed in their observance. Often they rationalized that they were merely moving to a different kind of Judaism, less intrusive but no less heartfelt.

That is the reason why some found Mordecai Kaplan's use of the term *crisis* in an article in the *Menorah Journal* in 1921 unduly alarming. He pointed out that "Western Civilization has become as necessary to him [the Jew] as breathing" but that in adoring it, his own religious culture was crowded out and left in "an appalling poverty of spirit." Indeed, those who imagined that a cultural net would catch "fallen" Jews had only to look at the result of the restrictive immigration laws of 1921 and 1924. Whereas almost half a million Jews had entered the country between 1902 and 1914, only 70,000 had done so between 1921 and 1927. The ethnic Yiddish culture secular survivalists like to imagine as a back up, was like other facets of American Jewish culture, carried by these immigrants. When they no longer came, the cultural energy weakened. Like so many other segments of secular Jewish culture, it was derivative. The Yiddish press and Yiddish theater, the shining exemplars of that culture, did in fact experience a sharp decline during the twenties, as did the Yiddish schools. Despite the fact that many of the second generation continued to read and speak Yiddish, it was Hebrew that became part of the high school curriculum in 1922. It was more acceptable because it was considered more modern and did not smack of the immigrant culture that Americanized Jews wanted to forget.

Predictably, it was the Orthodox community that was most reluctant to heed Kaplan's crisis warning, convinced, as they were, that rather than making the Torah fashion itself to the times, the times must be made "to harmonize with the Torah" (Agudath Harabonim, 1926). They preoccupied themselves with such matters as disciplining those Orthodox congregations who permitted mixed seating or the question of the permissibility of using a mechanical clamp (called a gomko) to perform circumcision. Not until June 1945, when a group of Orthodox rabbis tried to excommunicate Moredecai Kaplan, may it have occurred to some members of the ultra Orthodox rabbinic hierarchy (Agudath Harabonim) how serious the situation really was. Most Jews simply did not take their *cherem* (excommunication decree) issued against Kaplan seriously and rejected the authority of the rabbis to determine the definition of who was a Jew. They discovered again that their word counted for almost nothing among a people well on the road to secularization.

Orthodox Jews were not alone in their conviction that all that was required was to convince Jews to hang on to their faith. Most committed Jews bemoaned the visible manifestations of decline. That was as true of secularists, who berued the decline of Yiddish culture, as of observant Jews, who regretted the loss of faith in the younger generation. But they could not comprehend what they could not see, and the change in mind-set was as invisible as it was pervasive.

We need here only examine those facets of the secularization process that impacted on the formation of American Jewish group identity. Its historical impact has already been described. What American Jewry continued to experience was a secularization process that internalized and privatized the religious sensibility, compromised its sense of group belonging, and finally inhibited the ability to believe in a commanding voice outside of itself by a process of desacrelization and celebration of selfness. These familiar processes of secularization warrant further examination.

It should be understood that what is described here is the ideal model. In real life, most American Jews position themselves somewhere along an axis at one end of which was the totally secularized, autonomous individual and on the other a totally tribalized ultra Orthodox Jew, perhaps of the Agudath or Hasidic persuasion. The choice of place is based on comfort that is important in the day-to-day lives of those who are free to choose. Consistency is not its strong point. There are atheists who enjoy hearing a good cantor and members of Beth Dins (religious courts of law) who retrieve responsa by computer. Secular identity is multileveled rather than linear or organized around a core of beliefs.

American secularists are rarely fully committed to political and religious ideologies that demand a shaping role in life and thereby limit autonomy. They may call themselves Zionists but mean by it simply that they support Israel. Or they may call themselves Orthodox, but are not Sabbath observers. In the latter case, they mean that if they were not secular, they would be Orthodox, as their fathers were. Like most modernists, they place a high priority on rationalism and therefore are more intent on understanding than belief, which involves the supernatural or mythic. Secularization explains a great deal about the "practical" character of American Zionism. Historically it was more interested in developing a potash industry on the Dead Sea than in *chalutziut* (pioneering).

Those with a secular mind-set cherish a sense of autonomy and freeness. At the turn of the century, Jewish secularists often referred to themselves as "free thinkers." We can better understand that concept if we think of them as people not bound by the imperatives of the group, community, or tribe. Secularists' associations with these groups is voluntary and entered into on their own terms. That makes Jewish governance in the American Diaspora problematic. It is not only Halakha that secular Jews can disregard but all other types of fiat that have not proven persuasive. There is no power that can compell American Jews to be Jewish or Judaic, and a growing number choose to be neither. That individual autonomy also accounts for the troublesome lack of cohesiveness of the American Jewish polity. Leaders cannot lead, in the normal sense, because followers are not bound to follow. The quest to be free may go beyond ridding oneself of communal fetters. It is possible to imagine that it extends to family. That may be one reason for the astronomical divorce rates in highly secularized societies.

When a pervasive sense of individualism reigns supreme, it is bound to conflict with corporateness, a crucial characteristic of Judaism. In that conflict, religious ideologies come off second best. The need for self-actualization subverts all that would lay claim to having a dominant role in how life should be lived. Indeed, ideologies that maintain too insistent a claim on individuals and communities are inevitably broken. That is what the former Communist rulers have discovered. In America, one reason why political Zionism was replaced by a less demanding cultural Zionism, is that the praxis element in all modern ideologies, which insists that the theory must be bound to practice, inhibits autonomy and freeness. It therefore needs to be redefined or transmuted. The old wine is poured into new bottles. Sectarian religion is transmuted into universalized belief systems like ethical culture or socialism or secular humanism or, in the words of Joseph Blau, "moralism." For modern man, the wish for the Messiah may be transmuted into a desire for social justice. The deity may lose specificity and be transmuted into a generalized creative spirit or a pantheistic one. For diasporic Jews, the sense of exile may become a sense of personal alienation, the feeling of belonging nowhere and to no one. Heschel said it best: "Not only are all of us in Galut [exile], Galut is in us."

Once it is understood that the secular perception is organized around selfness, much of what has happened to Judaism and Jewishness in America comes into focus. Individuated secular Jews can be enlisted for communal objectives only when their first commitment to self has been satisfied or can be seen to correspond to their needs. That may include a need for transcendence that, among American Jews, is often fulfilled through philanthropic giving. They pick and choose those facets of the regnant ideology that fit their purposes. They have become their own tribal chieftains. Yet although individual secular Jews in effect comprise a tribe of one, when they recognize a Jewish interest and are mobilized in its behalf, they bring enormous talent and influence to bear. That kind of recognition and commitment did not happen enough during the bitter years of the Holocaust. Yet when fully mobilized, the power of secular Jews was evident in the decades after World War II. In some measure, their pressure on the Truman administration brought about the recognition of the State of Israel and its loving nurturing thereafter. It is largely their skills and support that keep the social service and organizational structure of American Jewry going. The question for survivalists is, how long can that memory of a memory that still enables secular Jews to recognize a Jewish interest be counted upon? Memories of peoplehood fade when there is nothing to support them.

Jewishness and Judaism

Can Jewishness survive without Judaism? That is really the dilemma secular survivalists have faced since the Enlightenment. At least part of the answer depends on the society in which the process is occurring. The problem of how to keep Judaism and Jewishness together has in fact been the major preoccupation of the various religious branches of American Judaism. At one end was classical Reform of the Pittsburgh platform period (1885), which viewed Judaism

JUDAISM AND JEWISHNESS 159

simply in denominational religious terms and, by stressing prophetic Judaism, established an attractive consonance with the principles of the Enlightenment. At the other end was the Orthodox camp, which responded to the force of modernity in a variety of ways but mostly by wariness and a determination to hold on to what was. If Reformists were reductive, the Orthodox community was deductive. Most interesting is the Conservative movement and its offspring, the Reconstructionists. Interesting because they recognized that secular Jewishness had gained the initiative and therefore had to be confronted. Under Solomon Shechter, the Conservative movement sought to enshrine Jewish ethnicity by such concepts as "catholic Israel." It wanted to become the "folk religion" of American Jewry and thereby provide a conduit for secularizing Jews to remain Jewish. Although both Mordecai Kaplan and Solomon Shechter supported cultural Zionism for ideological reasons, they were also aware that modern secular Zionism incorporated the peoplehood element in its most pristine form. It too could serve an instrument to keep de-judaizing Jews, Jewish. Kaplan, who was among the first to recognize that the loss of millions of secularizing Jews was a crisis of immense proportions, also thought in terms of Jewish peoplehood, which generated an evolving Jewish religious civilization. Judaism becomes a cultural expression, one among many, of the Jewish people. Similarly, when an alarmed Reform movement altered its vision in 1937 and stated in its new Columbus platform that "Judaism is the soul of which Israel is the body," it was responding to the chasm that had developed in the Reform movement between secularized Jewishness and Judaism that had caused it to lose momentum. But it would take more than rhetoric and eloquent metaphors to revitalize a radically bifurcated American Jewry.

The strategy of tightly binding Judaism and Jewishness together by ideological fiat, in the hope of reversing the very logic of modernity in America, was probably doomed to failure from the outset. Secularism is primarily a perception, a way of looking at the world and defining reality. It has become part of the culture and affects even those who most resist its embrace. Those who understand its full implications for faith and seek to neutralize its influence sometimes try skillfully to balance the claims of two worlds. Sometimes that is ingeniously achieved. But such balancing acts require will and energy, and there is loss of authenticity. We do not yet know the full story of attrition in the Orthodox community, but it must have been high because most American Jews who are now more or less secular can still remember their observant grandparents. Even during the current period of triumphalism, Orthodoxy has actually experienced a slower proportional growth than other branches and a decline in relation to the number of Jews who no longer affiliate at all. Similarly, the Conservative movement is plagued by a decline in observance. Their attempt to accommodate the modernization process, based, as it is, on a transaction in which each side has conceded something, has been less than successful. American Judaism has been as much altered as it has sought to alter, perhaps more. For some, even the changes such as ordination of women and adoption of patrilineal descent would be acceptable if they held out the promise of taming the secularization process. But clearly, the process is inexorable and the changes it requires, endless. One can negotiate the terms of living together and the concessions each side must make, but one cannot negotiate away the process itself.

Can there be a Judaism in America without the overwhelming mass of Jews who simply believe themselves to be Jewish but not religious? More precisely, can the proportionately small core of Orthodox Jews in America who have more or less resisted the blandishments of secular life survive without the mass of American Jews who have come to terms with it? Survival, as used here, means more than personal or small-group continuance. It means the generation of an American Jewish religious culture worthy of the name, rather than its becoming merely another religious sect on the already cluttered American landscape. Should the tension between Jewishness and Judaism that is at the heart of the secularization process cause either of the contestants to leave the arena, American Jewry would experience a more rapid decline. The tension is agonizing and increasingly uncivil, but it is a creative one that gives American Jewry measured change. Partly because of postemancipation Jewish history, partly because of the society with which it has cast its lot, American Jewry has inherited a secular spirit so certain of its vision that, if not checked by an equally determined force, it will generate life-styles that make communal life increasingly impossible. The turn-of-the-century Jewish secularists who celebrated Yom Kippur feasts before synagogues were not reasonable, and neither are their contemporary successors. Their passion for change is familiar to Jewish observers for whom it recalls nothing so much as the religious fervor of truly pious Jews. They have contended in the community since before the turn of the century and, in the process, have given American Jewry something more reasonable than either side proposes on its own. Who knows what will happen if the natural checks that we have been fortunate enough to inherit are dissipated.

Yet, Jewishness and Judaism seem to be growing further apart, with the result that the former no longer has much of a lease on life and the latter is barely holding its own. But historically the Jews have been a resilient people. Perhaps what we witness is not disintegration but transformation. It would be nice to be able to convince oneself of that. But then there is the historical reality that Jewish survival in the postemancipation Diaspora has not been natural but willed. That is even truer of the benevolent American Diaspora than of others. But to will survival, there must be a culture or a belief to generate it. For secular Jews there must also be a sense of the worthwhileness of that culture lest the question "survival for what?" remain unanswered.

11

The Charge of Rootless Cosmopolitan

IT OCCURRED TO ME only after I had decided to explore this topic that some readers would not recall the origin of the term *rootless cosmopolitan*. Early in the century, socialists used it to describe what they considered to be a major weakness in the class structure of the Jewish people. What was required was a greater development of so-called productive elements—like workers and peasants—and a diminution of "parasitic" ones, like petty merchants. It was imagined that furnishing the Jews with a peasantry would correct an abnormal class structure. Alumni of Zionist youth groups might recall the term being used in their all-night discussions about *chalutziut* and the need for an attachment to, and love of the land. My generation heard it in the 1950s when Khruschev used it to describe yet another thing Jews were guilty of. Undoubtedly, he meant that Soviet Jews were prone to resist the shaping influence of Communist ideology and were not fully committed to the regime. He need not have taken umbrage. We shall see that cosmopolitans display that kind of autonomy and unwillingness to plug into society fully, no matter in which nation they are ensconced.

You do not have to be Jewish to be a rootless cosmopolitan, but it describes a disproportionate number of Jews, whether they live in New York, Tel Aviv, or Moscow. That alone makes it sufficient to warrant our attention. I have since learned that the lot of the true rootless cosmopolitan is not an easy one, so that I hesitate to recommend it as a life-style. (In any case, one cannot choose to be a rootless cosmopoli-

This essay appeared originally in the *Jewish Studies Network* 2, no. 2 (Fall 1988), under the title "Rootless Cosmopolitanism: Defined and Defended."

tan. It takes years of deracination.) The quality of life rootlessness produces has its down side, which we all know about: alienation, loneliness, anomie, and the dozens of buzz words that we pick up in our social psychology courses. I think the Yiddish word *Einzamkeit* describes the malaise better than the words borrowed from psychotherapy. But here these personal malaises concern me less than what I observe from a Jewish survivalist perspective. I am not certain that a rootless cosmopolitan, which I view here as an advanced stage of secular identity formation, can carry the Jewish enterprise forward.

Can such Jews—who are by definition oriented to the cosmos rather than to a particular tribe that inhabits it—feel the pain of exile or otherwise make common cause with their brothers? Can they feel a separate and different Jewish value and rhythm to life? Finding answers to such questions is no simple task. Numerically, such secularized Jews predominate, but when they become rootless cosmopolitans some wonder whether they can be counted as Jews. By the very nature of what they aspire to be—individuated, uncommitted, detribalized—they appear on the historical stage singly rather than as a collectivity. Such secularized Jews have no rabbinic assemblies, no *Rosh Yeshivot*, no Federation *gedolim*, and certainly no charismatic leaders who speak for them. How could they, when by definition they belong only to themselves and to no one else? To speak then of the *community* of rootless cosmopolitans is the ultimate oxymoron.

Because they find their Zion everywhere, they are at home nowhere. They are Zionists who cannot settle in Zion, because their rootlessness denies them a sense of home from which they are exiled. Like Chaim Weizmann and Nahum Goldmann, they can understand the need of others for community; but, paradoxically, they cannot understand their own need. One can read the history of American Jewry as a denial of exile. There is affirmation of the *Galut* rather than negation. How many American cities have been proclaimed to be Jerusalem—Charleston, Cincinnati, perhaps even Brooklyn. There is good reason for such affirmation. American claims to share the hebraic heritage, and Jews are not strangers in the land, or at least they are not alone in being strangers. Known as a nation of nations, the land itself is peopled by strangers. America is a rational contrivance populated by dozens of subcultures of which the Jews are one. There is no one folk like the French. No one knows really precisely what Americans are supposed to be, and therefore a great deal of time and energy is expended in defining what they are not. In the French parliament they do not need an Un-French Committee, as we had a House Un-

American Activities Committee, to set the parameters of identity. Everyone knows what a French man or woman is. They are not Polish or Russian Jews living in Paris. They are the rooted French who have been baked in the same historical oven for centuries.

It was partly that multiplicity of tribes and cultures that brought pluralism into vogue. It served as a lubricant for America before it became a code word in the modern secular sensibility. Not accidentally, it was a Harvard-trained Jewish thinker and Zionist, Horace Kallen, who in 1915 legitimized the notion of cultural pluralism. In a democratic garden, he argued years before Mao, many flowers should bloom. It was a compelling rationale that could produce sufficient space for Jewish and other ethnic groups' particularism. Because it muted the stress that emanated from being strangers in the land, pluralism created a comfortable condition, and comfort is requisite for secular living. What Kallen did not foresee was the possibility that his symphonic analogy could also produce social tension and disharmony, a cacophony of sound and fury. More importantly, it could not be assumed that the granting of such cultural space would find secular Jews willing and able to create a home away from home or at least a cultural net to catch Jews who could no longer find meaning in the religious culture. They might not even recall what ought to be planted in a Jewish garden. But comfort there was, and that went far to diminish the pain of *Galut*. Today, their heart is not in the East. To find where it locates itself and to what it is devoted is our next order of business.

The seeming lack of passion in American Zionism is what made it so puzzling for the Jews of eastern Europe and for Israelis today. They do not understand that it is precisely the kind of Zionism produced by a highly secularized Jewry. Unlike the secularism of eastern European Jewry, the heart of American Jewry is constrained by the head. It is rarely totally given over to a cause or ideology or to a group. By definition, the secular mind-set is "cooler," more in quest of understanding than belief. In eastern Europe, where a different kind of secularism reigned, there was a preoccupation with *Galut*, if not with *g'ulah* (redemption). But for the most part, American Zionism never was preoccupied in this way, and those who tried to impose such a sensibility were consigned to the wastebin of history.

It is that misperception that was behind the debacle of the 1921 ZOA convention in Cleveland, where the secularized leadership group led by Louis Brandeis was unseated, so that, for a while, it seemed that American Zionism would develop along eastern European lines. Ostensibly, the reason for the conflict, which had been simmering for some time, had something to do with bookkeeping. Brandeis had not only lessened the number of dollars being sent to the World Zionist Organization center, he insisted on separating investments from donations for *Keren Hayesod*. He naturally preferred the latter. But bookkeeping was merely a metaphor for the cooler, more operational mind-set with which the Brandeis leadership approached Zionism. The supporters of Louis Lipsky, who succeeded Brandeis, referred to their predecessors as "Nordics," a term borrowed from the then raging debate over immigration restriction. In merely seven years, Brandeis transformed the Zionist movement into something they could not be comfortable with. It had become disciplined and efficient, but it lacked *heimishkeit*, passion and commitment. They were part-time Zionists and not the Jewish Jews with whom one could feel comfortable. A man who installed a time-clock at the Broadway headquarters of the ZOA obviously did not understand what it meant to be a Jew and a Zionist twenty-four hours a day. As Maurice Samuel said in addressing the delegates of the 1928 Pittsburgh convention in defense of the Lipsky leadership after the charge of incompetence and corruption had surfaced:

> You must have as the representatives of Zionism men who are Zionists not merely by conviction but by construction, men who have not reached Zionism by a method of logic, not logical Zionists, but biological Zionists, men who can be trusted instinctively to react correctly to any assault . . . upon that form of Judaism which is embedded in Zionism.

If one reasoned too much, one might discover how improbable the scheme for building a Jewish state really was. The still ideologically hot eastern Jew, whose visceral passion was not harnessed by rationality, was preferable. Yet, ultimately, they understood that such passions could not build lasting institutions that do the work of the world. By 1929, the year of the stock market crash, it was clear that Brandeis had been right. American Zionism was in disarray, membership was dropping, and the movement teetered near bankruptcy. The Brandeis-Mack faction was invited back to set the Zionist house in order. "Biological Zionists" were mostly a resonance of the first generation. The Americanized successors were those who, when they spoke of homeland, meant it not for themselves but for those who needed it, a Zionism for *yenem* (others). Yet such types were not strangers to the world Zionist movement. Theodor Herzl, Chaim Weizmann, Nahum Goldmann, and many other leaders of the movement fit neatly into the rootless cosmopolitan category.

So do many second- and third-generation Israelis. Not only do most American Jews steadfastly refuse to negate the *Golah* (the Diaspora), but an unseemly number of Israelis want to resettle there. A population exchange is happening around the axis of secularity. To Israel come those Jews most resistant to secularism, the religious and ideological survivalists. They resettle in Israel, the researchers tell us, in order to live more Jewish lives. Who are those who leave the homeland? Those who for whatever reason do not feel that there is a possibility for self-fulfillment in Israel. It is precisely self-realization, rather than the fulfillment of group goals, that is the driving force in secular life. That does not mean that *yordim* prefer the culture of their adopted countries. Many remain notoriously homesick and split in their attitudes. They will tell you at the drop of a hat that the quality of life, as measured by human relations, is better in Israel. But such things as human relations, religion, or culture play only a small role for secular Jews who are preoccupied with the development of self more than with the welfare of tribe or nation.

I must finally tell you what I mean by secularism, which at its maximal level produces our rootless cosmopolitan. I have said before that such secularists are unideological, questers for the rational, understanders rather than believers, and are committed primarily to development of self. The categories developed by social scientists may be helpful. They speak of the sense of autonomy in the secular mindset. Secular Jews consider themselves to be free and at the turn of the century simply called themselves "free thinkers." Of course, no one is totally free, and we would understand the concept better if we used the term *unbound* or *unlinked* to the imperatives of the group. That means that, if there were Jewish governance in the Diaspora, there would be no assurance that its laws would be obeyed. Secularists' associations with the Jewish community are voluntary and given on their own terms. With such loose governing structure, it is no wonder that the disorder in American Jewish political life made an effective response to the Holocaust extremely difficult.

Yet, on the level of the citizenship, secular Jewish citizens are generally law abiding. They pay their taxes and stop for red lights. When fully developed as a type, they are ideal citizens for the Marxist version of the "end of days," when government of people supposedly will give way to the administration of things. Because secularlists are self-governing and possess internalized controls, they need no government. Their quest is rather to free themselves of all fetters—that of tribe, nation, community, and, one suspects, family as well, or how else to account for the rising divorce rate in secularized societies? They prefer autonomy. That is why it is so difficult to enlist them in group causes. Because secularists understand that ideologies demand a role in shaping their lives and interfere with selfhood, ideologies lose their drawing power for them. Samuel is perceptive when he notes that Americanized Zionists are "logical" rather than "biological." Related to the need for autonomy is a relentless search for rationale. It leads to the separation of things that were once together. In the arena of Jewish identity, Judaism, the faith with its myriad laws, is separated from Jewishness, the ethnic peoplehood element. The simplest way to define secular Jews is to note that they believe that they can be Jewish without being Judaic. These separations and reclassifications are part of the scientific method, which seeks to explain and understand in order finally to control. Secular man desacrilizes. Things once held sacred and holy are removed from that category in order that they may be examined. Not only are sacred texts placed under the microscope but ultimately all extrarational or, as secularists would say, "nonscientific" forces are also. That includes political ideologies. When religious fundamentalists complain that "secular humanism" is in fact an idea-system that does not stop at questioning revelation but seeks to substitute its own explanation, they are, in some twisted way, on to something. Nothing can be shielded from modern science, and to be examined and explained and classified, it must first be desacrilized.

These are only two aspects of the secular mind-set. There are many others. But it occurs to me that there may be some who do not recognize that they too are subject to this process. To some degree we all are. It is in the air we breathe. What you have heard is a description of the ideal model. It is truer of some individuals and societies than of others. In real life, most secularists are neither totally rootless nor totally cosmopolitan. Most position themselves somewhere along the secular-modern-traditional continuum. The choice of position is based, not on consistency, but comfort, which is important in the day-to-day living of the free. Some have called American Jewry "the Jewry of comfort" or "air-conditioned Jewry." We have a Judaism without a yoke of Torah, just as we have a Zionism without the yoke of *aliyah*. It could not be otherwise in a secularized society. A monolithic logic and purity of category is rarely found in secular persons.

They are open-minded and operate on several levels. It is possible for them to believe one way, perceive another, and behave in yet a third. Secular identity formation, then, is multileveled rather than linear; we are no longer necessarily what we appear to be.

Although the way of perceiving reality changes, basic core problems do not. What has changed is not the questions but how we seek the answers. Modern secularists, no less than their predecessors, still need to know the meaning of their lives and perhaps even how to find a transcendent purpose in them. It is conceivable that secular persons become more intent on finding answers to such age-old quandaries than do the traditional pious or observant Jews, who, after all, have the comfort of learning the answer in their sacred texts. What occurs is a process of transmutation, by means of which old wine is poured into new bottles. It is, for example inaccurate to say that secularists are irreligious, even though we have seen that they are incapable of genuflecting obedience to an unseen force higher than themselves. Rootless cosmopolitans, especially, cannot be part of a flock of which God is the shepherd, much less accept the notion that God's special favor is invested in a particular church or people. That is why Reconstructionism, which is in a sense tailored to fit the mindset of modern secular Jews, eschews the idea of chosenness. Yet if religion has something to do with wonder about existential problems, then secularists are as religious as their predecessors. They have replaced a particular religion with a generalized or perhaps better universalized religiosity that allows interchangeability with other faiths by forming a so-called civil religion. How often have you heard modernists declaim that all religions are essentially alike? Yet some of our most outspoken secularists possess a sharply honed sense of justice and humanity, if not of Torah. Frequently, they outmatch their religious counterparts, if not in holiness, then in concern for others. Surely an André Sakharov or a Natan Sharansky possesses the moral stature of anything produced by the synagogue or church. What has happened is that the other-directed religious spirit has been internalized where such sensibilities were formerly ensconced. It is no longer linked to a particular church or a special people. It has been transmuted. The original quest for a Messiah may, in secular guise, appear as a desire for a more just social order or simply as the notion of progress.

Rootless cosmopolitans no longer fathom homelessness; nor do they live at ease in the world, especially if they are Jewish. Exile becomes transmuted into the modern phenomenon of alienation, the sense of belonging nowhere and to no one. Joshua Heschel said it best: "Not only are all of us in *Galut*, *Galut* is in us." The rootless cosmopolitan is no longer a commited Jew, but neither has he or she become an Esau.

Jewish corporateness, the hallmark of Judaism, is replaced by the secularists' pervasive sense of their individuality. That sense of self subverts ideologies as well. In America, political Zionism is replaced by cultural Zionism. The reason why that transmutation occurs is that all modern ideologies contain a praxis element that seeks to link theory and action, so that in order to be a Zionist one must heed the command to settle in Israel. But to accept such an imperative would inhibit autonomy and freedom, and it therefore needs to be redefined. As noted, life strategies for secularists are dictated by the potential for self-actualization, not by furthering a cause or faith. Where is the *chalutz* (pioneer) of yesteryear or the recruit for the Trappist monastery? Indeed, ideologies that maintain too insistent a claim on life and community are inevitably broken. That is what the Russians and the Chinese are discovering.

Once it is understood that, for secularists, the original tribal perception has been altered, their refusal to come home falls into place. It is not only that a secure and comfortable people rarely voluntarily chooses discomfort and danger. It is that individuated, secular rootless cosmopolitans no longer can be enlisted for purely communal objectives. Their home is everywhere. They pick and choose those facets of the regnant ideology that fit into their life goals. They are their own lonely tribal chieftain. It is as true of those American Jews who will never make *aliyah* as it is of those thousands of Israelis who have left home for homelessness in New York, Los Angeles, and even Berlin. It is also true of those Russian Jews who prefer life in the American Zion. Except for the different quotients of opportunity for self-actualization, these urban/urbane cities have become virtually interchangeable. In truth, the secular rootless cosmopolitans of New York, Tel Aviv, and Moscow have more in common with each other than they do with the folk of their own hinterlands.

So intent is this modern type of self-fulfillment that sometimes it seems that their desperate search for happiness has itself become a great source of misery. Can such self-involved Jews be useful for any greater purpose? Some conclude that, in the world of real power and conflict, rootless cosmopolitanism is dangerous in general to life and limb and Jewish survival. That much the fate of German and Soviet Jewry in the twentieth century can attest to. For the Jews of Germany,

Gershom Sholem observed that, "no benefit redounded for their status as classic representatives of the phenomenon of man's estrangement or alienation from society." Hannah Arendt came to the same conclusion when she condemned those Jews who eschewed involving themselves in the polis and settled rather for being "conscious pariahs," happy with the aura of fame.

Yet, there are those who find in them a model of what we should all become. As Hartley Alexander, president of the American Philosophical Society, wrote in an article in 1920,

> If there is today on earth a man who is both intensely and broadly cosmopolite; it is the Jew. He, more than any other man, has discovered the secret accommodations to the usages of fellow men without imitation of them, of cooperation without identification, of harmonization without mere unison. He lives in Rome, and is not as the Romans, he is in Asia, in Europe, in Africa, and is not Asian nor European nor African, but is everywhere a kindred spirit, related to all men, but confused with none—such a man, in short, as in the millennial day of the world's civilization, men of all races must become.[1]

The reason for Alexander's enthusiasm is not difficult to understand. Although the cosmopolites are not able to be mobilized for a greater cause, they are also refreshingly unfanatic and tolerant. They will not be found in modern mass movements. They are not seen cheering Hitler at the Nuremberg Partei Tag rallies, and they are strangers to rallies of the eye-bulging believers in contemporary Tehran. Nor do they lose themselves among the crowd-lovers of the Woodstock nation. Belonging only to a tribe of one, they are poor human material for crusades against other tribes. They resist the manipulation of the charismatic leader, be he Moses or Khomeini.

Because they are no longer fully ensconced in the culture of tribe, they are more prone to understand its myths and secrets. That is what has enabled them to contribute so disproportionately to the development of modern Western culture and science. Men and women like Einstein, Freud, and Kafka, and hundreds of others who composed the Jewish modernizing elite, were incubated in a cosmopolitan axis whose anchors were Berlin, Budapest, Vienna, and Prague. Their mentality is everywhere the same—urbane, tolerant, and creative. Modern life is not conceivable without such cosmopolitan cities, and predictably it is the Jews who are disproportionately their denizens.

What a paradox. There is awesome historical evidence to show that, during the Holocaust, it was precisely on such Jews that the well-being of the community depended. That was especially true in America. Most Holocaust researchers have their own agonizing "if onlies." Mine is, if only we had been more effective in activating the secular Jews around Roosevelt, the so-called "Jew Deal." But the Lubins and the Cohens, the Rosenmans and the Frankfurters could not identify with, much less advocate, a Jewish interest. They were marginally and, in a few cases, unhappily Jewish. They were decent men but not committed ones.

Yet even here, there is a glimmer of hope. Ultimately, the Jewish secretary of the treasury, Henry Morgenthau Jr., was reached. He became instrumental in establishing the War Refugee Board, which marked the zenith of the American rescue effort. Radicalized by the Holocaust, Morgenthau, under the tutelage of Henry Montor, remained active in Jewish causes for the remainder of his life. He serves as a model that secular Jews can be brought to the Jewish enterprise and even taught the sustaining Jewish values that undoubtedly contributed to their own achievements. For them, Jewish identity may be very thin, based only on a memory of a memory. They no longer learn its worth with their mothers' milk. But they do understand, as most modernists do, investment based on patrimony and cultural estate. These values can serve as the petals that draw the Jewish secularist to the rich cultural nectar beneath. Many rootless cosmopolitans need and would welcome such sustenance.

The secularization process is inexorable, and although its character changes from culture to culture, it is as much in Tel Aviv as in New York. But its peculiar nature is that it is open and can be influenced. It amalgamates and is tolerant. That much has been learned from the training of young leadership groups of the United Jewish Appeal (UJA) and the Federations. Secularized Jews, especially when they are young, can be taught to recognize and support a Jewish interest. Surely, it is by now clear to all that it is in the most highly secularized stratas of American Jewry that lie the very skills required to make our complex society operate smoothly. They are the lawyers and managers, the scientists and engineers, the poets and sundry opinion shapers. In America, it is also they who manage the Jewish interest. That is a natural and predictable development. There is a new kind of power in such knowledge, which gains in importance when daily the power of numbers, so crucial in democracy, becomes less available to American Jewry.

They prefer exile to homeland and investment in the human capital of themselves to ideology. I have heard them called checkbook Jews. But that misses who they are. The giving of money is what secular Jews, whose loyalty and commitment lie elsewhere, can do. In giving money they give life, love, health, power, and the myriad of things money has come to stand for in the secular world. It is no small gift, and it expresses their need to help others. Usually, they do not detest the tribe to which their ancestors once belonged. They are merely once removed from it. The need for transcendence does not disappear. It may, in fact, be more strongly felt in the inner spirit of the rootless cosmopolitans, which we have used here to designate the final stage of secular Jewish identity formation. It comes out in a familiar Jewish story:

A pious Jew finds himself on the road as the sabbath approaches. He makes his way to the nearest shtetl and asks the rabbi for shelter. But the rabbi is poor, and the traveler has arrived late. There are already more guests than can be fed without thinning the soup to water. The traveler is sent forth and told to find another Jewish household. With Rabbi's final words, "don't worry, God will help," still ringing in his ear, he approaches the first Jew he encounters with his request for a *shabbes*. It happens to be the town secularist, a staunch Bundist, who openly professes to be a nonbeliever. But the secular Jew takes him home and makes a Sabbath for the traveler that would satisfy even the most pious Jew. Finally comes that lazy time on a Sabbath afternoon where one can invite the soul. Curiosity gets the best of the traveler and he tells his story and his puzzlement. "Look, the Rabbi sent me forth assuring me that God would help, and you . . ." Here he is interrupted by the secularist: "What's the problem, it's precisely because I knew that God would *not* help, that I had to." The operative clause is those last four words *that I had to*. Whatever else secular Jews may have given up or lost, the moral imperative to help somehow often survives. So, too, does a sense of social justice. It is understandable that this should be so. The rootless cosmopolitans, like the Jews they once may have been, are, after all, strangers in the land. Who knows better than the stranger how tenuous are the bonds of civilization?

12

Can Secular Judaism
Survive in America?

SOME DAY AN IMAGINATIVE YOUNG SCHOLAR may view the history
of modern Jewry through the prism of laws and decrees enacted by
various host nations that shaped the destiny of their Jewish commu-
nities. Included would be the dozens of laws associated with emanci-
pation and those like the edict expelling the Jews from Spain (1492),
or the infamous May Laws in Czarist Russia (1882), or the more re-
cent Nuremberg laws in Nazi Germany (1935), I would caution that
scholar not to omit the American restrictionist immigration laws of
1921 and 1924. It would be easy to forget them because we are accus-
tomed to thinking of America as a benevolent host. Yet, these laws
may well have had the most negative impact of all on Jewish well-
being in the twentieth century.

During the Holocaust, restrictive immigration laws proved to be
a life and death matter for thousands of European Jews seeking to
flee Hitler's Final Solution. By dint of its tradition, ideology, and eco-
nomic capacity, the United States should have been a major receiving
country, serving as a model for the world. But during the restrictionist
1920s, the asylum provision could not withstand the onslaught of
"Nordicism." As Louis Marshall had forseen, these laws made no dis-
tinction between refugees in need of asylum and normal immigrants
seeking to resettle. From a historical perspective, failure to retain such
a provision in the law looms as profoundly significant in the destruc-

This essay appeared originally in the *Jewish Frontier* 66, no. 4 (July/Aug. 1989),
under the title "Where's the Net? Culture, Language and Survival in America."

tion of European Jewry. Failure to find a haven for these unwanted Jews contributed notably to Berlin's decision, in the fall of 1941, to make Europe *Judenrein* by mass annihilation.

The subsequent destruction of European Jewry was so traumatic that it has overshadowed the impact that the Final Solution had on the survival potential of American Jewry. There is a "dirty little secret" in American Jewish history. Before World War II, American Jewry was dependent for survival on the importation of Jews and their cultural contributions from Jewish communities abroad. The founding Sephardic community would surely have disappeared had it not been for the timely arrival of the Jews from central Europe in the 1820s. In its turn, the German-Jewish community would probably have melded into the majority culture had it not been for the timely arrival of the Jewish Jews of eastern Europe. In the twentieth century, that capital came from the overflow in eastern Europe. The question in the minds of survivalists is whether in turning with such special fury to destroy the Jewish community of eastern Europe, whose biological and cultural surfeit fed not only American Jewry but the *Yishuv*, Hitler did not also deliver a lethal blow to the survival possibilities of American Jewry and perhaps Israel as well. There are demographers who, after calibrating the attrition and intermarriage rate in this country, come precisely to that conclusion. They argue that American Jewry, barring some unforeseen infusion, will not sustain itself as a viable community beyond the middle of the twenty-first century. That projection may be unduly pessimistic.

It is in the impact that these restrictionist laws had on the ability to sustain an indigenous Jewish culture that the consequences were most dire. American Jewry never developed a separate culture and language such as we find in Jewish Poland or Spain. Judaism, the faith, and Jewishness, the ethnic identity, were carried here in the baggage of immigrants and were then reshaped to fit into the American environment. Not only was it biologically dependent, but it was also culturally derivative. Its religious enterprise (with the exception of the Reconstructionist movement), its labor movement, its now almost extinct *Landsmannschaften*, its shaping ideologies from Socialism to Zionism, all have "made abroad" labels attached to them. When restrictionism brought this supplementation to an end, the question faced by American Jewry was whether a separate survival was possible, given the strong solvent of American culture and its willingness to absorb the Jews. Unlike the situation in eastern Europe, a separate Jewish culture and language that could serve as a safety net to catch secularizing or falling Jews who no longer wanted to adhere to the religion had not developed.

Contemporary survivalists still argue back and forth about the possibility of sustaining a Jewish enterprise not fortified by a specific culture based on its own language. But today, all acknowledge that the hope for the development of such an indigenous Jewish culture is forlorn. It makes one think more fondly of the vital culture based on Yiddish that proved unable to withstand the shock of restrictionism during the twenties. As early as July 15, 1921, the *American Hebrew* noted that the Jewish immigrants were not only inclined to make their stay permanent but that they Americanized "even in the first generation." Three years later, Ludwig Stein noted that the Americanization process seemed to work much faster among Jewish immigrants in America than in Wilheminian Prussia. "American Jews," he observed, "have actually developed into Americans in physical appearance." They learned the native language faster than Jewish immigrants in France and Germany. It was not fast enough for nativist "uptown" Jews. One such suggested to Louis Marshall that the way to hasten acculturation was to push legislation to remove second-class mailing privileges from the Yiddish press. Marshall, who did not share the general disdain for Yiddish speakers, was appalled at the suggestion. He pointed out that some of the finest writers in English stemmed from Yiddish-speaking homes. "The younger generation," he observed "quickly forgets whatever Yiddish it may have learned at home and avoids the use of Yiddish."

Statistics that indicated that Yiddish cultural institutions were indeed moribund bore Marshall out. Although the census of 1930 showed the highest number of Yiddish speakers (1,750,000), the figure had not actually kept pace with the absolute increase in the Jewish population. The 1940 census showed a decline of one-half million who listed their mother tongue as Yiddish. Although there were more Jews who spoke Yiddish than ever before in 1930, the Yiddish press experienced a continued decline in circulation from its peak year of 1917, when it claimed 750,000 readers, a decline of 21.8 percent between 1916 and 1922 alone. The attempt to retain its readership by publishing English supplements barely affected the continuing decline. Moreover, a matching descent was manifest in all journals that dealt with Jewish subjects. Two Hebrew monthlies, two English weeklies, and one Yiddish weekly were forced to suspend publication between 1920 and 1921. Similarly the Yiddish theater, which had reached its zenith in 1927 when it attracted a weekly audience of

120,000, experienced a sense of crisis. Like the press and other cultural institutions such as Yiddish schools and teachers' institutes, they appeared to be a one-generation phenomenon.

That decline of Yiddish culture in America stood in sharp contrast to the Jewish experience in eastern Europe. There, after a struggle to legitimize it, Yiddish had given birth to a literature second to none in the world. Before its physical destruction, Yiddish culture gave every sign that it would be able to sustain itself. Indeed, it was the existence of that separate culture and language that was the major grievance of Polish nationalists. Yet in America, the culture and language could not prevail without being continually replenished from abroad. Every place where diasporic communities had survived, they had been able to do so partly by producing and then holding on to their own language, whether it was Ladino or Yiddish. There were of course other factors that helped them maintain cultural separateness. Neither Poland nor Spain beckoned Jews to enter their culture, and so Jews sustained their own. But in America, where acculturation was encouraged, the absence of such a culture surely lessened the possibilities of survival. No longer interested in observing the myriad rules of a law-obsessed religion, secularizing American Jews found no Jewish secular culture to break their fall, as in Poland. The most essential buttress to such a culture would have been the development of a separate language or the nurturing of one already in existence. The question of whether a Jewish culture can be generated in the language of the host culture remains unanswered. It is at the very center of the Jewish survival conundrum in America.

Survival anxiety was not confined to those in the process of abandoning the faith. There was something in the air of America, perhaps its freedom, that worked against piety and otherworldliness. Those observant Jews in Europe who warned their migrating brethren that America was a *tref medinah* (unpious society) seemed instinctively to have understood that. The attrition in the Orthodox community was high. It too depended on supplementation from abroad, especially for religious leaders. There were several instances in the first decade of the century when religious communities tried to import rabbis. The sad case of Rabbi Jacob Josef is merely one of several examples in the Orthodox experience in America. It is doubtful whether the current vitality of Orthodoxy could have been achieved without the biological supplementation it received during and after the Holocaust period. Clearly, American culture posed an unusual challenge, not only for secularists but also for those who adhered to the religious culture as well.

Left without a sustaining culture of their own and only halfway into the native American culture, which offered little that might make their lives meaningful, they were in great danger of total deracination, of becoming an anonymous mass that belonged nowhere and that would no longer connect with the millennial tradition of which they were once part. True, American Jewry developed a far-flung network of religious congregations, supplemented by an elaborate infrastructure of secular organizations to which thousands of Jews belonged. But the proliferation of congregations stood in sharp contrast to the decline in religious observance and passion. For the most part, the synagogues were half-empty except on the "high holy" days. By the 1930s, a growing percentage of Jews were not affiliated with any congregation. The organizational culture of secular organizations like the American Jewish Congress or B'nai B'rith was not designed to generate Jewish culture, although there were some unsuccessful efforts to "program" for it.

The truth of the matter was that the loss of group culture or the failure to develop a new one was both a personal and a group tragedy. The loss of comunity always is. Such a culture might have offered an extra measure of security for the individual Jew who was otherwise vulnerable to the vicissitudes that are everywhere the products of modernity. There was in America no buffer that Jewish communities sometimes develop in less seductive cultures to prevent the majority culture from bearing directly down on them.

Lest this be taken as a plea for a lost Yiddish culture that might have served as a redemption for secular Jews, let me hasten to add that although I count myself among those who sorely miss what was lost, I do not believe that such a culture could in any case have sustained itself in this country. What nettles a survivalist is that nothing has been generated by American Jewry to take its place. There is little Jewishly Jewish a secular Jew can hold on to. At the center of that kind of culture is the question of a separate language. Undoubtedly, the linguists, who Jews still produce in unseemly numbers, have elaborate explanation for its absence here and in other Western countries. But an explanation does not fill the space where language used to be. Without it, we are unable to think our separate thoughts, build our distinctive perceptions, mount our Jewish conspiracies to repair the world. Missing is that special sensibility based on language that marks off one people from another.

Possessing one's own language is no guarantee of survival, but it helps. It is possible for outsiders to break the language code and reveal the "secrets" of the culture as the well-known Palestinian writer Anton Shammas has done in Israel. He follows the path of those innumerable Jewish specialists on the writing of Goethe, Shakespeare, Ibsen, or Melville who interpreted these literary giants to the folk from which they had sprung. In pre-World War II Germany and Europe generally, the number of Jewish critics who "interpreted" major national writers was as embarrassingly disproportionate as were the number of Jewish writers, playwrights, journalists, and poets. Resentment that aliens had gained control of the national culture fed the anti-Semitic imagination. Yet, few Jewish critics were motivated by a need to open up or universalize the language in which they worked as has Shammas, who recently called for "de-Jewing" Hebrew. They understood the transaction in which they were involved. In order to understand the host culture, they had to become part of it. Like them, Shammas may discover that he has been as much Judaized or Israelized as he has "de-Jewed" Hebrew. Some critics have, in fact, detected a familiar Jewish sing-song in his thinking. Clearly, there is a trade-off in decoding the tribal language. The opening up of the language assures a worldwide audience and influence to Jewish writers. Isaac Bashevis Singer notwithstanding, our Bellows, Ozicks, Roths, Malamuds, and the host of American Jewish writers who are having such an impact would hardly be known if they wrote in Yiddish about exclusively Jewish concerns. A ghettoized culture is by definition directed internally. On the other hand, once Jewish writers address themselves to the larger audience in their language, their utility for preserving a specifically Jewish culture is diminished. That much the experience of the Jewish writers who turned to the Left in the 1930s teaches us.

But as things developed, American Jewry never had the luxury of facing such a threat to its integrity. At least the Jews in Israel have a language with which outsiders can tamper. The Jews of America have none, and the inner-tribal secrets over which it stood guard have long since been revealed. If Mr. Shammas' objective is really detribalizing Judaism and ridding it of its parochial cast, let him look to the American model. It has found a better way.

13

Jewry and America's Hard Secularism

TO BECOME MODERN, societies undergo a wrenching process of change in the way they are organized and view the world. The attitudinal aspect of modernity is sometimes called the secularization process. It takes different forms in different societies, but everywhere it requires the dethroning of traditional mind-sets. Because America is different, so is its secularism. I have called it "hard" secularism because of its libertarianism and the high degree of individuation and its lesser willingness to let old forms and institutions stand. It is that hardness that creates the powerful solvent that poses a survival challenge to all religious and ethnic cultures in America. The former are desacrilized, the latter, denuded. That is what has been happening to American Jewry since its origins in the seventeenth century.

To speak of secularism in a Jewish historical context poses almost insurmountable problems of definition because that term has prior usages in Jewish history. It implies irreligion or someone who adheres to a socialist-tinged ideology like Bundism. So I must state at the outset that the secularism I speak of here is only remotely connected to such ideologies as Bundism or Socialist Zionism. In secular persons there can be a religious sensibility that is internalized to become an integral part of the individual self. They may continue to enjoy the aesthetic celebratory aspects of formal institutionalized religion and even sing in the synagogue choir; but, being free, they are no longer ready to be commanded. The myriad structures of the Halakha (Jewish religious law) would impinge upon their autonomy,

This essay was presented at the Conference on Jewish Education, sponsored by the Melton Center at the Hebrew University of Jerusalem, January 1944.

which is central to secular persons. For the same reason, they do not lightly surrender themselves to the praxis element of modern ideologies, whether they preach the need to participate in the "revolution" or to halt the killing of whales. Secularists cannot long obey these exhortations because the secular mentalité is, in fact, already an ideology that preaches the development, or better, the liberation of self from all that would fetter it.

A separate study could be done on what the secular Jews choose to give up and what they retain. Life-cycle ceremonies, for example, are not easily surrendered. Even the most secular prefer to be married under a *chupa* (canopy) and buried in a Jewish cemetery. And many secular Jews light Sabbath candles before they attend a movie or turn on the TV. The choices are determined by the design of modern life in the particular community. If an automobile is a necessity rather than a luxury, then most Jews will drive to services; but there are many Orthodox exceptions. A favorite Jewish joke used to be that the difference between Orthodox, Conservative, and Reform Jews lies in the distance they park their cars from the synagogue.

Sadly, it is not a static process. As the secular spirit grows more intense, the distance from the religious and ethnic culture widens; and both are emptied of their content and deprived of their special language. Once particularity has been ground down, it becomes easier to commingle with other subcultures that have undergone a similar detribalization process. Intermarriage, which grows naturally out of such circumstance, is actually not the last step in the dissolution of a once distinctive and separate culture. It is merely part of a process of cultural dilution that is marked by a loss of communal memory. The member of the tribe no longer know who they are or why they should be.

Historians can best contribute to an understanding of the secularization process that acts as the motor force behind the changes in modern Jewish life by describing a specific instance of its workings. In this discussion, we begin with the growing "crisis of faith" during the interwar period, which was marked by a sharp decline of religious observance. We do so to gain a glimpse of the "hard" pervasive character of American secularism at work. The stage is then set for a broader discussion of how that process has shaped American Jewish life.

During the 1920s, the American Jewish "church" grew with startling rapidity. I use that alien term because it best describes the institutional structure, the seminaries, courts, rabbinic assemblies, and unions of congregations, in which the religion is housed. But supported by a divided and scattered people and having lost its hierarchical structure, the synagogue had less power to command than the Christian churches. Living in a society that developed in a post-Enlightenment setting, Jews could leave the fold with comparative ease. Indeed, they were often encouraged to do so by Christian missionaries. There was little that could coerce adherence or observance. Eventually, the idea of the church and synagogue holding on to its adherents by anything other than persuasion would prove impossible. The lack of direct power over its worshippers and the existence of a welcoming secular world enhanced the Jewish appetite for life outside the synagogue, a secular life. Jews ultimately became America's most avid secularists.

Thus, an increase in Jewish congregations, especially in its Reform and Conservative branches, occurred in the twenties. Both experienced a veritable "edifice complex" with the construction of houses of worship to shelter these newly organized congregations. The Orthodox branch lagged somewhat behind in imposing organizational structure. Its minyans (quorams required for prayer) were communities of faith that hardly required a fancy edifice and a "spiritual leader," but they were often also poor and transitory. Each branch had established a rabbinical seminary to produce an indigenous rabbinate. The Jewish church was establishing itself but did not seem to be able to avoid the plague of denominationalism that splintered the Protestant churches. That fragmentation became more apparent with the failure of the Jewish Theological Seminary and the Isaac Elchanan Yeshiva to unite in 1927. That failure forced the leaders of the Jewish Theological Seminary to think of themselves as a third, or middle, branch of American Judaism. It then rapidly expanded into areas of second settlement, where geographically mobile Jews were establishing new communities.

Rabbi Stephens Wise had established the Jewish Institute of Religion in 1921. In that same year, Mordecai Kaplan had established the Jewish Renascence Center, which soon evolved into the Society for the Advancement of Judaism. Based on an organizational principle copied from Felix Adler's Ethical Culture Society, it became the core for the Reconstructionist movement, which Kaplan envisioned merely as an influence, rather than another branch of Judaism.[1] Its ethos seemed to be fashioned to keep secularizing Jews in the fold. Jewish centers, also advocated by the Reconstructionist movement, proliferated. But the Jewish Center movement, which sought to combine all secular Jewish culture and religious activities, proved to be a failing strategy. In the centers, secular activities tended to overshadow purely religious ones, such as morning services.[2]

There was little in the economic situation of the children of immigrants, who were assuming leadership positions in the congregations and organizations, that suggested such a "crisis of faith." Most Jews knew about the anti-Semitic rantings of Henry Ford and the limitations policy of Harvard University. They understood that the restrictive immigration law of 1924 might have, despite denials, been aimed at excluding their brethren. But that was nothing to get excited about. There were no Black Hundreds, no pogroms, and why would Jews want to attend institutions where they were unwanted? One could establish one's own university or country club and even build one's own new neighborhood. That is in fact the path that American Jews often followed during the 1920s and after World War II.[3] Almost yearly, the *American Hebrew,* a popular Anglo-Jewish weekly, featured a review of the new posh Jewish country clubs all over the nation. "It's a free country" was a favorite observation of "alrightniks," the satirical term applied to those who acculturated too rapidly with often comical results. Most Jews of the jazz age had confidence in the American system and remained blithely unaware that it was the very freedom they so cherished that posed special problems for Judaism, a prescriptive faith based on Halakha (religious law). Free autonomous citizens could not be compelled to adhere to the long established ethical principles of their church. To be free meant that one could develop one's personal code of ethics and behavior and even a personalized idea of God.

At the grass roots, anti-Semitism was palpable and often painful to Jews seeking employment, especially with large firms. But by and large its proponents seemed unable to deny access to the instruments of socioeconomic mobility. Jews flooded into medical and law schools. A DDS, "disappointed doctor or surgeon," was usually available as a second choice for those who were rejected by medical school. The barriers to professionalism gradually crumbled. Perhaps it is more accurate to say that Jewish candidates for the professions worked their way around them. The proportion of Jews in the independent professions—law, medicine, accountancy—grew embarrassingly high. At the height of the Harvard quota debacle, President Abbott Lawrence Lowell liked to point to the fact that even after the new enrollment policy was implemented, the number of Jewish students at Harvard would remain disproportionately high.[4] That was also true in the new dependent professions like teaching and social work, which Jewish women found especially attractive. What Lowell could not fathom was that the drive to achieve middle class status that shaped the lives of these secularized Jewish students was so powerful that it would, like steam seeking to escape, find some way to come to the surface.

When a Harvard student accused Jewish students of underliving and overworking, he was probably unaware of the enormous pressure to achieve these students had imposed upon themselves. Such students were actually doubly driven. Achievement through learning was inherent not only in the Judaic culture from which they were often distancing themselves but also in the quest for self-realization peculiar to the secular spirit of America. This doubly motivated drive for professionalism among second-generation Jews was, in fact, only the beginning. It could also be observed in the higher aspirations of the Jewish work force that, during the interwar years, experienced an occupational upgrading that converted a finisher into a cutter and a filing clerk into a secretary. A second perhaps larger stream used small business to achieve middle class status. The result was that no other immigrant group was so successful in sharing the prosperity of the twenties. It was as if Jews knew instinctively how to prime themselves to function in the emerging complex market economy. When the economy collapsed in 1929, Jews were already better equipped than other immigrant groups to sustain themselves through the lean years and then to recover their former position. It was the inordinate drive to rise out of the ghetto and to achieve a secure place in America's middle class that was the most powerful motivational force that shaped the lives of second-generation American Jews. That spirit of self-improvement, of viewing oneself as incomplete but perfectible, associated here with American secularism, released enormous new energies and ultimately altered the way Jews saw themselves and the world. What these driven Jews could not foresee was that the priority given to self-development carried with it the potential for asociality, which would have a profound impact on Jewish communalism.

Beyond the prosperity of America that second-generation Jews shared fully, beyond the proliferation of temples and synagogues, a communal and religious crisis was brewing. The noted historian Lucy Dawidowicz observed that a religious depression preceded the economic one. Religious observance was less important in the secular worldview. Paradoxically, although that secular spirit was pervasive, its impact remained hidden from most observers, just as the weaknesses in the economy were not fully realized until the great market crash and the depression that followed. Mordecai Kaplan had first sensed something amiss while counseling troubled rabbinical students at the seminary who often complained that they could get little meaning or guidance from their faith to confront the challenges of their daily lives. Their malaise, which was rooted in the dissonance between the demands of the faith and the requirements of daily life, was not limited to them. To remain observant often meant having to give up not only the material comfort of middle class life but also its promise for self-betterment.

By the 1930s, the massive synagogue building crusade tapered off; and with the deepening depression there was concern about how the mortgages would be paid. But the decline in observance and synagogue attendance could not be attributed to the high annual cost of synagogue membership alone. The decline in piety and observance, much in evidence in the old country, was hardly a new phenomenon. What was new in the America of the twenties and thirties was that second- and third-generation Jews no longer possessed backgrounds that rooted them firmly in the religious culture. By the thirties, almost everyone had become an "alrightnik." Most knew less of Judaic texts and religious laws and customs than their parents. Often, they no longer knew how to pray. There was thus even less to pass on to their children, who would be compelled to carry on the tradition armed with only a memory of a memory. Most important, something in the new mind-set prevented them from seeing themselves as members of a special tribe. By the mid-twenties complaints by rabbis that their synagogues were empty were frequently heard. An editorial in the *American Hebrew* recommended the building of accordian shaped synagogues because they had the possibility of expansion during the high holy days, when everyone attended services, and contraction for the weekly Sabbath and daily services, when comparatively few did.[5]

There remained much that was recognizably Jewish in the daily lives of the Jews of the interwar period. They ate Jewish foods and told Jewish jokes. But the Yiddish press would be forced to convert to English, the preferred language of the "alrightniks." In the late twenties, a sharp decline in attendance occurred at the Yiddish theater, the "jewel in the crown" of immigrant culture. And the decline in religious observance and synagogue attendance occurred in tandem with the weakening of Jewishness, the ethnic culture. In contrast to the situation in eastern Europe, in America, the ethnic secular culture to hold them was thin; Yiddish, its language, was falling into disuse.

That falling away could take various forms. Some became involved in Jewish organizational life or the Zionist movement, which could delay the assimilation process for a generation or two. Sometimes it seemed as if the familiar Jewish zeal for faith and *mitzvot* (good deeds) was transmuted to political idealism embodied in the doctrines of socialism, often in only one generation. Led by college students, whose mobility had been blocked by the collapse of the economy, young Jews flocked in disproportionate numbers to the social justice and peace movements that proliferated during the interwar period. The familiar role of Jews as the most conspicuous activists on the Left of the political spectrum began in earnest during the thirties. But the quest for social justice was not sought through Jewish institutions or organizations like the American Jewish Congress or the Reform movement, whose theology had made a special place for it. Young Jews became active through secular nonsectarian parties and groupings. Jewish students were conspicuously present in the American Student Union, the American Youth Congress and the Young Communist League.[6] The peace strikes and protest rallies in which Jewish students participated with such fervor may have had a familiar religious enthusiasm about them, but they were secular and espoused radical universalism. Ultimately "falling" Jews fell out of Jewish space and into the cosmos. Jewish cosmopolitans were concerned for the world, not a particular tribe within it.

In 1942, a rudimentary "state of the faith" survey of New York Jewry found that over 40 percent checked none of the items customarily associated with practicing Judaism, such as the lighting of Sabbath candles, the observance of *kashrut*, or the giving to charity. When the puzzled interviewers asked what then made them Jewish, the response was inevitably that they felt "Jewish in their heart." They were promptly dubbed "cardiac Jews."[7] It was apparent that it was not a heart that beat very strongly. Zionism, a secular ideology that served in other democratic Western democracies to break the fall of the newly secularized, also reached a low point in America during the early thirties. Having already found its Zion, American Jewry understood little of Zionist ideology and fairly neglected the agencies and organizations that were associated with the world Zionist movement.

Generally, American Jewry's response to the Holocaust, especially by native-born Jews, was unorganized and largely ineffective. The closer Jews were tied to families in Europe, that is, the less acculturated they were, the more visceral the response. It was the American Jewish Congress, whose membership was composed of the secularized children of "downtown" Jews, who organized and attended the rallies to protest what Berlin was doing to its brethren. For native-born, secularized Jews who came under the influence of universalist left-wing ideologies, the response was different. They fought the "scourge of fascism," not in a proposed Jewish army, which was much spoken about after 1940, but in the Lincoln Brigade. They fought and died in Spain for universal right and justice for all mankind.[8] The specific threat that Nazism posed for the Jews of Europe was merely part of that. Later, American Jews enlisted in the American armed services in disproportionate numbers. A special agency was created to remind the nation of the Jewish contribution to the war effort. It was, they believed, the failure to do that during the First World War that led to charges of malingering and war profiteering. The use of public relations to ward off the slings and arrows of a hostile host culture, even the notion that they could be counteracted, had been developed by Louis Marshall in his fight to stop Henry Ford's campaign of anti-Semitism in the 1920s.[9] It was a matter of manipulating images that were infinitely malleable. Even defense strategies had become modernized. But there were no strategies to counteract the negative impact of secularism on the religious culture. That required commitment and faith that secularized Jews committed to the development of self.

Was American Jewry's crisis of faith inevitable? Secularization, the kind we speak of here, entails less willingness to allow life to be shaped by command of faith or ideology. American Jewry's survival conundrum would be better managed if the link between temporality, so much part of secularism, and the remarkable success of Jews in business and the professions were understood. Secularization's this worldliness, the privatization and distancing from tribal identity it brings in its wake, impacts on everything on the Jewish agenda, from the way Jewish leadership responded to the Holocaust, to the Jewish performance in the business arena. Nothing is left untouched. How modern American Jews see themselves and the world has undergone a profound change, especially since World War I. That change stems from the continuing impact of America's "hard" secularism on its vision. To grasp it fully, its principles and value orientation deserve our special attention.

We note at the outset that, unlike the single unifying sensibility of the observant, premodern Jews, their modern counterpart have a multileveled identity and matching plural loyalties that are often in conflict with religious observance. The secular world of work knows not of sacred time. An emergency call to a doctor or lawyer, the tax season for an accountant or the possibility of overtime for a cutter in the garment industry may conflict with Sabbath observance. Secular identity formation also differs from the premodern in that it is not organically of one piece. The secular persona is necessarily split and divided to enable Jewish men and women to function in the complex modern world. The tensions involved in this multiplicity of roles is for secularizing Jews only partially solved by the post-Emancipation response that calls for duality, being Jews at home and men and women in the world. Of all the roles they play, it is the professional or vocational role, rather than the notion of a caring watching God, that is the integrative one. Ask modern men and women who they are, and they are likely to tell you what they do.

A tribe unto themselves, they are autonomous. The guidance of family and community are diminished. The quest for self-actualization becomes the prime organizing principle of secular life, playing the role that tribe or church did for premoderns. They choose their mates on the basis of romantic love rather than the need to enhance the family position and coffers. They can choose to be unencumbered by communal, church, and even family ties and increasingly do so. They must be persuaded to affiliate or give to charity, and then they do so voluntarily and on their own terms. Because democracy is the secular spirit's favorite offspring, the well-being of the laity becomes more urgent than placating the deity. Secular persons cannot be commanded, they must be persuaded. Tribal bonds have been replaced by voluntary association. The family ceases to be the arena of primary association and soon loses its role as an agency of social control.

Though some of these elements may be familiar, there are few who touch all bases of "compleat" secular Jews. A composite portrait of such Jews would show them as neither totally secular nor traditional. Most station themselves somewhere on the axis between the two poles. They find what is comfortable by picking and choosing from religious and secular modalities, as if in a cafeteria. Some rules are obeyed, others are disregarded, still others are transmuted. Exile becomes priestly mission. Exodus, a search for freedom. Prophetic exhortation, a quest for social justice. The religious garment is retailored to fit. The important thing is that individual secular Jews, not the community, are the tailors. The centrality of the individual person is quintessentially what America's "hard" secularism is about.

Secularism, then, is the attitudinal core behind modernity. It shapes the identity of its advocates and alters their sense of self and place in the world. Moderns, we have seen, are more concerned with the present and less with the hereafter, more with material well-being and less with things of the spirit. In 1691, anxious to save souls, the college of William and Mary petitioned the Lords of Treasury for a charter. Back from London came an exasperated reply: "Souls, damn your souls; make tobacco."[10] That appeal for material wealth might be the cry of a secular priesthood, were it possible for secular people to cherish a priesthood.

But the actual profile modernization would assume and the character of the transition differed widely from culture to culture. Israel, Spain, and England, for example, do not make a fetish of the separation of church and state, as is done in America. Although the motor force of America's hard secularism is individual self-realization, the former Soviet Union sought class well-being and preoccupied itself with creating an egalitarian society. Russia, without socialism, remains strongly collectivist and egalitarian, while America is still passionately libertarian and individualistic.

The high degree of individuation and freedom that produces America's hard secularism is related to its historical proximity to Calvinist Protestantism. There we find the separation of public from private behavior, indeed with our first notion of behavior as differentiated from feeling. America's tolerance of pluralism also can be traced back to its Protestant roots. In a sense, what we have witnessed in the American Jewish experience is the gradual Protestantization of its Judaism. That is what American Jews acculturated to. It went beyond the concern of Charleston Reformers with decorum and family pews.[11] What was important was how things looked and how people behaved, which was not necessarily linked to how they felt. That is directly linked to another bifurcation of modernity, that of ethics from etiquette, what is believed to be right from what looks right. Premodern Jews cared little for such concerns, and many of the ultra-Orthodox still do not. It also separated Jewishness, the tribal, ethnic, folk culture, from Judaism, the religious aspect. That also was a distinction unknown in Ancient Israel.

The transitional immigrant culture weakly continued to nourish the Jewish spirit and culture of the second- and third-generation. In the 1920s and 1930s, one could still feel Jewish by going to the Yiddish theater, or reading a Yiddish newspaper, or eating "Jewish" food. But clearly that culture would not live beyond the life of the language, whose users were passing from the scene. Oddly, though mutually antagonistic, the religious and the secular-ethnic culture were in the same boat and somehow dependent on each other. They were both challenged, as noted by the sociologist Talcot Parsons, by the spirit of "universal otherhood," which secularism sought to put in the place of "tribal brotherhood." But all attempts to bridge the chasm between them, including Mordecai Kaplan's Jewish Center movement, failed. They preferred to wage the uphill battle to sustain themselves alone.

So unobtrusive yet pervasive, so seemingly natural, was the gradual acceptance of the spirit of secularism that few realized that it had penetrated the inner recesses of even the most religious communities. The speed and intensity with which the children of immigrants adopted secular values and aspirations and abandoned the synagogue startled and worried religious leaders, who saw it as a cause of Jewish crime and political radicalism. Some have speculated that the special Jewish penchant for the secular spirit may be attributable to the early place it found in Jewish history. One scholar traces it to the split life maintained by generations of Marranos that gave them a strong "this worldly" disposition, a fragmented religious identity, and other characteristics of the modern mind-set. It was already manifest in the thinking of philosophers like Baruch Spinoza (1632–1677), centuries before the Enlightenment and Emancipation.[12]

Yet in contrast to eastern Europe, American Jewish secularism was not embodied in a particular ideology. Rather it was something in the air, a way of seeing, a *mentalité* that shaped the perception of reality. At its core was the idea of self-fulfillment, the notion that all citizens had the right and the obligation to develop their talents, to be what they could be. Such a scheme required that citizens be fully assured of their freedom, today interpreted as the right to unencumbered access to opportunity for education or business enterprise. That is the promise of liberalism, some form of which is America's preferred political ideology in both political parties.

Liberalism, which also has become the most distinctive fingerprint of what remains of a distinctive American Jewish identity, is a peculiar ideology when compared to those of eastern Europe because its primary burden is not to shape behavior but rather to make free, to liberate. Extending opportunity or access whether to former slaves or to the handicapped is a strong force in American politics. The individuation that such a libertarian secularism brings in its wake has special implications for the Jewish enterprise. It makes the intrusive legalistic and corporate character of Judaism difficult to sustain. It is also a key to the survivalist dilemma of American Jewry. Jews might legally be someone born of a Jewish mother, but they cannot be forced to assume the responsibility of their birthright. They can reject membership in the corporation. Being free, they must be persuaded to associate themselves voluntarily. It is in that sense that all secular Jews in America are "Jews by choice," not merely regarding the degree of affiliation but whether they want to be affiliated at all.

A mind-set that places self-realization at its center was bound to pose a challenge to any intrusive religious dogma or political ideology that insisted upon praxis, a linkage between theory and action. Understandably, free secular citizens could not easily permit their newly won freedom to be refettered by the claims of ideology. Churches and political movements that insisted on claiming such control did not fare as well with American Jewry as those that managed to make room for the free secular spirit by what Henry Kissinger called "creative ambiguity." The comparative success of the Conservative movement in the 1930s and 1950s is attributable in part to the very uncertainty of its ideology, which some bemoan today. Conversely, the ultimate failure of Orthodoxy to attract and hold American Jewry can be traced directly to its need to intrude deeply into the personal lives of its adherents.

Most interesting is how Zionism, which in its socialist incarnation contained an imperative to resettle in Palestine, was refashioned by Louis Brandeis to fit the American reality. Brandeis understood that the secular American Jew could no longer be commanded, as were his ancestors at Sinai. He had to be persuaded. Often what is most persuasive is what is believed to bring happiness or contentment in contemporary vogue. It could be the ownership of a Cadillac or a Ph.D. The point is that individual Jews, wisely or foolishly, determine the content of their lives. Their power goes beyond choosing the rabbi and determining his salary. They also choose what to consider sacred or profane. The church is democratized, the "people" stand where once was the deity. It is they who command and they who choose to obey.

The democratic command structure of modern secular American society is profoundly at variance with the one in which the synagogue was born and grew to maturity. Predictably, in the American Jewish world it was the Orthodox branch that was least able to accommodate the change. It takes some getting used to, and some rabbinic leaders never did. In the 1920s, the Vaad Harabonim, fearing that the Isaac Elchanan Yeshiva was being tainted by secularism, tried several times to intervene. Earlier, in 1902, a similar group had brought Rabbi Jacob Josef here to be chief rabbi. Both attempts, and others as well, to revert to a premodern command structure failed.

For some, this secular outlook, especially the notion of freedom, brought confusion; but for the majority, it brought personal confidence and a release of new energies. The feeling of being at the center of the cosmos brought with it a sense of being in control, accompanied by a willingness to assume risks that is requisite for the entrepreneurial spirit associated with business enterprise. But once having mastered the temporal world of the professions or business, secularists can no longer easily view themselves as a mere speck of dust before a commanding God. They can neither pray nor obey. The humility and sense of proportion that ultimately forms the essence of faith is lost to them. It is in that sense that they have become irreligious. But that does not mean that they are unspiritual or immoral. It simply means that the religious spirit, once housed in the church or synagogue, has been privatized or internalized. In our time, one can name few moral giants that have stemmed from the synagogue. André Sakharov and Nathan Sharansky, who fit that description, stem from intensely secular backgrounds.

All of America's religions have been affected by its hard secular spirit; but for Jewry, the subculture that has embraced secularism with an adoration their ancestors reserved for their commanding God, the impact seems amplified. We have witnessed a remarkable release of new energy and talent in American Jewry. It now boasts the highest per capita income and the greatest degree of professionalism in the nation. But Jews are also the first to confront the growing disorder in personal and communal life that unbridled secularism leaves in its wake.

For American Jewry, the decline in the strength of the family has special significance because it is the traditional incubator of identity and social controls. The internalization of these controls is especially important because, without such a process, there can be no communal life. Like all communities, Jewish communal life is based on the assumption that the process of maturation is based on widespread self-governance, rather than communal authority. Good citizens stop for red lights and pays their taxes without having to be policed to do so. Jews were particularly good at such internalization. But lately, we have seen traces that all is not well. As community, synagogue, and family life weaken, the internalization process is disrupted. Predictably, some Jews, like the cohort of Jewish inside traders, have gone too far in the quest for self-actualization. They and thousands of other Jews who have broken the law were too avid in the "pursuit of happiness," which for them meant the accumulation of wealth. They did not possess the internal controls, the moral compass, to prevent themselves from tipping into crime.

But they are the exception rather than the rule. Generally, Jews in America have successfully combined remarkable success, achieved in acceptable secular terms, while assuming a high degree of civic responsibility. They are self-governing. But it is predictable that, as the secularization process continues and the influence of institutions like family, community, and synagogue continues to weaken, American Jewry will be faced with an increase in asocial behavior. Paradoxically, the community itself might be too fragmented to concern itself with it. After all, in secular terms, what an Ivan Boesky or any of a group of indicted inside traders did, they did as free modern secular individuals, not as Jews.

It is then virtually predictable that America's most upwardly mobile group, its Jews, is also its most avidly secular one. Jewry's secularity is linked to its formidable success in achieving middle class status through business and professionalism. Understandably, that success is written almost exclusively in secular terms. One can actually graph the reverse correlation between the rise of its annual per-capita income and the decline of religious observance. Secularization, as used in this essay, explains the relationship between the two.

Properly understood, the impact of hard secularism throws new light on virtually every problem area of contemporary Jewish life in America. The decline of observance is merely one example, probably the most direct one, that can be presented to illustrate the impact of secularization. The burgeoning intermarriage rate is but its latest manifestation. But there are less direct linkages also. The sequence of problems that shook the synagogue in the last few decades, from the ordination of women to the organization of gay congregations, even the move to prosletyze among the unchurched, is related to it. Each of these extensions of freedom to previously excluded or partially excluded groups, pushed forward by secular liberalism to extend the bounds of freedom, requires yet a new accommodation that entails a difficult alteration of founding principles.

In another arena, the failure of the world Zionist movement to generate mass *aliyah* from America and the related massive *yerida* from Israel cannot be understood apart from the comparative opportunities for self-realization. As I have noted, that desire is central to the secular imagination; and until now, it has been more realizable in America. It goes without saying that, if the conditions for self-realization through business or education were expanded and personal security were assured in Israel, *yerida* would decrease and immigration would increase. These are the necessary preconditions of the secular life-style.

Like the weakening of the synagogue and the Jewish all-purpose organization, the weakening of the Jewish family is related to the new secular mind-set that leaves nothing untouched. Secularists often feel a need to free themselves of all fetters, including those of community and family. They become a lonely tribe of one. The contemporary contraction of Jewish organizational life can also be laid at secularism's doorstep. Secularized and therefore autonomous, American Jews prefer to organize their own social lives and to purchase their medical insurance and cemetery benefits individually. At one time, these matters drew Jews to the large fraternal orders. Secularists have become sufficiently universalized to socialize with similarly reprocessed Gentiles. There is no longer much that actually differentiates the two groups. In a word, a pervasive spirit of secularism, whose meaning goes far beyond merely being irreligious, effects every aspect of modern personal and communal life. It dictates the values, the style, and the basic content of modern life.

Ever since the Jewish Population Survey was published in 1990, Jewish communal organizations have placed great hope in "Jewish education" to restore the missing Jewish ingredient destroyed by modernity. Seeking "continuity," the budgets of the local federations hope to strengthen the local Jewish day school. Some are considering subsidizing enrollment for those who cannot afford the tuition. Their rationale is simple. Survey research clearly indicates that graduates of Jewish day schools retain a much higher degree of affiliation with the Jewish community generally and with the synagogue particularly.

Can contemporary Jews be taught a culture they once learned naturally with their mother's milk? There is no satisfactory answer historians can give to that question, but of one thing we can be fairly certain. If the Judaism that emerges from a Jewish education system bears only a tenuous relationship to what went before, if the connection is allowed to be completely severed by the sheer force of secularism, then there is little hope. A great deal will depend on how much of its basic beliefs and practices can be transmuted or otherwise altered while still authentically retaining a strong link to the original culture as it was laid down in Judaic texts. The fundamental question then is not whether a Jewish education system can teach the culture and thereby enhance identity. It is whether, on the one hand, it can ever be made strong enough to tone down, to mute, the most extreme demands of secularism so that a recognizable Jewish/Judaic culture remains. On the other hand, much also depends on whether Jews on the observant side of the spectrum can be convinced to accept these secularized Jews as Jews.

The first mentioned alternative can be dismissed. The education system that can reverse the values of modernity has not been invented yet and probably never can be. American schools seem to pick up and transmit secular values and style earlier than most communal institutions. But the open secular society prides itself on its tolerance. It encourages pluralism and change. Space for the development of a separate culture is offered by society. The problem is that American Jews no longer know what to plant in that space. Ultimately, it may be the second problem that involves gaining acceptance by the observant, which poses the more serious obstacle to revitalizing American Jewry.

First, the notion that identity can be taught or enhanced by education is itself a secular notion. It assumes the existence of a human spirit and intellect infinitely malleable or improvable. The very idea of a separate psychological identity related to the self, is modern. One rarely hears mention of problems of "Jewish identity" in premodern texts. Identity was a given, stemming directly from the life lived within the Jewish community and family. They were Jews because they lived as Jews, together with other Jews. Each member of the Jewish community was an identifiable part of the whole. Clearly, such a community and family no longer exists in America. What we do when we link Jewish education to survival is to assign a ramshackle school system the impossible task of doing what the community and family can no longer do. It is a set-up for failure. Even the most effectively organized and adequately funded Jewish education system, armed with the best curricula, methodology, and teachers, cannot create Jewish identity from scratch. That much we can learn from the failure of the far-flung Catholic school system, now in the process of being dismantled. It did not produce better Catholics. Group identity stems from belonging to the group. That is the reason why the Orthodox branch in America consistently creates people with stronger Jewish identities than other branches. It has retained a sense of community especially in the need to live in close proximity to each other and to the shul. When the group feeling no longer exists, there is little purpose in contriving and teaching an identity for it. It is not possible to mimic the resistance to secularism of ultra Orthodox communities. That entails a price that most "modern" Jews are unwilling to pay. Given the choice, and secularists insist that there be such choices, most American Jews would not surrender their freedom.

If no system of education strong enough to withstand the basic values of America's hard secularism is conceivable, then what kind of Jewishness can be enhanced by Jewish education? It will have to be one that fits into the postsecular world. That world is still composed of highly individuated people who not only strive for self-fulfillment and resist any kind of fetters that curtail their individual freedom but also find a place for subcultures that do not infringe on the freedom of others. In such a world, many things are permissible, but few are mandated. The Jewish day school is especially appropriate, not because it is successful in teaching a culture that is no longer lived. We have seen that its success in this area is problematic. But nothing prevents such schools, while they are teaching Jewish culture and values, also to teach skills that enhance the possibility of self-realization in the secular world. It is precisely in the area of self-realization that there is a confluence between Judaic and secular values. It is conceivable that secular Jews enrolling their children in the subsidized day school will be attracted more by the SAT scores of the graduating class than the Jewish content of the curriculum. But given the continued failure of the public school system, secular Jewish parents will have no choice but to place their children in an environment that is willy-nilly Jewish. The problem for Jewish educators will be to conceive and implement a Jewish education that does not dislocate the students in the secular environment in which they have to live. If they cannot do that, these students will abandon the Jewish school the way their grandparents abandoned the cheder and the yeshiva.

Despite its pervasiveness and inexorability, room can be found within this hard secular environment for the thriving of a Judaic religio/ethnic culture, many of whose basic tenets and practices do not fit easily into modernity. It does not require great prescience to predict that a movement away form the more extreme forms that American secularism has taken will occur in the twenty-first century, even as its underlying assumptions remain in place. The rising violence of American urban life, with which American Jewry has cast its lot, suggests that national life organized around the extreme selfness at the core of America's hard secularism cannot be sustained. The percentage of citizens who do not internalize controls or allow the quest for fulfillment to get out of control is simply too great. For whatever reason, too many people cannot heed the basic commandments of the secular mind-set: "Invent thyself" but also "control thyself." The primary goal of the secular person, self-realization, which is usually thought of in the sense of achieving economic security or professional fulfillment, may be less possible in the economy of the future. The next generation of American Jews may need to modify some of their basic aspirations.

Despite their avid secularism, most Jews will continue to belong to the religious congregation and blithely disregard the fact that they are no longer believers and know little of Jewish culture. Such a disjuncture is possible because America's secularism, unlike its eastern European counterpart, does not demand atheism or view the church as the "opiate of the people." It becomes merely another formerly sacral, but now largely social activity that secular Jews partake in more out of habit than reason. A free society leaves ample room for inconsistent and even irrrational behavior. That may be its most important advantage.

The secular spirit of American Jewry has served it well. Its social status, its affluence, the central role its adherents play in the operational and scientific and cultural elites of the nation attest to that. They enjoy a measure of tolerance and belonging unprecedented in Jewish history. Yet clearly, America's hard secularism has exacted a price in community adhesion and coherence. Jewish educators need to be aware of the primary assumptions that shape America's unique form of secularism. Its two primary ingredients, libertarianism and individuation, might be reshaped in the years to come, but they cannot be eliminated. It is what Americans of all faiths want. Recent events indicate that these aspirations have become universal. As long as they remain in place the "old time religion" based on faith and obedience will remain outside the life options for most American Jews. That is the real price America's hard secularism is exacting from the American Jewish enterprise. What Jewish educators need to think about is how to deal with tribes of one, with an individuated and often deracinated people. We need to learn how the negative impact of American secularism can be minimized while the benefits it bestows are maximized.

Notes

Selected Bibliography

Index

Notes

1. Jewish Survival in America

1. Hanoch Bartov, *Forum* 46 (Winter 1980/1981): v, 19–20.

2. Jewish Exceptionalism

1. Quoted in D. J. Boorstin, *The Americans: The Democratic Experience* (New York: Vintage, 1974), iii.

2. H. L. Feingold, *Zion in America: The Jewish Experience from Colonial Times to the Present* (New York: Hippocrene, 1974), preface.

3. M. Davis, "Centers of Jewry in the Western Hemisphere: A Comparative Approach," *Jewish Journal of Sociology* 5 (1963): 4 ff.

4. For a discussion of the pitfalls of the Weimar analogy, see H. L. Feingold, "German Jewry and the American Jewish Condition: A View from Weimar," *Judaism* 20 (Winter 1971): 108–19.

5. S. W. Baron, *History and Jewish Historians: Essays and Addresses* (Philadelphia: Jewish Publication Society of America, 1964), 39.

6. See M. Rosenstock, *Louis Marshall, Defender of Jewish Rights* (Detroit: Wayne State Univ. Press, 1965) 128–200.

7. C. A. Lindbergh, *The Wartime Journals of Charles A. Lindbergh, 1937–1945* (New York: Harcourt, 1970); Wayne Cole, *Charles A. Lindbergh and the Battle Against Intervention in World War II* (New York: Library of Social Science, 1974).

8. B. W. Korn, *American Jewry and the Civil War* (New York: Atheneum, 1970), 121–55.

9. L. Dinnerstein, *The Leo Frank Case* (New York: Dell, 1956).

10. T. Weiss-Rosmarin, "The Cultural Tradition of the American Jew," in Stanley M. Wagner, ed., *Traditions of the American Jew* (New York: Ktav, 1977), 1–19.

11. S. Lubell, *The Future of American Politics* (New York: Anchor, 1956).

12. G. Smith, *To Save a Nation: American Countersubversives, The New Deal and the Coming of World War II* (New York: Basic, 1973).

13. H. L. Feingold, *The Politics of Rescue: The Roosevelt Administration and the Holocaust, 1938–1945* (New Brunswick: Rutgers Univ. Press, 1970); Saul Friedman, *No Haven*

for the Oppressed: United States Policy Toward Jewish Refugees, 1938–1945 (Detroit: Wayne State Univ. Press, 1973).

14. Lucy S. Dawidowicz, *The War Against the Jews, 1933–1945* (New York: Holt, 1975).

15. J. R. Marcus, "The Periodization of American Jewish History," in J. R. Marcus, *Studies in American Jewish History* (Cincinnati: American Jewish Archives, 1969).

16. A. M. Greeley, "American Catholics, Making It or Losing It?" *Public Interest* (Summer 1972), 26–37.

17. S. Thernstrom, *The Other Bostonians: Poverty and Progress in the American Metropolis, 1800–1915* (Cambridge, Mass.: Harvard Univ. Press, 1973), 143; T. Kessner, *The Golden Door: Italian and Jewish Immigrant Mobility in New York City, 1880–1915* (New York: Oxford Univ. Press, 1977), 161–77; S. Hertzberg, "Unsettled Jews: Geographic Mobility in a Nineteenth Century City," *American Jewish Historical Quarterly*, 47 (Dec. 1977): 125–39; N. Glazer, "The American Jew and the Attainment of Middle Class Rank: Some Trends and Explanations," in Marshall Sklare, ed., *The Jews: Social Patterns of an American Group* (New York: Free, 1958), 138–46.

18. Stephen Birmingham, *"Our Crowd": The Great Jewish Families of New York* (New York: Harper, 1967).

19. B. E. Supple, "A Business Elite: German-Jewish Financiers in Nineteenth Century New York," *Business History Review* 31 (Summer 1957): 143–78; V. P. Carosso, "A Financial Elite: New York's German-Jewish Investment Bankers," *American Jewish Historical Quarterly* 46 (Sept. 1976): 67–88; L. R. Rachman, "Julius Rosenwald," *American Jewish Historical Quarterly* 46 (Sept. 1976): 89–104; K. Grunwald, "Three Chapters of German Jewish Banking History," *Leo Baeck Yearbook* 22 (1977): 191–208.

20. J. S. Auerbach, "From Rags to Robes: The Legal Profession, Social Mobility and the American Jewish Experience," *American Jewish Historical Quarterly* 46 (Dec. 1976): 249–84; S. M. Lipset and E. Ladd Jr., "Jewish Academics in the United States: Their Achievement, Culture and Politics," *American Jewish Yearbook* 72 (1971); R. S. Willis, *The College of the City of New York, A History, 1847–1947* (New York: City College Press, 1949); S. Steinberg, *The Academic Melting Pot: Catholics and Jews in American Higher Education* (New York: Carnegie Foundation, 1974). For a personal account, see N. Podhoretz, *Making It* (New York: Random, 1967); "Professional Tendencies Among Jewish Students in Colleges, Universities and Professional Schools," *American Jewish Yearbook, 1920–1921*, 383–93.

21. J. R. Marcus *Early American Jewry* (Philadelphia: Jewish Publication Society of America, 1953), 3:53.

22. N. Glazer and D. Moynihan, *Beyond the Melting Pot* (Cambridge, Mass.: Harvard Univ. Press, 1969) 155. See also "The Egghead Millionaires," *Fortune* (Sept. 1960), 172 ff.

23. E. Mendelsohn, "The Russian Roots of the American Jewish Labor Movement" in E. Mendelsohn, ed., *Essays on the American Jewish Labor Movement, YIVO Annual of Jewish Social Science* 16 (1976): 150–76; M. Rischin, *The Promised City: New York's Jews, 1870–1914* (New York: Harper, 1970), 25–31, 125–94.

24. M. Hillquit, *Loose Leaves from a Busy Life*, (New York: Macmillan, 1934), 15–40; see also R. Sanders, *The Downtown Jews: Portrait of an Immigrant Generation* (New York: Harper, 1969) chaps. 4 and 5; Feingold, *Zion in America*, chap. 11.

25. Joseph Brandes, "From Sweatshop to Stability: Jewish Labor Between Two World Wars," in E. Mendelsohn, *Essays*.

26. Ibid., 7.

27. Robert Asher, "Jewish Unions and the American Federation of Labor Power Structure, 1903–1905," *American Jewish Historical Quarterly*, 45 (Mar. 1976): 226.

28. Brandes, 62.

29. Ibid., 68–69.

30. Ibid., 76–77; see also M. Rischin, "The Jewish Labor Movement in America: A Social Interpretation," *Labor History* 4 (Fall 1963): 231 ff.

31. Brandes, 77.

32. Rischin, "Jewish Labor Movement" 234; see also J. B. S. Hardman, "The Jewish Labor Movement in the United States: Jewish and Non-Jewish Influences," *American Jewish Historical Quarterly* 41 (Dec. 1952).

33. S. Polishook, "The American Federation of Labor, Zionism and the First World War," *American Jewish Historical Quarterly* 45 (Mar. 1976): 228–44.

34. R. P. Ingalls, *Herbert H. Lehman and New York's Little New Deal* (New York: New York Univ. Press, 1975), 131–42.

35. Asher, 227.

36. For a description and analysis of Jewish organizational life, see D. Elazar, *Community and Polity: The Organizational Dynamics of American Jewry* (Philadelphia: Jewish Publication Society of America, 1976); C. S. Liebman, "American Jewry: Identity and Affiliation," in D. Sidorsky, ed., *The Future of the Jewish Community in America* (Philadelphia: Jewish Publication Society of America, 1973), 127–52; Feingold, *Zion in America*, 208–27.

37. G. Lenski, *The Religious Factor* (New York: Anchor, 1963), 37; M. Sklare and J. Greenblum, *Jewish Identity on the Suburban Frontier* (New York: Basic, 1967), 280–81.

38. B. Lewis, "The Meaning of Jewish History," in *Land of Immigrants*, Proceedings, B'nai B'rith Commission on Adult Education (Mar. 1976), 10.

39. A. A. Goren, *New York Jews and the Quest for Community: The Kehillah Experiment, 1908–1922* (New York: Columbia Univ. Press, 1970), 3.

40. Ibid., 7–12

41. Naomi W. Cohen, *Not Free to Desist: A History of the American Jewish Committee, 1906–1966* (Philadelphia: Jewish Publication Society of America, 1972), chap. 1.

42. Quoted in C. S. Liebman, "Reconstructionism in American Life," *American Jewish Yearbook* 71 (1970): 3–100. For additional information, see M. M. Kaplan, *Judaism as a Civilization: Toward a Reconstruction of American Jewish Life* (New York: Schocken, 1967), parts 2, 4, 5; M. Scult, "Mordecai M. Kaplan, Challenges and Conflicts in the Twenties," *American Jewish Historical Quarterly* 46 (Mar. 1977): 401–16; S. M. Cahn, "Religion Without Super Naturalism," in R. A. Brauner, ed., *Shiv'im: Essays and Studies in Honor of Ira Eisenstein* (New York: Ktav, 1977), 225–29.

43. M. Curti, *The Roots of American Loyalty* (New York: Atheneum, 1968), 184 ff.

44. J. Higham, *Strangers in the Land: Patterns of American Nativism, 1860–1925* (New York: Atheneum, 1968), 236–39.

45. H. M. Kallen, *Cultural Pluralism and the American Idea* (Philadelphia: Univ. of Pennsylvania Press, 1956), 100. See also "American Jews: What Now?" *Jewish Social Service Quarterly* (Fall 1955), 22.

46. That is an observation made by A. Hertzberg, "Some Reflections on Zionism Today," *Congress Monthly* 44 (Mar./Apr. 1977), 5–6.

47. M. I. Urofsky, *American Zionism: From Herzl to Holocaust* (New York: Doubleday, 1975), 123–24, 128–30; "Zionism, An American Experience," *American Jewish Historical Quarterly* 43 (Mar. 1974): 215–30; N. W. Cohen, *American Jews and the Zionist Idea* (New York: Ktav, 1975), 16–17.

48. See Elazar; Cohen, *American Jews*; Urofsky; Yehuda Bauer, *My Brother's Keeper: A History of the American Jewish Joint Distribution Committee* (Philadelphia: Jewish Publication Society of America, 1974), 1–18.

49. T. A. Bailey, *The Man in the Street: The Impact of American Public Opinion on Foreign Policy* (New York: Macmillan, 1948), 187–90; G. Almond, *The American People and Foreign Policy* (New York: Praeger, 1960), 185; A. O. Hero, *American Religious Groups View Foreign Policy* (Durham: Duke Univ. Press, 1973), 201–4; Louis L. Gerson, *The Hyphenate in Recent American Politics and Diplomacy* (Lawrence: Univ. of Kansas Press, 1964), 86–87.

50. According to Rabbi A. Hertzberg, it is far higher and more intense for foreign concerns. A. Hertzberg, "Some Reflections," 5–6.

51. Elihu Bergman, "The American Jewish Population Erosion," *Midstream* 23 (Oct. 1977): 9–19.

3. Jewish Refugeeism

1. Stephen Steinberg, *The Ethnic Myth: Race, Ethnicity, and Class in America* (New York, Atheneum, 1980); "Letters from Readers," *Commentary* 72 (Nov. 1981): 18, 20.

2. Jonathan D. Sarna, "The Myth of No Return: Jewish Return Migration to Europe 1881–1914," *American Jewish History* 71 (Dec. 1981).

3. Irving Howe, *World of Our Fathers* (Touchstone, 1976), 137–41, 145.

4. Selma Berrol, "Education and Economic Mobility: The Jewish Experience in New York City 1880–1920," *American Jewish Historical Quarterly* 65 (Mar. 1976): 257–71.

4. Studying the Problem

1. Ben Halpern, "What Is Antisemitism?," *Modern Judaism* 1 (Dec. 1981): 251–62; see also "Antisemitism in the Prospective of Jewish History," in *Jews in the Mind of America*, ed. Charles Stember et al. (New York, 1966), 273–301.

2. Jonathan D. Sarna, "Anti-Semitism and American History," *Commentary* (Mar. 1981): 42–47; Michael Dobkowski, *The Tarnished Dream: The Basis of American Anti-Semitism* (Westport, Conn., 1979).

3. Naomi Cohen, ed., "Anti-Semitism in the United States," *American Jewish History* 71 (Sept. 1981): 9.

4. Oscar Handlin, "American Views of the Jews at the Opening of the Twentieth Century," *Publication of the American Jewish Historical Society* 40 (June 1951): 324–25.

5. Edward H. Flannery, *The Anguish of the Jews* (New York, 1964), 249.

6. John Higham, "American Anti-Semitism Historically Reconsidered," in Stember et al., 237.

7. The term "radical ambiguity" belongs to Harold Fisch, *The Dual Image* (London, 1971), Introduction. Almost all researchers fall back on the term *ambivalence* to describe anti-Semitic images. It is especially commonplace in the work of Louis Harap, *The Image of the Jew in American Literature* (Philadelphia, 1974). For an exhaustive examination of the ambivalent theme, see Louise A. Mayo, "The Ambivalent Image: The Perception of the Jew in Nineteenth Century America," Ph.D. diss., The City University of New York, 1977.

8. Halpern, 252.

9. See Timothy L. Smith, "Religion and Ethnicity in America," *American Historical Review* 83 (Dec. 1978), 115–85.

10. Will Herberg, *Protestant, Catholic, Jew: An Essay in American Religious Sociology* (New York, 1955).

11. Higham, "American Anti-Semitism," 237–58.

12. Leo Pinsker, *Autoemanzipation* (Berlin, 1936), 5. The digestion metaphor is frequently used in the literature of anti-Semitism. Anna L. Dawes, *The Modern Jew* (Boston, 1886), 41, sees them as "an indigestible substance" in all societies. Reference cited in Mayo, 467.

13. Jonathon D. Sarna, "Nineteenth Century American Christian Mission to the Jews"; and Morton Borden, "Jews and American Sunday Laws, with Special Reference to the Newman Case." Both papers, unpublished, delivered at the American Historical Association Annual Convention, Apr. 5, 1984, in Los Angeles.

14. See, for example, John Higham, *Strangers in the Land: Patterns of American Nativism, 1860–1925* (New Brunswick, 1955); and also "Religious Conflict in Ante-Bellum Boston," in Oscar Handlin, ed., *Boston's Immigrants* (Cambridge, 1959), 178–206.

15. See Roger Daniels, *The Politics of Prejudice: The Anti-Japanese Movement in California and the Struggle for Japanese Exclusion* (Stanford, 1962); Anthony B. Chan, *Gold Mountain: The Chinese in the New World* (Vancouver, 1983); Carl Wittke, *German-Americans and the World War* (New York, 1936).

16. John J. Appel, "Jews in American Caricature: 1820–1914," *American Jewish History* 71 (Sept. 1981), 109–10.

17. For the considerable variation using similar archival sources, see, for example, Alan Kraut, Richard Breitman and Thomas W. Imhoof, "The State Department, The Labor Department, and German Jewish Immigration, 1939–1940," *Journal of American Ethnic History* 3 (Spring 1984): 5–38; and Henry L. Feingold, " 'Courage First and Intelligence Second': The American Jewish Secular Elite, Roosevelt and the Failure to Rescue," *American Jewish History* 72 (June 1983), 424–60.

18. David Brody, "American Jewry, the Refugees and Immigration Restriction, 1932–1942," *Publication of the American Jewish Historical Society* 45 (June 1956), 219–47.

19. Halpern, "What is Antisemitism?," 256, notes that the term "the Jews" alone "contains a vast range of information."

20. A review of the criticism of Theodor Adorno et al., *The Authoritarian Personality* (New York, 1950) is presented in Melvin M. Tumin, *An Inventory and Appraisal of Research on American Anti-Semitism* (New York, 1961), 7–10. Also Herbert H. Hyman and Paul Sheatsley, "The Authoritarian Personality—A Methodological Critique," in *Studies in the Scope and Method of "The Authoritarian Personality,"* ed. Richard Christie and Marie Jahoda (Glencoe, 1954).

21. "Antisemitism in the United States: A Study by Yankelovich, Skelly & White, Inc.," 1981, 4 (of American Jewish Committee Summary Report). A full statistical analysis is presented by Geraldine Rosenfield, "The Polls: Attitudes Toward American Jews," *Public Opinion Quarterly* 46 (Fall 1982): 431–43.

22. Higham, "American Anti-Semitism," 238.

23. Gunnar Myrdal, *An American Dilemma: The Negro Problem and Modern Democracy* (New York, 1962), Foreword.

24. Higham, "American Anti-Semitism," 238.

25. Morton Keller, "Jews and the Character of American Life Since 1930," Stember et al., *Jews in the Mind*, 259–71. Quote is from the Introduction, 15.

26. Gertrude J. Selznick and Stephen Steinberg, *The Tenacity of Prejudice, Anti-Semitism in Contemporary America* (New York, 1969), 184–93.

27. Noting the increase in proportion of the populace with formal education since 1935, George Gallup concludes that "the college-educated segment in each survey has consistently been found to be more tolerant than those with less formal education."

George Gallup, "Anti-Semitic Acts Not Symptoms of Increased Prejudice in U. S." *The Gallup Poll*, News Release, Apr. 16, 1981.

28. Lucy S. Dawidowicz, "Can Anti-Semitism Be Measured?," *Commentary* (July 1970); See also Charles Stember, "Anti-Semitism and the Study of Public Opinion," in *Jews in the Mind*, 31–47.

29. See also Michael R. Marrus, "The Theory and Practice of Anti-Semitism," *Commentary* (Aug. 1982): 39.

30. Ibid.

31. Milton Himmelfarb, "No Hitler-No Holocaust," *Commentary* (Mar. 1984).

32. Sarah Gordon, *Hitler, Germans, and the "Jewish Question"* (Princeton, 1984), 296–316.

33. Marrus, "Theory and Practice," 42.

34. See Gideon Hausner, *Justice in Jerusalem* (New York, 1966), 352–73; Hannah Arendt, *Eichmann in Jerusalem, A Report on the Banality of Evil* (New York, 1963), 36–55, 276–79; "Eichmann Tells His Own Damning Story," *Life* (Nov. 28 and Dec. 5, 1960). See also *Eichmann Interrogated: Transcripts from the Archives of the Israeli Police*, ed. J. Von Lang and Claus Sybil (New York, 1983).

35. Gitta Sereny, *Into That Darkness, An Examination of Conscience* (New York, 1983).

36. Christopher Browning, *Ordinary Men: Reserve Police Battalion 101 and the Final Solution in Poland* (New York, 1992).

37. Hanna Arendt, *Antisemitism* (New York, 1968) and *The Origins of Totalitarianism*, pt. 1, vii–xiii, 11–53.

38. Arendt, *Origins*, 42–50; See also Paul Johnson, "Marxism vs. the Jews," *Commentary* (Apr. 1984), 28–34.

39. John A. Hobson, *Imperialism, A Study* (London, 1902), 30–32, "Moral and Sentimental Factors."

40. See, for example, the character of Prince Cabano (née Jacob Isaacs), whose objective is to reestablish "the ancient splendors of the Jewish race" in Ignatius Donnelly, *Ceasar's Column* (Cambridge, 1960).

41. For a description of the character and role of American Zionism, see Naomi W. Cohen, *American Jews*, 147–50. See also Ben Halpern, "The Americanization of Zionism, 1880–1930," in *Solidarity and Kinship, Essays on American Zionism*, ed. Nathan M. Kaganoff (Waltham, 1980), 37–55.

42. Leonard Dinnerstein, *Leo Frank* (New York, 1968).

43. Joachim C. Fest, *Hitler* (New York, 1974), 3–9.

44. For the Jewish aspect of the civil religion concept, see Jonathon Woocher, "Civil Judaism, The Religion of Jewish Communitas," *Policy Studies 79*, National Jewish Conference Center (May, 1979).

5. The Struggle for Middle-Class
Status and Acceptance at Harvard

1. The term "courageous enterprisers" is used by Jacob R. Marcus to describe the pioneering commercial activity of colonial Jews. See Jacob R. Marcus, *Early American Jewry* (Philadelphia, 1953), 530.

2. John Bodner, *The Transplanted: A History of Immigrants in Urban America* (Bloomington, Ind., 1985), 196.

3. The rise in Jewish enrollment actually began several years earlier. See table, "Enrollment of Jewish Students in American Colleges and Universities in 1915–1916,"

American Jewish Yearbook (5678) 19: 407–8. The term "Jewish invasion" was also employed then. See Nitza Rosovsky, *The Jewish Experience at Harvard and Radcliffe* (Boston, 1986), 6–7. It is a recognizable pattern in the postemancipation Jewries in the West, especially those of Germany, France, and England, where, as in the United States, a disproportionate share of the "invasion" was composed of Jewish students from eastern Europe.

4. Multiplier industries are those that, by virtue of their size and business volume, stimulate the growth of related industries. They act as economic pump primers. Until World War I, the railroad was such an industry, but its influence was on the wane. The automobile industry was a welcome new multiplier in the twenties.

5. Arthur S. Link, *American Epoch* (New York, 1955), 300–306; William E. Leuchtenburg, *The Perils of Prosperity, 1914–1932* (Chicago, 1958), 178–203.

6. Editors of *Fortune Magazine, Jews in America* (New York, 1936), 15.

7. The clothing business was dominated early by German Jews and continued to be 85 to 95 percent Jewish owned in the thirties. Ibid., 7.

8. *American Hebrew,* Oct. 14, 1921, 597.

9. Ibid.

10. Ibid., 7; Vincent P. Carosso, "A Financial Elite: New York's German Jewish Investment Bankers," *American Jewish Historical Quarterly* (Sept., 1976), 84–87.

11. I. M. Rubinow, "The Economic and Industrial Status of American Jewry," in the *Proceedings of the National Conference of Jewish Social Service* (Philadelphia, 1932), 8 (typescript copy in folder "Jews in the United States, Economic Conditions, 1932–1957," Library of American Jewish Committee.)

12. Lawrence P. Bachman, "Julius Rosenwald," *American Jewish Historical Quarterly* 66 (Sept. 1976), 96–97.

13. Henry Citroen, for example, was called the Henry Ford of France, Ande Manners, *Poor Cousins* (New York, 1972), 298.

14. *Jews in America,* 9.

15. Manners, *Cousins,* 298.

16. *Jews in America,* 9. The figure is for 1924 and includes ferrous and nonferrous metals.

17. Rubinow, "Economic and Industrial Status," 6; Nathan Reich, "Economic Trends," in *The American Jew: A Composite Portrait,* ed. Oscar Janowsky (New York, 1942), 167–69. The advent of processed foods triggered an expansion in the kosher food industry, even as the percentage of *kashrut* observers decreased. In 1934 in New York City alone, kosher food sales, not counting meat and poultry, amounted to $200 million. See Harold P. Gastwirt, *Fraud, Corruption and Holiness* (New York, 1974), 7–9.

18. L. Harris, *Merchant Princes: An Intimate History of Jewish Families Who Built Great Department Stores* (New York, 1979), xv. For the negative image of the Jewish petty merchant in the thirties, see Judd L. Teller, *Strangers and Natives* (New York, 1968), 147–49.

19. *Jews in America,* 11; Link, *American Epoch,* 310–11.

20. *Jews in America,* 10.

21. Daniel Pope and William Toll, "We Tried Harder: Jews in American Advertising," *American Jewish History* 72 (Sept. 1982), 45–46.

22. *Jews in America,* 13.

23. Ibid., 11; Larry May and Elaine May, "Why Jewish Movie Moguls: An Exploration in American Culture," *American Jewish History* 72 (Sept. 1982), 6–8. Harry Cohn (Columbia) had been a cobbler, trolley car conductor, and vaudevillian; Jesse Lasky, in

the shoe business; Carl Laemmle (Universal), a clothing salesman; Louis B. Mayer (MGM), in the junk business; the Warner brothers, cobblers and bicycle repairmen; Marcus Loew, the theater chain owner, a factory worker and an owner of nickelodeons; and Samuel Goldwyn, a glovemaker.

24. Nathan Glazer, *American Judaism* (Chicago, 1972), 81.

25. Selma Berrol argues, for example, that education could not have been a primary mobility instrument for the first generation and for much of the second. The observations in this discussion apply to the twenties, when a change did in fact occur. See Selma Berrol, "Education and Economic Mobility: The Jewish Experience in New York City, 1880-1920," *American Jewish Historical Quarterly* (Mar. 1976), 259-70.

26. The term *commercial* or *business* elite is used by Barry Supple to describe the "our crowd" phenomenon. "A Business Elite: German-Jewish Financiers in Nineteenth Century New York," *Business History Review* 31 (Summer 1957), 143-78.

27. Nathan Glazer and Daniel P. Moynihan, *Beyond the Melting Pot*, lv; Thomas Kessner, *The Golden Door: Italian and Jewish Immigrant Mobility in New York City* (New York, 1977), xi-xvii. See also Jacob Lestchinsky, "The Position of Jews in the Economic Life of America," in *Jews in a Gentile World*, ed. I. Graeber and S. H. Britt (New York, 1942), 402-16.

28. For the complexity of developing professionalism, see Barton J. Bledstein, *The Culture of Professionalism: The Middle Class and the Development of Higher Education in America* (New York, 1976).

29. Nathan Goldberg, "Economic Trends Among American Jews," *Jewish Affairs* (Oct. 1, 1946): 11-14, 17; Nathan Reich, "The Role of Jews in the American Economy," *YIVO Annual* 5 (1950): 116; Simon Kuznets, "Economic Structure of the U.S. Jewry: Recent Trend," (Jerusalem, 1972) (pamphlet in Economic Condition File, Library of the American Jewish Committee); Lestchinsky, "Position of Jews," 406-10. A 1937 survey of 924,258 wage earners, done for the Committee on Economic Adjustment sponsored by the American Jewish Committee, gives the 7.4 percent figure for "professional" and finds that 13.5 percent were unemployed. See Ronald Bayor, "Italians, Jews, and Ethnic Conflict," *International Migration Review* 4 (Winter 1972), 380.

30. Barry R. Chiswick, "The Earnings and Human Capital of American Jews," *The Journal of Human Resources* 17 (Summer 1983), 313-36. By 1957, 28.5 percent of Jews had graduated from college as compared to 10 percent for the general population. Kuznets, "Economic Structure," 5-7; See also Glazer, *American Judaism*, 81 and Nathan Goldberg, "Economic Trends," 11.

31. Eli Ginzberg, "Jews in the American Economy: The Dynamics of Opportunity," in *Jewish Life in America*, ed. Gladys Rosen (New York, 1978), 114; Reich, "Role of Jews," 170.

32. Irwin Rosen, "The Economic Position of Jewish Youth," American Jewish Committee Library, Jews in U. S. Economic Conditions, 1932-1936, mimeographed (1936). Barry R. Chiswick and June A. O'Neill, eds., *Human Resources and Income Distribution* (New York, 1977), 91-93, 172-73.

33. Chiswick, "Earnings," 313-14; Lestchinsky, "Position of Jews," 313-14, 414.

34. Chiswick, "Earnings," 313.

35. Ibid.

36. In 1918, Columbia experienced a whopping 40 percent, slightly lower than NYU's 42 percent, which it lowered to 22 percent in two years by quietly imposing a quota. Syracuse registered 15 percent and Dartmouth and Princeton, not located near large Jewish population centers, a mere 7 percent and 9 percent. Stephen Steinberg, *The*

Academic Melting Pot: Catholics and Jews in American Higher Education (New York, 1974), 19–20. The fullest overall account is Marcia G. Synnot, *The Half-Open Door: Discrimination and Admissions at Harvard, Yale, and Princeton: 1900–1970* (Westport, Conn., 1979), 11 ff.

37. Morris R. Cohen, *A Dreamer's Journey* (Boston, 1949), 151; See also Stephen Steinberg, "How Jewish Quotas Began," *Commentary* 52 (Sept. 1971), 67–76.

38. Nathan C. Belth, *A Promise to Keep* (New York, 1979), 101–2.

39. Ibid., Harvard officials were convinced that Jews would agree to self-limitation and were astonished at the attitude of the Menorah Society, headed by Harry Starr, *American Hebrew*, Sept. 22, 1922, 537.

40. Samuel Eliot Morison, *Three Centuries of Harvard* (Boston, 1936), 147, cited in Steinberg, *Melting Pot*, 5.

41. Steinberg, *Melting Pot*, 14. Of Norwegian stock, Veblen had little use for such criteria, but he appreciated the cultural sources of the Jewish academic performance. See "On the Intellectual Preeminence of the Jews," in *Essays in Our Changing Order*, ed. Leon Ardzrooni (New York, 1939). For the historic roots of the Protestant posture, see E. Digby Baltzell, *The Protestant Establishment: Aristocracy and Caste in America* (New York, 1964).

42. *American Hebrew*, Aug. 25, 1922, 352.

43. Ibid., Mar. 24, 1922, 497 (editorial). Jewish students did create their own fraternities, Zeta Beta Tau, Sigma Alpha Mu, Kappa Nu, and Tau Epsilon Phi.

44. *American Hebrew*, Mar. 24, 1922, 497.

45. Ibid., July 8, 1921, 193 (editorial), and Aug. 5, 1921, 273. See also Judd L. Teller, *Strangers and Natives*, 90. When the Hakoah Soccer team, wearing its blue and white colors, played at the Polo Grounds, a holiday atmosphere prevailed in Jewish neighborhoods.

46. They did not do too badly in campus sports either, according to a special study made by Zeta Beta Tau, probably in response to the charge that Jewish students did not go out for athletics. In the 1922 academic year in the ten major universities, excluding those three that practiced limitation, Jewish students earned 7 percent of the varsity letters awarded. Interestingly, in the category of honors for publications, they earned 16.7 percent. *American Hebrew*, Dec. 29, 1922, 207.

47. Alexander Bloom, *Prodigal Sons: The New York Intellectuals and Their World* (New York, 1986), 29–30.

48. Steinberg, *Melting Pot*, 17.

49. William T. Ham, "Harvard Students on the Jewish Question," *American Hebrew*, Sept. 15, 1922, 406.

50. Ibid., Sept. 22, 1922, 537.

51. Cohen, *Dreamer's Journey*, 224.

52. Steinberg, *Melting Pot*, 12–13; Rosovsky, *Harvard and Radcliffe*, 7.

53. Nitza Rosovsky, *The Jewish Experience at Harvard and Radcliffe* (Boston, 1986), 13.

54. *American Hebrew*, Sept. 29, 1922, 530.

55. Walter P. Eaton, "Jews in the American Theater," *American Hebrew*, Sept. 22, 1922, 464.

56. Besides the Schiff donation, the Warburg family gave $200,000 for a new administration building in 1924, and the Lehman, Straus, and Sachs families contributed $700,000 for the 1924 fund-raising campaign. *American Hebrew*, June 20, 1924, 200, and June 27, 1924, 214.

57. Ibid., Oct. 6, 1922, 551, 564, column "From a Graduate's Window."

58. Harry Starr, "The Affair at Harvard: What Students Did," *Menorah Journal*, 8 (Oct. 1922): 264–65. See also Belth, *Promise*, 5. Starr had surmised correctly. The figure that Lowell had in mind beyond which Harvard would no longer be able to absorb the "Menorah boys" was 15 percent. That is what he revealed in his now famous conversation with a Harvard alumnus on Christmas Eve aboard a delayed New York Central train. Victor A. Kramer, "What Lowell Said," *American Hebrew*, Jan. 26, 1923, 391.

59. Charles Reznikoff, ed., *Louis Marshall: Champion of Liberty* (Philadelphia, 1945), 1: 268 (Marshall to J. L. Magnes, Aug. 10, 1922).

60. Steinberg, *Melting Pot*, 11.

61. *American Hebrew*, Sept. 22, 1922, 515.

62. Walter Lippmann, "Public Opinion and the American Jew," *American Hebrew*, Apr. 14, 1922, 575.

63. Stern was a Harvard graduate, class of 1922. His letter first appeared in Philadelphia's *Jewish Exponent* and then was mentioned in an editorial in the *American Hebrew*, July 28, 1922, 258.

64. *American Hebrew*, July 14, 1922, 447.

65. *American Hebrew*, June 23, 1922, 151.

66. Julian Morgenstern, "American Judaism Faces the Future," *American Hebrew*, Sept. 22, 1922, 447.

67. *American Hebrew*, June 9, 1922, 109 (editorial). But for the next three years, the idea of a Hebrew university, which had gained some support as a result of the Harvard affair, was rejected by the *American Hebrew* as an undesirable form of self-segregation. See, for example, the editorials of Dec. 15, 1922, 163, and Mar. 9, 1923, 521.

68. Reznikoff, *Marshall* 1: 267 (Marshall to A. C. Ratshesky, June 17, 1922).

69. Steinberg, *Melting Pot*, 28.

70. The work that captures the flavor of Jewish student life most completely is Cohen, *Dreamer's Journey*. See also Irving Howe, "The New York Intellectuals," in *Decline of the New* (New York, 1970) and *World of Our Fathers* (New York, 1976), 280–86. Of the NYU downtown campus, one observer noted "quickness of speech," casualness of dress, little interest in athletics and general extracurricular activities and little of the spirit generally associated with student life. See Felix Morrow, "Higher Learning on Washington Square: Some Notes on New York University," *Menorah Journal* (Apr. 1930), 346–57.

71. Sept. 29, 1922, 529 (editorial).

72. James G. Heller, "Americanizing Our Universities," *American Hebrew*, Oct. 10, 1922, 636.

73. *American Hebrew*, Apr. 20, 1923, 745 (editorial).

74. The concern about "covert devices" undoubtedly referred to the admissions application, which requested information on race, religion, and family background and then inquired if there had been a family change of name. See *American Hebrew* editorials for Sept. 29, 1922, 529, and Apr. 13, 1923, 744. See also Rosovsky, *Harvard and Radcliffe*, 20.

75. *American Hebrew*, Apr. 13, 1923, 744; Synnot, *Half-Open Door*, 96 ff.

76. Rosovsky, *Harvard and Radcliffe*, 23; Belth, *Promise*, 108 ff.

77. The term "shoe string capitalism" was employed by Burton J. Hendricks in a series of anti-Semitic articles published in *World's Work* in Dec. 1922 and Jan. 1923. It is quoted in Max J. Kohler, "Reply to an Insidious Attack," *American Hebrew*, Mar. 9, 1923, 522. Originally the term "egghead millionaires" referred to those Jews who started

businesses in electronics and other highly technical areas in which professional training was required. It was first used in "The Egghead Millionaires," *Fortune* (Sept. 1960), 172 ff., and then picked up by Glazer and Moynihan, *Beyond the Melting Pot*, 155.

78. Industrial research was formalized by the establishment of the Mellon Institute of Industrial Research in 1913. Three years later, the National Academy of Science established the National Research Council. By 1927, 999 corporations were involved either in independent or cooperative research for product and cost improvement; Link, *American Epoch*, 306.

6. Sources of Jewish Liberalism

1. That observers regard Jewish "liberal" proclivities as permanent, rather than as part of an ongoing search for suitable systems, is nowhere better indicated than in a work by Mark R. Levy and Michael Kramer, *The Ethnic Factor: How American Minorities Decide Elections* (New York: Simon & Schuster, 1973). The chapter devoted to Jewish political behavior is titled "The Jews: Forever Liberal Wherever They Are."

7. The Changing Liberalism of American Jewry

1. Woodrow Wilson, *Congressional Government: A Study in American Politics* (Boston: Houghton Mifflin, 1913); Michael Kammen, *Spheres of Liberty: Changing Perceptions of Liberty in American Culture* (Madison: Univ. of Wisconson Press, 1986). The problems posed by libertarianism for liberalism are examined by James A. Monroe, *The Democratic Wish: Popular Participation and the Limits of American Government* (New York: Basic, 1990).

2. François Furet, "From 1789 to 1917 and 1989: Looking Back at Revolutionary Traditions," *Encounter* (Sept. 1990): 3–7.

3. John M. McFaul, *The Politics of Jacksonian Finance* (Ithaca: Cornell Univ. Press, 1985).

4. See Arthur Goren, "The Tradition of Community," in *New York Jews and the Quest for Community: The Kehillah Experiment (1908–1922)* (New York: Columbia Univ. Press, 1970), 6–9.

5. George Will, "The Presidency in the American Political System," *Presidential Studies Quarterly* 14, no. 3 (1984): 324.

6. Melvin Urofsky, *Louis D. Brandeis and the Progressive Tradition* (Boston: Little, Brown, 1981), 71–86.

7. Moses Rischin, *Promised City* (Cambridge, Mass.: Harvard Univ. Press, 1962), 221–35; Goren, *Kehillah*, 4, 24, 186; John D. Buenker, *Urban Liberalism and Progressive Reform* (New York: Scribner's, 1973).

8. Michael A. Meyer, *Response to Modernity: A History of the Reform Movement in Judaism* (New York: Oxford Univ. Press, 1988), 286–89.

9. Morris Frommer, "The American Jewish Congress: A History" (Ph.D. diss., Ohio State Univ., 1978).

10. *American Jewish Yearbook* 27 (1919–1920): 599; 39 (1937–1938): 735; 40 (1938–1939): 529.

11. Alan Fisher, "Continuity and Erosion of Jewish Liberalism," *American Jewish Historical Quarterly* 66, no. 2 (Dec. 1976): 322–62.

12. See Samuel Lubell, *The Future of American Politics* (New York: Harper, 1966), 35–43.

13. A portrait of the social-class background of the Progressive reformer is presented by George C. Mowry, *The California Progressives* (Berkley: Univ. of California Press, 1951).

14. Quoted in Arthur Liebman, "The Ties That Bind: The Jewish Support of the Left in the U.S.," *American Jewish Historical Quarterly* 66, no. 2 (Dec. 1976): 285–321.

15. Allen L. Kagedan, "The Formation of Soviet Jewish Territorial Units, 1924–1937" (Ph.D. diss., Columbia Univ., 1985).

16. Will Herberg, "The Jewish Labor Movement in the U.S.," *American Jewish Yearbook* 53 (1952–1953): 5 ff.

17. Nathaniel Weyl, *The Jews in American Politics* (New Rochelle, N.Y.: Arlington House, 1968), 116–19.

18. Others attribute it to Samuel Rosenman. See Edward J. Flynn, *You're the Boss* (New York: Viking, 1948), 183.

19. Alonzo L. Hamby, *Liberalism and Its Challengers: FDR to Reagan* (New York : Oxford Univ. Press, 1985), 22 ff.

20. Steven M. Cohen, *The Dimensions of American Jewish Liberalism*, Jewish Political Studies Series (New York: American Jewish Committee, 1989), 1–4.

21. For an elaboration of this dilemma, see Edward Alexander, "Liberalism and Zionism," *Commentary*, Feb. 1986.

22. Hasia Dinner, "In the Almost Promised Land: Jewish Leaders and Blacks, 1915–1935" (Ph.D. diss., Univ of Illinois, Chicago Circle, 1975), xii–xvii, 237.

23. Cohen, *Dimensions*, 14.

24. The term "suicidal altruism" is used by Leonard J. Fein, "Liberalism and American Jews," *Midstream* 19, no 8 (Oct. 1973): 12.

25. For an elaboration of how the race question has been exploited to alter liberal assumptions from equality to preference, see Jim Sleeper, *The Closest of Strangers: Liberalism and the Politics of Race* (New York: Norton, 1990).

26. Alan Fisher, "Are We Changing?," *Comment and Analysis* 2, no. 1 (Feb.1991): 1–2.

27. Cohen, *Dimensions*, 14–20.

11. The Charge of Rootless Cosmopolitan

1. Hartley Alexander, "The Jew, Exemplar of the Future Cosmopolite," *Menorah Journal* 6, no. 1 (Feb. 1929).

13. Jewry and America's Hard Secularism

1. Mel Scult, *Judaism Faces the Twentieth Century: A Biography of Mordecai Kaplan* (Detroit: Wayne State Univ. Press, 1993), 53, 237, 261.

2. Ibid., 165–66.

3. Deborah D. Moore, *At Home in America: Second Generation New York Jews* (New York: Columbia Univ. Press, 1981), 19–58.

4. For a full examination of the Harvard debacle, see Marcia G. Synnott, *The Half Opened Door: Discrimination and Admissions at Harvard, Yale and Princeton, 1900–1970* (Westport, Conn.: Greenwood, 1979).

5. *American Hebrew*, Oct. 7, 1921, 553; May 29, 1925, 100.

6. Robert Cohen, *When the Old Left Was Young: Student Radicals and America's First Mass Student Movement, 1929–1941* (New York: Oxford Univ. Press, 1993), 24–38.

7. I. Steinbaum, "A Study of the Jewishness of Twenty New York Families," *YIVO Annual of Jewish Social Science* 5 (Sept. 1942).

8. Haim Avni, *Spain, the Jews, and France* (Philadelphia: Jewish Publication Society, 1982), 50.

9. Henry L. Feingold, *A Time for Searching: Entering the Mainstream, 1920–1945* (Baltimore: Johns Hopkins Univ. Press, 1993), 8–13.

10. Quoted by Willaim L. Sperry, *Religion in America* (Boston: Little Brown, 1963), 36.

11. For the fullest description of the Charleston Reform movement, see James W. Hagy, *This Happy Land: The Jews of Colonial and Antebellum Charleston* (Tuscaloosa: Univ. of Alabama Press, 1993), 128–60; Michael Meyer, *Response to Modernity: A History of the Reform Movement in Judaism* (New York: Oxford Univ. Press, 1988).

12. Yirmiyahu Yovel, *Spinoza and Other Heretics: The Adventures of Immanence and the Marrano of Reason* (Princeton: Princeton Univ. Press,1989); Robert M. Seltzer, *Jewish People, Jewish Thought: The Jewish Experience in History* (New York: Macmillan, 1980), 407, 504–5, 550–55.

Selected Bibliography

Part One: History

Baron, Salo W. *History and Jewish Historians: Essays and Addresses.* Philadelphia, 1964.
Elazar, Daniel. *Community and Polity: The Organizational Dynamics of American Jewry.* Philadelphia, 1976.
Glazer, Nathan. *American Judaism.* Chicago, 1972.
———, and Daniel Moynihan, *Beyond the Melting Pot.* Cambridge, Mass., 1969.
Kallen, Horace M. *Cultural Pluralism and the American Idea.* Philadelphia, 1956.
Kessner, Thomas. *The Golden Door: Italian and Jewish Immigrant Mobility in New York City, 1880–1915.* New York, 1977.
Marcus, Jacob R. *Studies in American Jewish History.* Cincinnati, 1969.
Meyer, Michael A., *Ideas of Jewish History.* New York, 1974.
Seltzer, Robert M. *Jewish People, Jewish Thought: The Jewish Experience in History.* New York, 1980.
Steinberg, Stephen. *The Academic Melting Pot: Catholics and Jews in American Higher Education.* New York, 1974.
Urofsky, Melvin I. *American Zionism: From Herzl to Holocaust.* New York, 1975.

Part Two: Anti-Semitism

Belth, Nathan C. *A Promise to Keep.* New York, 1979.
Dinnerstein, Leanord. *Antisemitism in America.* New York, 1994.
Dobkowski, Michael. *The Tarnished Dream: The Basis of American Anti-Semitism.* Westport, Conn., 1979.
Gerber, David A., ed. *Anti-Semitism in American History.* Urbana, Ill., 1986.
Higham, John. *Strangers in the Land Patterns of American Nativism, 1860–1925.* New Brunswick, N.J., 1955.
Rosovsky, Nitza. *The Jewish Experience at Harvard and Radcliffe.* Boston, 1986.

Stember, Charles H., ed. *Jews in the Mind of America.* New York, 1966.
Synnot, Marcia. *The Half Open Door: Discrimination and Admission at Harvard, Yale and Princeton, 1900–1970.* Westport, Conn., 1979.

Part Three: Political Culture

Bodner, John. *The Transplanted: A History of Immigrants in Urban America.* Bloomington, Ind., 1985.
Buenker, John D. *Urban Liberalism and Progressive Reform.* New York, 1973.
Cohen, Steven M. *The Dimensions of American Jewish Liberalism.* New York, 1989.
Feingold, Henry L. *A Time for Searching: Entering the Mainstream, 1920–1945.* Baltimore, 1994.
Gerson, Louis L. *The Hyphenate in Recent American Politics and Diplomacy.* Lawrence, Kan., 1964.
Hamby, Alonzo. *Liberalism and Its Challengers: FDR to Reagan.* New York, 1985.
Hero, Alfred O. *American Religious Groups View Foreign Policy.* Durham, N.C., 1973.
Howe, Irving. *World of Our Fathers.* New York, 1976.
Kammen, Michaek. *Spheres of Liberty: Changing Perceptions of Liberty in American Culture.* Madison, Wis., 1986.
Levy, Mark, and Michael Kramer. *The Ethnic Factor: How American Minorities Decide Elections.* New York, 1973.
Urofsky, Melvin. *A Voice That Spoke for Justice: The Life and Times of Stephen S. Wise.* Albany, 1982.
———. *We Are One: American Jewry and Israel.* Garden City, N.Y., 1978.

Part Four: Secularism

Bledstein, Barton J. *The Culture of Professionalism: The Middle Class and the Development of Higher Education in America.* New York, 1976.
Chiswick, R., and June O'Neil, eds. *Human Resources and Income Distribution.* New York, 1977.
Cohen, Morris R. *A Dreamer's Journey.* Boston, 1949.
Cohen, Steven M. *American Assimilation or Jewish Revival?* Bloomington, Ind., 1988.
———. *American Modernity and Jewish Identity.* New York, 1983.
Eisen, Arnold M. *The Chosen People in America: A Study of Jewish Religious Ideology.* Bloomington, Ind., 1983.
Furman, Frieda K. *Beyond Yiddishkeit: The Study for Jewish Identity in a Reform Synagogue.* Albany, 1887.
Gastwirt, Harold. *Fraud, Corruption and Holiness.* New York, 1974.
Herberg, Will. *Protestant, Catholic, Jew: An Essay in American Religious Sociology.* New York, 1955.

Jick, Leon A. *The Americanization of the Synagogue, 1820–1870.* Hanover, N.H., 1976.

Kaplan, Mordecai. *The Future of the American Jew.* New York, 1948.

Lederhandler, Eli. *Jewish Responses to Modernity: New Voices from America and Eastern Europe.* New York, 1984.

Manners, Ande. *Poor Cousins.* New York, 1972.

Meyer, Michael A. *Response to Modernity: A History of the Reform Movement in Judaism.* New York, 1988.

Moore, Deborah D. *At Home in America: Second Generation New York Jews.* New York, 1981.

Sarna, Jonathan D. *JPS: The Americanization of Jewish Culture.* Philadelphia, 1989.

Seltzer, Robert, and Norman J. Cohen, eds. *The Americanization of the Jews.* New York, 1995.

Silberman, Charles. *A Certain People: American Jews and Their Lives Today.* New York, 1985.

Weber, Max. *The Protestant Ethic: The Spirit of Capitalism.* New York, 1958.

Index

Adams, Henry, 80
Adams, John, 136
Adler, Felix, 181
African Americans: American polity excludes, 3, 150; and anti-Semitism, 9, 76–77, 81; Jewish Americans outnumbered by, 18; as victims, 76–77, 88
Agudath Harabonim (ultra Orthodox rabbinic hierarchy), 156
Alexander, Hartley, 170
Aliyah (U.S. Jewish immigration to Israel), 58, 144, 146, 167,192
"alrightniks," 182, 184
Amalgamated Clothing Workers, 42
America: and anti-Semitism, 5, 7–10, 16, 24, 71–90, 98, 100–105, 116, 123, 151, 182–84; Catholics in, 8, 46, 149–50; and Christianity, 6–8, 71–72, 74–75, 149–51; and conservatism, 118–19, 135; and the Diaspora, 7, 30, 35, 67, 148, 151, 161; and the Enlightenment, 3, 11, 135, 150; and the Holocaust, 15, 18, 52, 56, 61, 112, 116, 146, 173–74, 176, 185–86; and Israel, 13, 15, 52, 57, 66, 82, 84–86, 112, 129–30, 131, 157–59, 169; and Judaism, 15–20, 25–29, 47–48, 148–95; and liberalism, 9–14, 113–14, 117–38; and libertarianism, 12, 16, 118–19, 123–24, 127–28, 131–38; and modernity, 1–4, 14–

20, 26, 46, 144, 150, 167–72, 179–96; and the New Deal, 12, 111, 119–21, 123, 126–27, 130, 133–34, 137–38; and pluralism, 48–49, 54–56, 58–59, 73–77, 102, 147, 149–51; and Protestantism, 39, 74, 76, 96, 141, 149, 188; and secularism, 14–20, 141–96; and *Yerida*, 58, 64, 192–93; and Yiddish culture, 15–16, 122, 155–56, 175–76, 184, 188; and Zionism, 47, 49, 54, 111, 129, 144, 157, 164–67, 174, 190, 192–93
American Federation of Labor (AFL), 41
American Hebrew (Anglo-Jewish weekly): on "Americanization" of Jewish immigrants, 175; Hebrew universities opposed by, 208n. 67; high school fraternities opposed by, 97; Jewish country clubs and, 182; on Judaism in America, 153; Lippmann editorial in, 100–101; public schools promoted by, 102–103; on religious observation of American Jews, 184; scholarship results published by, 96
American Israelite (periodical), 110
American Jewish Committee, 32, 50, 76, 114, 122
American Jewish Congress: decline during 1920s of, 49; formation of, 50; and Holocaust opposition, 185–86; and incorporation of Jewish Ameri-

Federal Order Number 11 (1862). *See* General Order Number 11 (1862)
Federal Reserve System, 120
Federal Social Security Act (1935), 44
Federation of American Zionists. *See* Zionist Organization of America
Fein, Leonard J., 210n. 24
Feinstein, Diane, 133
Feinstein, Michael, 133
Felter, William, 97
Fiddler on the Roof, 15
Final Solution, 56–57, 79, 173–74
Fisch, Harold, 202n. 7
Flannery, Edward H., 71
Ford, Henry: as American hero, 36, 89; and anti-Semitic articles in *Dearborn Independent*, 16, 36, 87, 88, 123, 182; Jewish perspective on, 5, 36; Marshall opposes, 186; *Protocols of the Elders of Zion* published by, 36, 88–89; public apology of, 123
Fort Ontario (Oswego, NY), 57
Fortune (magazine), 89–90
Forverts (Forwards), Yiddish daily, 43, 125, 132
Fourier, Charles, 81
Fourteenth Amendment, 119
Frank, Leo, 36, 78, 83, 88
Freedmen's Bureau, 119
Free Synagogue, 142
French Revolution, 117, 118, 135
Freud, Sigmund, 146, 170

Gallup, George, 203–204n. 27
Galut (exile), 158, 163, 164, 169
General Order Number 11 (1862), 8, 36, 78
Germany: anti-Semitism in, 8; under Nazis, 50–51; 56–57
Glanz, Rudolf, 35
Glass-Steagal law, 89
Glazer, Nathan, 92, 104
Gleason, Philip, 54
Gobineau, Joseph, 80
goldeneh medinah (promised land), 5, 55, 60
Goldenwasser, A. A., 101

Goldmann, Nahum, 146, 163, 166
Goldman-Sachs (Jewish investment team), 89
Goldwyn, Samuel, 206n. 23
Gompers, Samuel, 41, 42
Gordon, Milton, 61
Gordon, Sarah, 79
Grant, Ulysses S., 36, 78
g'ulah (redemption), 164

Halakha (Jewish religious law), 146, 153, 157, 179, 182
Halpern, Ben, 71, 72
Hamilton, Alexander, 11, 121
Handlin, Oscar, 60, 71
Harrington, Michael, 126
Harvard Graduates' Magazine, 100
Harvard University, 73, 95–105; and *numerus clausus* case, 8–10, 16, 88, 93, 99–103, 123, 182; Semitic Museum at, 99
Hausner, Gideon, 80
Hebraism, 74, 150–51
Hebrew, 155, 178
Hebrew Union College (HUC), 101, 153, 154
heimischkeit (passion, commitment), 165
Hellenism, 17
Hendricks, Burton J., 208n. 77
Herberg, Will, 73, 151
Hertz, John D., 91
Hertzberg, Rabbi A., 202n. 50
Herut (freedom), 137
Herzl, Theodor, 67, 146, 166
Heschel, Abraham Joshua, 158, 169
Higham, John, 71, 76, 78
Hillman, Sidney, 43–44
Hillquit, Morris, 125
Hispanic Americans, 18, 75
Hitler, Adolf, 79, 174
Hobson, John A., 81
Holocaust, the: and American anti-Semitism, 173–74; American Jewish Congress organizes rallies protesting, 185–86; and American Jewry, 15, 18, 52, 61, 112, 116, 185; anti-Semitism in relation to, 82; Israel a result of, 7,

Zionism, Zionists (*cont.*)
190; and *chalutziut*, 162; and cultural
pluralism, 54, 164; cultural Zionism
as expression of, 47, 157, 159, 169;
and the Diaspora, 30–31, 82; as Euro-
pean import, 174; and the Holocaust,
57, 82; and Jewish corporateness, 6;

Samuel on, 165, 167; and secularism,
14, 56, 142, 164–67, 185; and social-
ism, 44, 179, 190; Soviet persecution
of, 124
Zionist Organization of America (1918),
50, 164–65

Other books in the Modern Jewish History series

Bearing Witness: How America and Its Jews Responded to the Holocaust
HENRY L. FEINGOLD

Bondage to the Dead: Poland and the Memory of the Holocaust
MICHAEL C. STEINLAUF

The Golden Tradition: Jewish Life and Thought in Eastern Europe
EDITED BY LUCY S. DAWIDOWICZ

Our Crowd: The Great Jewish Families of New York
STEPHEN BIRMINGHAM